DATE DUE

THE PSYCHOPATHOLOGY OF LANGUAGE AND COGNITION

COGNITION AND LANGUAGE
A Series in Psycholinguistics • Series Editor: R. W. RIEBER

A Continuation Order Plan is available for this series. A continuation order will bring delivery
of each new volume immediately upon publication. Volumes are billed only upon actual
shipment. For further information please contact the publisher.

THE PSYCHOPATHOLOGY OF LANGUAGE AND COGNITION

ROBERT W. RIEBER
*John Jay College of Criminal Justice
   and Graduate Center
City University of New York
New York, New York*

HAROLD J. VETTER
*University of South Florida
Tampa, Florida*

Plenum Press • New York and London

Library of Congress Cataloging-in-Publication Data

Vetter, Harold J., 1926-
    The psychopathology of language and cognition / Robert W. Rieber
and Harold J. Vetter.
        p.   cm. -- (Cognition and language)
    Includes bibliographical references (p.) and index.
    ISBN 0-306-44757-6
    1. Mentally ill--Language. 2. Psycholinguistics.   I. Rieber, R.
W. (Robert W.) II. Title. III. Series.
RC455.4.P78V48   1994
616.89--dc20   94-44347
                                                         CIP

ISBN 0-306-44757-6

An earlier version of Chapter 4 appeared in the *Journal of Psycholinguistic Research, 23* (1), 1–28, 1994. An earlier version of Chapter 6 appeared in the *Journal of Psycholinguisitic Research, 23* (2), 149–195, 1994.

© 1995 Plenum Press, New York
A Division of Plenum Publishing Corporation
233 Spring Street, New York, N. Y. 10013

10 9 8 7 6 5 4 3 2 1

Printed in the United States of America

Preface

A quarter century ago, one of the authors (Vetter, 1969) undertook the task of surveying research and theory in an area that, for lack of a more precise designation, was called "language behavior and psychopathology." The book published under the same title addressed those precincts of language behavior wherein the interests of the psychologist, psychiatrist, linguist, and speech pathologist showed some tendencies toward convergence. The principal focus was on aspects of language and paralanguage—variously, and on the whole, indifferently referred to as "deviation," "anomalies," "aberrations," or "disturbances"—that occur with sufficient frequency in relation to certain categories of personality disorders that they have long occupied a prominent (and controversial) place in the psychodiagnostic process.

Language Behavior and Psychopathology (1969) made clear to the reader that it did not deal with such primary patterns of language disturbance as aphasia and stuttering. This was not to deny the relevance of psychopathological considerations in such language disorders. The importance of emotional conflict in the pathogenesis of stuttering had been amply documented, and there was abundant clinical evidence that aphasic patients might react adversely to their lowered or altered capacities in symbolizing and communicating, even to the extent of exhibiting what Kurt Goldstein called a "catastrophic reaction." Regardless, however, of any psychopathological factors that may be present in aphasia or stuttering, both are essentially *linguistic* disorders. Their principal symptoms are manifested in vocal speech, and their treatment requires some or a great deal of speech therapy and retraining.

On the other hand, as the book sought to emphasize, the linguistic and paralinguistic phenomena that occur as concomitants to conventional psychiatric syndromes might be characterized more accurately as language symptoms than as language disturbances. Clinical descriptions of personality disorders prominently feature descriptions of language and paralinguistic behavior. Anyone questioning this statement need only try to imagine the difficulties presented by the psychodiagnostic assessment of a patient bereft of speech. Much, if not most, diagnostic test behavior is language behavior, and among the chief criteria for gauging therapeutic progress is change in language behavior.

If there was a common orientation toward language and communication behavior in the psychopathological context, it expressed itself in two objectives. The first was an attempt to arrive at a precise description of the way or ways that individuals diagnosed as belonging to a particular nosological category—schizophrenia, for example—differed from those in other diagnostic categories or from normals. The second objective, which was much more complex, dealt with attempts to utilize language and communication to advance our understanding of the psychopathological processes involved in various psychiatric disorders. One of the major and continuing sources of complexity in this area of inquiry was—and still remains—the relationship between language and thought. These objectives were expressed succinctly by Forrest (1968):

> Little description is needed with which to recognize the utterances of schizophrenics as such; and were its recognition the only interest in such speech, much of the extensive description that has been attempted would be useless. But psychiatry, having as its concerns a system of response whose circuits are beyond tracing and probably beyond chemistry in their ordering, has had little from these circuits by way of data, and is consequently based on the study of communication. If the study of schizophrenic communication is the principal means by which the disease may be understood, its course known, and its causes discovered, then precise description of schizophrenic language is valuable. (p. 153)

A good deal of the material covered by *Language Behavior and Psychopathology* was directed toward assessing the efforts among investigators to attain the two objectives identified above. It will be seen that these objectives were also significantly involved in the further investigations covered by the present volume, organized into three parts.

Reflecting back across the gulf of two and a half decades, it is possible to discern some areas of significant change and others in which the passage of time does not appear to have had any significant effects. Among the former can be noted the revision in the DSM-III that eliminated both the term *neurosis* and nearly all the problems and issues involving nosology. Among the latter, nearly every study dealing with language behavior in schizophrenia raised nearly as many questions as it answered, and we have only reached the point at present that we can begin to identify some of the more promising leads for future research.

We have not attempted to rewrite *Language Behavior and Psychopathology*. At the time the original volume was published, psycholinguistics was a new specialty, and all those who identified themselves as psycholinguists could probably have been comfortably accommodated in a minivan. Other specialty areas such as sociolinguistics were also new, and we were at the very advent of the computer age. We have sought in the present book to sketch some of the progress that has taken place over the past quarter century in research and theory on language and communication in the psychopathological context and to identify what appear to us as potentially promising avenues of further inquiry for the future.

ROBERT W. RIEBER
HAROLD J. VETTER

REFERENCES

Forrest, D. V. (1968). Poiesis and the language of schizophrenia. In H. J. Vetter (Ed.), *Language behavior in schizophrenia* (pp. 153–181). Springfield, IL: Thomas.

Vetter, H. J. (1969). *Language behavior and psychopathology*. Chicago: Rand McNally.

Acknowledgments

We wish to express our appreciation to Aileen Clark as a contributing author to this manuscript. The concluding section of Chapter 6 headed "Vocal Acoustic Studies of Schizophrenic Speech" quotes directly from her own original research on language behavior in affective disorders and schizophrenia, as well as from her critical review of theoretical and research initiatives in these important areas of systematic inquiry. We are also indebted to Murray Alpert for his generous assistance and support in surveying recent developments in computer-based voice analysis systems which bear the imprint of his significant and continuing contributions.

A special note of thanks is due to Eva M. Fernández. Without her diligence, hard work, linguistic skills, and thorough acquaintance with the professional literature in diverse fields of psycholinguistic investigation, this project could not have reached completion.

Finally, we must acknowledge the material contribution made to this manuscript by Trudy Brown, Senior Production Editor at Plenum Publishing Corporation. Her meticulous and painstaking review of the text managed to produce a timely identification of many items requiring improvements in scholarship and literacy. She does not share the blame for any of those we may have missed.

Contents

1

Historical Roots

Curiosity about the relation between language and thought is of long standing, going back to the earliest philosophical speculations. Language was of interest to the pre-Aristotelian philosophers because it distinguished human beings from other creatures and appeared intrinsically linked to every aspect of being human: the physical, intellectual, and spiritual self. Pre-Aristotelian philosophers were the first systematic investigators of language, speculating on its origin, the relationship between words and their meanings, and the applications of principles of logic to grammar. It was they who were to lay the foundations of classical European grammar.

Philosophical discussions among Hellenic scholars were often directed toward linguistic problems. For instance, the question of whether language was a gift of nature (i.e., a distinct physiological function based on sound production) or an extension of human functions such as reasoning and memory generated a great deal of debate. The "analogists" maintained that there existed a perfect correlation between human sound and the meaning of words, an assumption that led to examining the extent to which language is rule governed. The "anomalists" rejected this view in support of an idiosyncratic, "imperfect" etiology of language, implying that language was unpredictable in nature.

Aristotle (384–322 B.C.) integrated both views, proposing that the sound component of language was part of the natural order (*physis*) while the meanings of words were manmade (*thesis*). He based the difference between human and animal sound production on a difference in the locus of sound production and instrument of articulation. Adult language differed from the sound production of animals and children because of the muscular action of the human tongue, which required training to function properly. Aristotle also classified language units according to function. Nouns (*onoma*) and verbs (*rhema*) were designated as the fundamental units of language since they had meanings of their own. The remaining words functioned as links between logical associations of ideas.

During the Alexandrine period in the West and on the basis of developments of the classical era, two distinct schools of thought with respect to the study of language had emerged, the Alexandrines and the Stoics. In Alexandria, Dionysius Thrax (c. 100 B.C.) developed a grammar of the Greek language spoken at the end of the pre-Christian era. His contention that grammar is the empirical study of prose and poetry (*empeira*) ought to be considered a foreshadowing of what would later become common praxis in the field of linguistics. On the other hand, the Stoics (beginning c. 300 B.C.) were developing a more technical and abstract approach to the study of language, basing their work on the assumption that language is a way of understanding the inner workings of the mind. They revised the *onoma/rhema* distinction established by Aristotle and recognized more basic units in the system of language, including participles, articles, pronouns, prepositions, adverbs, and conjunctions in the repertoire of parts of speech. The debate between these two traditions would continue until the sixth century A.D., when Alexandrian empiricism became the established approach to the study of language.

THE CARTESIANS

The Stoic practice would be taken up again long thereafter in the Port Royal School founded in the mid-17th century at the University of Paris. The Port Royal scholars based their study of language on attempts to identify universal aspects of grammar. Working on an elaborate empirical base that included many known facts about Latin and Greek, the Romance languages, the Semitic languages, and German, they began to develop the idea that, while words vary across languages, concepts do not. They defined the mind as comprising three levels: that of conceiving, that of judging, and that of reasoning. These levels were then connected to grammatical concepts; a proposition with a verb or a copula, for instance, was related to the judgment level. As Chomsky (1972) has pointed out, the Port Royal School was the precursor to the generative grammars developed in the twentieth century. One of the most important developments in the Port Royal *Grammar*, published in 1660, was its recognition of constituent phrases within sentences or other phrases as grammatical units, something earlier grammars had never considered in their descriptions of language (Chomsky, 1972, p. 16).

It was not until Descartes (1596–1650) that philosophy and science became separated with respect to language (Marx, 1967). Although he did not write extensively about language, Descartes's division of the mind and body into separate entities influenced much of the later speculation involving language. A tenet of Cartesian philosophy with strong repercussions for subsequent language theory was the postulation that the existence of innate thoughts (e.g., God, self, conceptions of time and space) made language possible. Descartes equated language with thought, viewing speech as proof of thought's existence. This contention did much to foster the popular belief that deaf persons were idiots because of their inability to acquire language.

The study of deaf and blind people by 17th-century phoneticians such as Holder (1669) and Wallis (1653, 1670, 1698) would do much to discredit these notions as well as to challenge the belief that language developed only in those capable of producing and hearing human sound. Dalgarno (1661, 1680), a phonetician acquainted with the work of Holder and Wallis, proposed that the five senses were equally capable of instructing human beings about their world, thus advancing their knowledge. Dalgarno believed the five senses were also equal in their communication function. Language was not based on any particular sense or physiological function, nor were any sense productions naturally symbolic of anything. Nevertheless, debate on the relation between sense function (e.g., hearing) and language development continued into the 19th century.

Max Müller (1887, 1890, 1907) was the major advocate of the concept that thinking is not possible without language. Sir Francis Galton, a prominent psychologist of the time, vehemently denied Müller's contentions, arguing that a careful study of congenital deaf individuals would prove him wrong. But Galton never carried out the study himself, and it was not until the 20th century that experimental cognitive psychologists were able to demonstrate what Galton had anticipated. Galton's (1883) warning to Müller is worth quoting, for it is as pertinent now as then: "Before a just knowledge can be attained concerning any faculty of the human race, we must inquire into its distribution among all sorts and conditions of men on a large scale, and not among those persons who belong to a highly specialized literary class."

EARLY PHYSIOLOGICAL RESEARCH

In the 18th century, a physiological approach to the problem of language and thought came to the fore. The shift from metaphysical categories (i.e., faculties) to a view of the brain as the source of language and thought, owed much to Gall's doctrine of phrenology. Gall's system postulated that localized physiological functions of the brain were responsible for the psychological strengths and weaknesses of the individual. These functions affected the growth of the skull and could be determined from a careful inventory of the skull's shape.

Ironically, the experimental psychophysiology that stood diametrically opposed to Gall's conception of the functions of the brain and that reverted to the psychological tradition that he opposed derived its belief in cerebral localization from Gall's postulations. The views of his primary proponents, Broca and Hughlings Jackson, grew historically out of phrenology.

Broca's center for "the faculty of articulate language" was the first localization of a function in the brain hemisphere to meet with general acceptance from orthodox scientists. By drawing on Gall's early descriptions of motor aphasia, Broca's studies clearly demonstrated this localization at a time when the scientific community was at last prepared to take the issue seriously. By 1863, Broca and his colleagues had collected 20 cases showing some pathological change in the left half of the brain, 19 of them in the third frontal convolution. No exact location of the cortical center was given.

Hughlings Jackson (1879) recognized the impact of Broca's work and agreed that "Broca's area was the part of the brain most often damaged in patients suffering from aphasia." However, he pointed out the danger of the trend of claiming exact localized centers: "To locate the damage which destroys speech and to locate speech are two different things."

Perhaps the single most important contribution to the study of language and brain mechanism was made by Kurt Goldstein (1948). Using concepts based on Gestalt psychology, Goldstein believed that "to every mental performance, there corresponds a dynamic process which concerns the entire cortex. The function of a specific region is characterized by the influence which the particular structure of that region exerts on the total process." Current work in the neuropsychology of language continues to explore such problems as lateralization of brain function and related problems (Rieber, 1976).

Toward a Psychiatric Approach to Language Study

The application of scientific inquiry to psychological questions on language was furthered in the late 19th century by the work of Wilhelm Preyer (1841–1897). A German professor of physiology at the University of Jena, Preyer's studies helped establish the field of developmental psychology. His most important work, *Die Seeles des Kindes*, written in 1881, was translated into many languages (including English, in 1894) and directly affected two of the most influential psychological theorists of our time, Jean Piaget and

Sigmund Freud. Freud had been motivated by Preyer's ideas when he established as part of his theoretical system (1) the notion of the study of abnormal development and (2) the value of using stages of development as a better means of understanding the psychological growth patterns of the child.

It was in 1903 that psychiatry took a serious interest in the relations among language, thought, and mental illness (Liebmann & Edel, 1903). Although psychiatrists had acknowledged the importance of such phenomena, they were primarily understood as a means of communicating in everyday life. Liebmann and Edel's book was the first attempt in the field to set the stage for future contributions in this area. The literature before the publication of the monograph was mostly anecdotal in nature, as a few examples will illustrate.

Wyllie (1895) gave a fine review of the literature during the period of the 19th century. He pointed out that in mental illness the function of thought appears to be more damaged than that of speech and language. According to Wyllie, the functions of both thinking and speaking must be directly related to the operations of the mind, both normal and abnormal. His first task was to demonstrate the manner in which the various disorders of the mind are mirrored in the language of the mental patient. Second, he pointed out that auditory-verbal hallucinations in mental illness must be related to the disturbances in the cortical speech centers. His third suggestion was that the scientist should look at language and thought disturbance in mental illness as an important area of study in itself.

One of the forerunners of a modern viewpoint of language behavior was Southard, who suggested in a pair of interesting papers (1916a, 1916b) that standard grammatical categories might be applied to the description of psychopathological conditions with greater accuracy and reliability than was afforded by conventional psychiatric terminology. Such elements as verb tense and mood, Southard proposed, could be used to depict aspects of the patient's subjective relationship with his environment. Southard confined himself to speculation on these possibilities; he did not attempt to explore his hypotheses with reference to the actual speech of his patients. Nevertheless, his observations on the potential meaningfulness of grammatical categories clearly foreshadows the thesis that the language behavior of individuals reflects their general adjustment.

About a decade later, Busemann (1925) provided the empirical complement to Southard's speculative essays. In what became the first in a series of *psychogrammatical* studies, he presented data that purported to demonstrate a relation between emotional stability and the relative frequency of verbs and adjectives in carefully gathered samples of speech. Using shorthand transcriptions of narratives related by children of various ages on a variety of subjects, Busemann counted the number of "active" and "qualitative" constructions.

The former category contained all verbs except auxiliaries; the latter category included adjectives, adjectival nouns, and all participles used as adjectives. He then divided the number of active constructions by the number of qualitative expressions to obtain an "action quotient" (AQ). The AQ, according to Busemann, varied from year to year for a given child. Moreover, he found that a relative increase in the number of verbs paralleled an increase in emotional instability, as rated by teachers. Among the 26 children who exhibited changed AQs, those with a higher quotient received ratings of more unstable, while those with a lower quotient were rated as more stable than at the time of the previous test. For the four children whose AQs showed no change, the ratings by the teachers were also unchanged.

In 1926 William Alanson White published a critical review of language research in schizophrenia that set forth the essential conditions for a program of systematic inquiry into schizophrenic-language phenomena. According to White (1926):

> A complete understanding of the language of schizophrenia would imply an understanding of language in general, of which schizophrenic language is only a part. This would further imply an understanding of thought in general, of which language is largely an expression. Because of its extent this program is quite impossible, but certain principles need to be clearly in mind in order to avoid the taking over, in any attempt to understand the language of schizophrenia, of certain misconceptions in both of those territories which are still rife, not having been as yet fully replaced by the newer ways of thinking about the matters involved. (pp. 411–412)

Four years later, White (1930) pointed out the importance of such factors as intonation pattern, modulations of voice, and gestures in the study of psychotic language. These statements provided a remarkably clear and prophetic description of the task awaiting research in the field of language behavior in schizophrenia and other psychoses, and it is not without merit as an assessment of the situation that still confronts researchers. White cannot be fairly accused of undue pessimism in viewing the aims of the program he announced as impossible to attain. The developments that were to raise linguistics to the status of a rigorous behavioral science still lay ahead in the 1930s and 1940s, and the interests of academic psychologists in fashioning an attack on problems of language and cognition had to be deferred until even later, when American psychology had recovered from its overdose of crudely reductionist behaviorism.

By 1938 enough observations of the gross characteristics of language behavior in manic-depressive and schizophrenic patients had accumulated to permit Eisenson (1938) to sketch "linguistic profiles" for these syndromes. The manic patient is described by Eisenson as talking rapidly and incessantly and tending to be telegraphic in style, with the rapidity of speech frequently producing mispronunciations. Such an individual flits from topic to topic, with little concern for the listener, omitting many connective constructions. Depressed patients, on the other hand, speak in a manner consistent with their feelings of dejection and dysphoria. Talk of almost any kind seems as though it were a crushing burden to bear. Where the speech of the manic is variegated and telegraphic, the speech of the depressive is stereotyped and discursive. The patient speaks slowly, with monotony, and exhibits little variety of voice, tempo, or subject matter. Schizophrenics show contempt for the listener in their frequent use of neologisms, whose meanings are impossible to discern from the context. Speech forms are distorted, content is often purely idiosyncratic, and the overall effect may be one of strangeness verging on unintelligibility. Despite the frequent occurrence of polysyllabic words and overly pedantic expressions, the language of schizophrenics demonstrates a low order of abstraction. They may even exhibit the ultimate in scorn for the listener by choosing to remain mute.

Such descriptions convey the impression that psychotic speech presents a rough analogy with other forms of psychotic behavior. In Eisenson's (1938) terms a "disorder in the use of speech of any type or degree reveals a disorder in personality" (p. 166). In addition, "we should realize . . . that any personality change and any appreciable deviation from the norm in the mentality of an individual will be revealed in his speech" (p. 190).

The manifold inadequacies of such vague and generalized descriptions led Newman and Mather (1938) to attempt a more precise and systematic analysis of psychotic-language behavior. In a study that is remarkable for the sophistication of its methods, the speech of a group of patients with affective disorders was recorded phonographically as they read aloud from certain selections and as they spoke spontaneously. These speech samples were then analyzed according to such variables as pitch, emphasis, articulatory movements, pauses, tempo, resonance, and so on. The results of the analysis show clear differences among the three syndromes described by the authors as classical depression, manic syndromes, and states of dissatisfaction, self-pity, and gloom.

In their conclusion Newman and Mather state that "except in a purely formal sense, speech is not a self-contained category of behavior. Together with other behavioral forms it provides external symbols of human functioning, and one can therefore expect and find relations between speech and other modes of behavior" (p. 939).

In retrospect, it seems rather unusual that the Newman and Mather study failed to produce a host of emulators. This carefully executed piece of research marked a major advance in conception and methodology over practically all the studies that preceded it. However, it remained a solitary achievement until nearly two decades later, when technological advances in phonometry and sound spectrography encouraged renewed interest in problems of acoustic measurement. In the meantime, further psychogrammatical studies proceeded in several directions (Brengelmann, 1960).

1. *Active/Qualitative Constructions*: In addition to Buseman's (1925, 1926) findings of a positive correlation between high verb index and "emotional instability" in the language of children, the "verb/adjective quotient" (VAQ) was employed in a number of studies with patient groups: neurotics, including conversion hysterics, obsessive-compulsives, and anxiety states (Balken & Masserman, 1940); "normal" individuals with elevated scores on the manifest anxiety scale (Benton, Hartman, & Sarason, 1955); manic and hysteric patients (Lorenz & Cobb, 1953); and schizophrenics (Fairbanks, 1944; Mann, 1944). Research generally supported a relation between "activity" level, as measured by a high VAQ, and various clinical manifestations of abnormality. These findings are summarized in Brengelmann (1960).

2. *Pronouns*: Studies of pronoun usage involved both counts of general pronominal usage and the incidence of first-person pronouns and self-referential statements. Fairbanks confirmed an hypothesized higher frequency of first-person pronouns (I, me, myself) and self-referrals in the speech of schizophrenics. Mann, however, failed to obtain comparable results with written language in a sample group of schizophrenics. It seems premature to conclude whether the inconsistencies that have been reported in research on pronominal usage (Conrad & Conrad, 1956) are due primarily to differences in the types of patients studied or in the mode of response employed in the research, that is, written and verbal language. In addition, Goldman-Eisler (1943) cautioned that pronoun scores may vary according to examiner.

3. *Vocabulary Inflexibility*: Johnson (1944) introduced a research technique called the type/token ratio (TTR), the ratio of different words (types) to the total number of words (tokens) in a particular passage. Fairbanks found significantly lower TTRs for schizophrenics than for normals in spoken-language samples. Mann (1944) reported similar findings for written language among schizophrenics. Fairbanks and Mann considered their results to be independent of intelligence. According to Brengelmann (1960), results of TTR studies have shown rather consistently that vocabulary usage is less flexible in schizophrenics than in normals.

In 1942, Fillmore H. Sanford surveyed a wide range of problems in research and theory in areas that would today be characterized as part of psycholinguistics. Although research in language behavior and psychopathology only formed part of his broader concern with the interrelations of speech and personality, Sanford provided an incisive cumulative frequency curves analysis of the problems awaiting attention:

> If the investigation of the linguistic side of personality is going to amount to a great deal, the problem of choosing and defining significant variables must be met and solved. Grammatical categories are available, but they are not psychologically conceived and may not be of maximal use in the psychological study of language. For one thing, there is great difficulty in fitting everyday speech into grammatical rubrics which were tailored to fit formal prose. For another, the grammatical category, as is possibly the case with adjectives and verbs, may include constructions which, psychologically conceived, are of a different and maybe an incompatible nature. Researchers have shown that the grammatical categories are useful in the study of individuality in speech. But there is no evidence that they are the most useful categories or that a better way of classifying linguistic phenomena cannot be found. (Sanford, 1942, p. 831)

Among the key questions he asked were these:

> What sort of variables can be used most profitably in the analysis of speech? The grammarians give us a multitude of analytical categories, but this may not be much of a gift, for the grammatical rubrics are of untried objectivity and may be of limited psychological significance. Is the individuality of speech too delicate a thing to submit to quantification and analysis? Will statistics blur and obscure personality, or bring it out into the open where we can come to grips with it? What sort of speech should be studied if we are hunting for personality; does the individual reveal himself more in oral or written language? In any sample of speech, how much of the response is attributable to the stimulus situation and how much to "personal" determinants? Must we remain on the level of specific variables and specific correlations, or are there general factors and broad dimensions of linguistic individuality? (pp. 840–841)

THE QUEST FOR A PSYCHOLINGUISTIC APPROACH

Before the 1950s, the search for functional units of language behavior in psychopathology neglected the potential contributions of linguistic science, or, perhaps more accurately most psychiatrists and psychologists were unaware of such potential contributions. This neglect stemmed in large part from the minimal degree of overlap between the two disciplines up until that time. Under the influence of J. B. Watson, human behavior (of which language was considered a subset) was regarded as a set of stimulus-response reactions determined by prior conditioning. B. F. Skinner, the most recent and influential proponent of the behaviorist view, claimed in his monograph *Verbal Behavior* (1957) that verbal responses are directly attached to stimuli without any need for intervening variables such as meaning, ideas, or grammatical rules. This antimentalistic model of language clearly had little use for grammar other than taxonomic purposes.

Linguistics, on the other hand, was being shaped into an autonomous, scientific discipline by Leonard Bloomfield (1887–1949), who adhered to behavioristic principles in defining a framework for linguistic description

(Lyons, 1970). However, apart from using an empirical methodology, Bloom-field (1955) referred to the behaviorist point of view only when dealing with meaning. He believed that the analysis of meaning was "the weak point in language study," and the subject was defined to be outside the purview of "Bloomfieldian linguistics" (Lyons, 1970).

In the 1940s, the study of language disorders in schizophrenics and other psychotics served to underline the weaknesses of the behaviorist model of language in favor of viewing language as a set of complex processes. Toward the end of the decade, it became apparent that a great knowledge of linguistic theories could help provide guidelines by which to test psychological language models.

In the summer of 1951, the Social Science Research Council (SSRC) sponsored an interdisciplinary seminar on language behavior at Cornell University that brought together three psychologists and three linguists. The conferees found themselves sharing a solid foundation of methodology and interests in language phenomena. One of the consequences was the grass-fire rapidity with which the term *psycholinguistics* entered the lexicon of psychologists and linguists alike.

Further SSRC conferences were held during the next several years at various locations on such topics as comparative psycholinguistics, bilingualism, content analysis, associative processes in verbal behavior, dimensions of meaning, style in language, aphasia, and language universals. With the publication of Sol Saporta's (1961) anthology, *Psycholinguistics: A Book of Readings*, it became apparent that psycholinguistics was established, both as a term and as an important area of interdisciplinary effort.

During most of the decade between the first SSRC conference and the appearance of Saporta's reader, language analysis was largely dominated by the structural-linguistics viewpoint as it had been developed and elaborated by Bloomfield, Fries, Hockett, Pike, and others. Verbal behavior theory, which maintains that language is acquired through social conditioning, complemented structural grammar models, in which sentences are thought to be generated by means of a series of choices made from left to right, with every subsequent choice being limited by the immediately preceding words, for example, the model of a finite-state grammar described in Lyons (1970).

Phrase-structure grammar, an elaborated model of fine-state grammar, postulates that sentences are organized according to grammatical function (e.g., subject, verb, object) as well as linear sequence. In the 1950s and early 1960s, linguistic research based on phrase-structure models concentrated primarily on words as the grammatical units that determined both a sentence's linear and hierarchical order. Studies by Osgood, Suci, and Tannenbaum (1957) involved the measurement of meaning responses to individual words but neglected to consider how word meanings are combined to form meaningful statements. Psycholinguistic studies followed the lead of linguistic experiments, and, beginning with the work of Weckowitz and Blewett (1959), more than 100 studies used words in isolation, in lists, and as targets in sentences to measure the schizophrenic person's ability to attend to stimuli (Rochester and Martin, 1979, p. 12).

Laffal (1963, 1965a) conducted word-association studies as a method of analysis of contextual associates in free speech. According to Maher (1966), three assumptions that derived from the study of word association underlie Laffal's approach. First, when a particular stimulus word is presented to a subject, there are high probabilities that some, and not other, words will occur to the subject as associates of the stimulus. Second, in the absence of pathology, unusual motivation, or unusual sets, the response most likely to be produced is the one given by a large random population to the same stimulus word. Third, where there are unique sets or motivations, an unusual response will occur, the character of this response being determined by the set or motivation (Maher, 1966, p. 406).

According to Laffal (1965b):

> Two types of fault in free speech are of special interest, providing illustrations of the application of word-association models to free speech. The first is the facilitation of an unusual response by some immediately precedent response, and the second is the tongue slip. The notable feature of the response in these situations is that, despite an intention generated by the speaker, stimuli irrelevant to that intention influence the response in question. The response then, although appropriate to the generating intention, is also the product of another, incidental stimulus. (p. 79)

Laffal provides as an example an analysis of the intrusory associational processes that resulted in the inadvertent witticism "he worked in a bakery but quit because he was not rising." The appendix to Laffal's (1965b) book on pathological and normal language contains a lexicon of approximately 5,000 words listed under 114 vocabulary entries that permits an analysis of contextual associates in free speech. According to Maher (1966):

> Given this method of categorizing speech, it is possible to select a topic word—such as "female"—and tabulate all other associates that occur in conjunction with it. Laffal has applied this method to the autobiography of Daniel Schreber . . . using it to identify the contextual significance of certain key concepts in the account. . . .
>
> So far, this technique has been used to study internal significance of individual speech or writing and has not been applied to the characteristics of schizophrenic language pathology in general. However, the rationale behind it gives promise for application to that problem. (p. 407)

Raven (1958) attempted to develop empirically based categories of "verbal dysfunction" in psychotic patients, on the basis of vocabulary responses to

17 words selected from the Mill Hill vocabulary scale. Although some types of response characterized all the clinical groups, for the most part the "verbal dysfunctions" tended to be more individual and more characteristic of specific patients. Deviant tendencies and the categories of patient in which they occurred are given by Raven as follows:

Disordered syntax occurred most frequently in organic psychosis and senile dementia. For example, a patient suffering from the after-effects of a head injury said the word "View" meant: "What you can see on your own eyes as you look and regard everything you can see in the space of your own eyes."

Preservation occurred most frequently in senile dementia, but it also occurred frequently in hebephrenia, chronic leucotomotized schizophrenics, and was found to be common to, but less frequent in, all classes of mental illness. It can in fact occur under any conditions of fatigue or exhaustion.

Patients often elaborated some recurrent idea in successive responses. Thus one patient said for:—"Cruel"—"To try and believe what you really are. It's cruel sometimes to be kind." "Near"—"To cure kindness you've got to be keen on kindness. Sometimes it's cruel." "Shrivel"—"You shrivel up if you don't believe in what you say." "Chivalry"—"It's sometimes more cruel to act age instead of beauty."

Bizarre content was typical of hebephrenia, but occurred in other groups also. A good example of this is a patient who, for the word "Mingle" said: "You could say 'mingle your eyebrows with mine.'"

Rigidity of expression was noted if the same construction was used throughout successive responses. It was frequent among manic depressive patients, and occurred in manic as well as depressed phases. To a lesser extent it occurred among chronic leucotomized schizophrenics.

Poverty of expression, in which a patient's response amounted to little more than a monosyllable, was found chiefly in depressive psychosis.

Circumstantial talk occurred most frequently in seniles, and, to a lesser extent, in arteriosclerotic dementia. These were talkative, superficial, often long, unstructured responses, which never got around to the meaning of the word the patient was asked to explain or use, and sometimes digressed into childhood anecdotes.

Structurally vague responses were general to all the clinical classes. They differentiated them from healthy people, but did not differentiate one clinical class from another. These were ambiguous explanations of a word which could not be said to be grammatically incorrect, although they were comprehensible, if at all, only in an attenuated, metaphorical or esoteric sense, as for example when a patient said "Liberty" meant "Having no difficulty about doing a thing. You can do what you like on a thing. Liberty is the thing I find very easy to do. It's very easy to manage."

Distractions due to intrusions of psychological or geographical origin were general to all classes of patient. They formed a large and interesting group of responses in which either the patient's thoughts or his surroundings appeared to *distract* him from giving a satisfactory explanation of a word's meaning, or made it difficult for him to use it as other people do. It was as if excessive introversion or extraversion interfered with a person's normal explanation and use of a word. A woman, for example, said that "Virile" meant: "Manly, a person that's virile can frighten the thoughts, but they can't obey them always." Another patient said that "Perpetrate" meant: "To mess about, to waste. At times everybody perpetrates because their mind is disturbed and they can't concentrate on what they are doing"; also that "Verify" meant: "Thinking of turning round which was in his mind." As an example of an intrusion of geographical origin, one patient said "Mingle" meant: "A thing you could take—that's easy—the thing on the table," and another patient said that "Construe" meant: "you try out holding that form on a sensible rest!"

Chain Associations, Telescoped Ideas, Nonsense Words, Dissipated and Echo responses occurred in several groups, but with low frequency. Stylized Language and Negativistic responses occurred more than in some groups. (Raven, 1958, pp. 223–225)

Miller and Selfridge (1950) and Taylor (1953) investigated the "left to right" properties of structural grammar in a series of experiments using sequential constraints. Subjects were asked to complete sentences such as "The bright _____ shone for _____ first time _____ three days" in order to test their knowledge of English grammar rules. By the 1960s many studies predicated on these procedures had been conducted to test schizophrenic "verbal behavior" (Rochester & Martin, 1979, p. 15).

The studies based on structural-grammar models have been subjected to various criticisms. Although of psychological significance, these experiments are not based on linguistic models that explain how people generate or perceive language in a comprehensive, systematic way. By concentrating on subjects' responses to individual words, the studies may conceivably tap specific skills while neglecting general language processes. The underlying assumption of both the vocabulary and sequential constraint studies is that people learn the rules of English by exposure to a large repertoire of standard English sentences. However, as George Miller (1962) points out, reducing language to conditioning "treats only the simplest one percent of the psycholinguistic problem" (Rochester & Martin, 1979, p. 10).

Generative Grammar and Psycholinguistics

The foremost critic of structural linguistics has been Noam Chomsky, whose (1957) *Syntactic Structures* revolutionized the discipline of linguistics. What Chomsky did in this volume and in a subsequent critique of Skinner's *Verbal Behavior* (Chomsky, 1959) was to effectively challenge the psychological and linguistic premises underlying structural linguistics and proceed to redefine the scope and aims of grammar.

One of Chomsky's primary points is that verbal learning theory provides an inadequate and inefficient account of how people acquire language. Six-year-old children, notes Chomsky, are able to generate sentences that they have never heard uttered, and the range of their grammatical ability can, with difficulty, be accounted for by social conditioning. Chomsky stresses that language is a creative act and that the number and type of sentences that can be generated is infinite. He attributes the astounding rate and breadth of human language acquisition to an innate biological propensity that involves both conscious and unconscious processes. Grammar should, therefore, be generative and should describe the knowledge of a language that provides the basis for the formulation of all potential sentences. At best, a grammatical model should also match a native speaker's intuitions about semantic relations and distinctions. Chomsky points out that "any interesting generative grammar will be dealing, for the most part, with mental processes that are far beyond the level of actual or even potential consciousness; furthermore, it is quite apparent that a speaker's reports and viewpoints about his behavior and his competence may be in error. Thus, a generative grammar attempts to specify what the speaker actually knows, not what he may report about his knowledge" (Chomsky, 1965, pp. 109–122).

In *Syntactic Structures*, Chomsky demonstrates the inability of the left-to-right hypothesis to meet such a grammatical criterion by pointing out that syntactic associations can operate between words that are not adjacent to each other in a sentence. An example of such a sentence would be "Anyone who says that people who deny the existence of leprechauns are wrong is foolish," in which "anyone" and "is foolish" are related, although separated by a grammatical phrase. Furthermore, structural grammar gives a poor account of people's ability to process structurally ambiguous sentences, such as "Flying planes can be dangerous" or "The shooting of the hunters was awful" (Lyons, 1970).

In his generative-grammar model (Chomsky, 1957), Chomsky proposes that an adequate grammar makes most use of a small number of basic elements or kernel sentences from which an indefinitely large number of derived sentences can be generated by means of rules (called *transformations*) that rearrange the components of a word string. Such transformations involve operations like additions, deletions, permutations, and combinations that convert a sentence with a given constituent structure. For instance, specific rules change kernel sentences into their passive or negative forms.

In the modified version of his model (Chomsky, 1965), Chomsky added a semantic component that screens the output of syntactic rules and comprises "dictionary entries for individual words and projection rules for combining them according to the syntactic structure of a sentence" (Greene, 1972, p. 89). This semantic component or lexicon assigns features such as count, mass, humanness, sex, and so on to words and specifies in which syntactic contexts words can occur. As Green points out, a syntactically correct but meaningless sentence such as "Green ideas sleep furiously" would not be classified as ungrammatical at the selectional rule level, since sleep presumably requires an animate object while green can only apply to physical objects.

These rather radical observations on the nature of human language and its relation to thought led to an explosive period of research. Questions that had been thought to be impertinent during the behaviorist era suddenly became quite pertinent, and entire areas of scholarly work on language and thought had to be reevaluated. Another important event in this period was the invention of the sound spectrograph and other devices to either analyze or reproduce human speech. The ideas of the structure of language held by the behaviorists predicted that it would be feasible to design a machine that would perceive human speech and analyze it into discrete phonemes consisting of bundles of phonological features. In fact, a great deal of money and time was spent during the 1940s and 1950s on the development of such machinery, projects that continuously failed, leading the experts to conclude that human speech is much more complicated than they had imagined. The featural composition of a words such as "stop" makes it easily discerned on a sound spectrograph; on the other hand, a word such as "yellow" is not as easy for a machine to divide into distinct segments, since the spectral representation of vowels and sonorant consonants almost blend into each other in the speech signal.

During the 1960s and 1970s a great deal of growth took place in the field of psycholinguistics. First came the application of linguistic theory (in the form of generative grammar) in studies dealing with the workings of the human mind. Later came the harsh realization that, although linguists were providing relatively productive descriptions of the structural system of language, such descriptions were not really meant to be models of production. This in turn led psycholinguists, the new breed of researchers in the discipline of language and thought, to move away from the theories proposed by syntacticians, phonologists, and the like by devising their own psychologically real models and scientific approaches. Many of the experimental techniques in psycholinguistic research in use today were in fact developed during the 1960s and improved in the 1970s.

Modularity and Autonomy

The shift from purely linguistic models in psycholinguistic research led to conclusions about language and the mind that incorporated the postulation that language ability is an interactional process involving a synthesis of different informational levels in producing or perceiving language. Current research in psycholinguistics has delved deeply into the question of exactly how the processing of information takes place in the mind, and the newest models have eschewed the interactionalist theory proposing that language use is modular and the modules of grammar are autonomous (Fodor, 1987; Frazier, 1988). The perception and production of language have been shown to operate more like reflexes than like other complex cognitive processes such as problem solving. Understanding any uttered sentence is often an unstoppable process taking place almost unconsciously, even if one is engaged in a different conversation or activity.

Although theoretical linguistics does not play the essential role in psycholinguistics today it played in earlier decades, new developments in the general theory of syntax and phonology are of great pertinence to the work of the psycholinguist. The newest modification to the modern understanding of the system of language is the theory of principles and parameters, whereby language is conceived as being governed by a set of universal principles—rather than transformational rules—that determine what is and what is not an utterance with well-formed components. The parameters of human language are variables set language specifically that further delimit the set of possible well-formed strings in a given language. As Chomsky explains:

> We no longer consider UG [universal grammar] as providing a format for rule systems and an evaluation metric. Rather, UG consists of various subsystems of principles; it has the modular structure that we regularly discover in investigation of cognitive systems. Many of these principles are associated with parameters that must be fixed by experience. (1986, p. 146)

The aspects of language determined by the principles and parameters of UG are termed by Chomsky as constituting the *core* grammar, while the rest of the knowledge of language actually represented in the mind makes up the *peripheral* language. The oddities exhibited in the abnormal speech of an individual suffering from schizophrenia, to take an example, may well be components of the periphery and not the core of the grammar.

Throughout the rest of this volume we shall delve into such questions as we have raised in this chapter: how research in the field has explored the possible answers or solutions and what awaits in store for future research. This introduction will, we hope, serve as a catalyst for focus in the present, although credit to the past must admittedly be given, insofar as it is on the basis of earlier work—the accomplishments, the leaps forward, the distractions, the setbacks—that we have come to this point in current research. We also intend this analysis of the psychopathology of language and thought to serve as a starting point for others looking for insight into this and other related disciplines.

References

Balken E. R., & Masserman, J. H. (1940). The language of phantasy: III. The language of the phantasies of patients with conversion hysteria, anxiety state, and obsessive-compulsive neuroses. *Journal of Psychology, 10*, 756–786.

Benton, A. L., Hartman, C. H., & Sarason, I. G. (1955). Some relations between speech behavior and anxiety level. *Journal of Abnormal and Social Psychology, 51*, 295–297.

Bloomfield, L. (1955). *Language.* New York: Holt, Rinehart & Winston.

Brengelmann, J. C. (1960). Expressive movements and abnormal behavior. In H. J. Eysenck (Ed.), *Handbook of abnormal psychology.* New York: Basic.

Busemann, A. (1925). *Die Sprache der Jugend als Ausdruck der Entwicklungsrhythmik.* Jena: Fisher.

Busemann, A. (1926). "Über typische und phäsische Unterschiede der kategorialen Sprachform. *Zeitschrift pädagogischen Psychologie, 27*, 415–420.

Conrad, D. C., & Conrad, K. (1956). The use of personal pronouns as categories for studying small group interaction. *Journal of Abnormal and Social Psychology, 52*, 277–279.

Chomsky N. (1957). *Syntactic structures.* The Hague: Mouton.

Chomsky, N. (1959). Review of *Verbal behavior* by B. F. Skinner. *Language, 35*, 26–58.

Chomsky, N. (1965). *Aspects of the theory of syntax.* The Hague: Mouton.

Chomsky, N. (1972). Linguistic contributions to the study of mind: Past. In N. Chomsky (Ed.), *Language and mind* (enlarged ed., pp. 1–23). San Diego: Harcourt Brace Jovanovich.

Chomsky, N. (1986). *Knowledge of language: Its nature, origin, and use.* New York: Praeger.

Dalgarno, G. (1661). Ars Signorum, vulgo. *Character universalis et lingua philosophica.* London.

Dalgarno, G. (1680). *Didascalophus or The deaf and dumb man's tutor to which is added a discourse on the nature and number of double consonants.* Oxford.

Eisenson, J. (1938). *The psychology of speech.* New York: Crofts.

Fairbanks, H. (1944). Studies in language behavior: II. The quantitative differentiation of samples of spoken language. *Psychological Monographs, 56*, 41–74.

Fodor, J. A. (1987). Modules, frames, fridgeons, sleeping dogs, and the music of the spheres. In J. L. Garfield (Ed.), *Modularity in knowledge representation and natural language understanding* (Chap. 1). Cambridge, MA: Bradford/MIT Press.

Frazier, L. (1988). Grammar and language processing. In F. Newmeyer (Ed.), *A survey of linguistic science* (Vol. 2, pp. 15–34). Cambridge, MA: Cambridge University Press.

Galton, F. (1883). *Inquiries into the human faculty and its development.* New York: Macmillan.

Goldman-Eisler, F. A. (1943). A study of individual differences and of interaction in the behavior of some aspects of language interviews. *Journal of Mental Science, 100*, 97–117.

Goldstein, K. (1948). *Language and language disorders.* New York: Grune & Stratton.

Greene, J. (1972). *Psycholinguistics: Chomsky and psychology.* Baltimore: Penguin Education.

Holder, W. (1669). Elements of speech: An essay of inquiry into natural production of letters: with an appendix concerning persons deaf and dumb. London.

Jackson, H. (1879). An affectation of speech from views of the brain. *Brain, 1*, 304–330.

Johnson, W. (1944). Studies in language behavior: I. A program of research. *Psychological Monographs, 56*, 1–15.

Laffal, J. (1963). The use of contextual associates in the analysis of free speech. *Journal of General Psychology, 69*, 51–64.

Laffal, J. (1965a). Pauses in the speech of a schizophrenic patient. *Journal of General Psychology, 73*, 299–305.

Laffal, J. (1965b). *Pathological and normal language.* New York: Atherton.

Liebmann, A., & Edel, M. (1903). *Die Sprache der Geisteskranken nach stenographischen Aufzeichnungen.* Halle a.S.: Marhold.

Lorenz, M., & Cobb, S. (1953). Language behavior in psychoneurotic patients. *Archives of Neurology and Psychiatry, 69*, 684–694.

Lyons, J. (1970). *Chomsky.* New York: Viking.

Maher, B. A. (1966). *Principles of psychopathology.* New York: McGraw-Hill.

Mann, M. B. (1944). Studies in language behavior: III. The quantitative differentiation of samples of written language. *Psychological Monographs, 56*, 41–74.

Marx, O. (1967). The history of the biological basis of language. In E. H. Lenneberg (Ed.), *Biological foundations of language* (pp. 340–359). New York: Wiley.

Miller, G. (1962). Some psychological studies of grammar. *American Psychologist, 17,* 748–762.

Miller, G., & Selfridge, J. A. (1950). Verbal context and the recall of meaningful material. *American Journal of Psychology, 63,* 176–185.

Müller, F. M. (1887). *Science of thought.* London: Longman's Green.

Müller, F. M. (1890). *Three lectures on the science of language.* Chicago: Open Court.

Müller, F. M. (1907). *Three introductory lectures on the science of thought.* Chicago: Open Court.

Newman, S., & Mather, V. G. (1938). Analysis of spoken language of patients with affective disorders. *American Journal of Psychiatry, 94,* 913–942.

Osgood, C. E., Suci, G. J., & Tannenbaum, P. H. (1957). *The measurement of meaning.* Urbana: University of Illinois Press.

Preyer, W. (1894). *The mind of the child.* New York: Appleton.

Raven, C. J. (1958). Verbal dysfunctions in mental illness. *Language and Speech, 1,* 218–225.

Rieber, R. W. (Ed.) (1976). *The neuropsychology of language.* New York: Plenum.

Rochester, S., & Martin, J. R. (1979). *Crazy talk: A study of the discourse of schizophrenic patients.* New York: Plenum.

Sanford, F. H. (1942). Speech and personality. *Psychological Bulletin, 39,* 811–845.

Saporta, S. (1961). *Psycholinguistics: A book of readings.* New York: Holt, Rinehart & Winston.

Skinner, B. F. (1957). *Verbal behavior.* New York: Appleton-Century-Crofts.

Southard, E. (1916a). On the application of grammatical categories to the analysis of delusions. *Philosophical Review, 25,* 424–455.

Southard, E. (1916b). On descriptive analysis of manifest delusions from the subject's point of view. *Journal of Abnormal Psychology, 2,* 189–202.

Taylor, J. A. (1953). A personality scale of manifest anxiety. *Journal of Abnormal and Social Psychology, 48,* 285–290.

Wallis, J. (1653). Grammaticae linguae anglicanae cui praefigitur de longue la sive sonorum formatione. *Tractatus grammaticus physicus.* Oxford.

Wallis, J. (1670). A letter of Doctor J. Wallis to Robert Boyle, Esq. *Philosophical Transactions, 5*(61), 97–1087.

Wallis J. (1698). A letter of Dr. John Wallis to Mr. Thomas Beverly concerning his methods for instructing persons deaf and dumb. *Philosophical Transactions, 30*(245), 60–353.

Weckowitz, T. E., & Blewett, D. B. (1959). Size constancy and abstract thinking in schizophrenia. *Journal of Mental Science, 105,* 909–934.

White, W. A. (1926). The language of schizophrenia. *Archives of Neurology and Psychiatry, 16,* 395–413.

White, W. A. (1930). The language of the psychoses. *American Journal of Psychiatry, 9,* 697–718.

Wyllie, S. (1895). *Disorders of speech.* London: Oliver & Boyd.

Yongue, V. A model and an hypothesis for language structure. *Proceedings of the American Philosophical Society, 104,* 444–466.

Language and Cognition in Mental Retardation

Heber (1958) defines mental retardation as "subaverage general intellectual functioning which originates during the developmental period and is associated with impairment in adaptive behavior." Others, such as Sloan (1954) and, more recently, Ingalls (1978), have extended the nomenclature to include defects in the psychological and social spheres resulting from environmental deprivation. Ingalls (1978) points out that the second or "functionally" retarded group that suffers from mild retardation comes almost exclusively from the lower strata of society and constitutes a larger group than that made up by organically impaired retardates.

The extension of the nomenclature has had certain beneficial effects. For instance, it has improved the prognosis for most retardates (both organic and functional) by bringing attention to the environmental and social factors operating in language acquisition and communication. It should be noted that the view of mental retardation as an improvable condition is relatively recent. Doll, as late as 1947, held that mental retardation was "incurable." This is essentially the classical, medical (and pathological) orientation that has tended to dominate the field of mental retardation. At one time such an "incurable" interpretation was further supported by the dogma of "IQ constancy" in the field of psychological measurement. The inherent pessimism of such a pathological orientation all but obliterated the meager attempts to treat mental subnormality before the 1960s. The custodial and nonacademic approaches were direct corollaries of such a narrow interpretation of all mental retardation. It is highly questionable whether the medical diagnoses of mental retardation as resulting from "brain damage" or "neurological dysfunction" are empirically justified in the less extreme cases of intellectual impairment. Such classifications have few, if any, pragmatic implications for the treatment of the behavioral problems of concern here. Rather, a new emphasis is in order that concentrates on both the abilities and disabilities of the mentally retarded and the improvement or facilitation of the latter through the former.

Until a more reliable and valid system of classification is developed, the mentally retarded must continue to be differentiated on the basis of their performance on standard tests of general intelligence. In terms of this criterion, the mentally retarded have traditionally comprised that group of individuals with tested IQs of about 70 or below. Four levels of mental retardation have been suggested by the American Association of Mental Deficiency (Heber, 1958, p. 57): profound, severe, moderate, and mild retardation. The profoundly mentally retarded have IQs of below 20; the severely retarded, IQs of 20–35; the moderately retarded, an IQ range of 36–52; and the mild retardates, IQs of 53–68.

Stevens (1964) has characterized the profoundly retarded as exhibiting extensive impairment of the central nervous system and has noted the presence in this group of considerable organic pathology. Handicapping conditions other than mental retardation (e.g., blindness, deafness, epilepsy) are also present in the profoundly retarded. Motor development among these individuals is very poor and speech is absent. The profoundly retarded are considered "incapable of profiting from any type of training or education," and most "require life-long residential care" (Stevens, 1964, p. 4).

The severely retarded share some of the same characteristics of the profoundly retarded but to a lesser degree. Many of the severely retarded may also require intensive care. Language, speech, and motor development are also retarded in the severe group. Stevens (1964) notes further that many severely retarded individuals, particularly those with IQs between 25 and 35, can respond to and profit from systematic training in self-help skills.

The moderately retarded group presents a less complicated neuropathological picture and fewer additional handicaps than the profoundly and severely retarded groups. Language and speech show capabilities of being "developed," and potentialities for motor behavior approach normal. Self-help skills and social awareness can be taught to this group with organized formal programs of systematic training.

The mildly retarded make up the largest group among the mentally retarded—possibly as much as 85 percent of all retardates. According to Stevens (1964):

> They are usually slow in development in walking, talking, feeding themselves, and toilet training. . . . [H]andicapping conditions appear in a frequency higher than in the average general population. Motor development is relatively normal. Eye-hand coordination is somewhat retarded below normal expectancy. (p. 5)

Stevens suggests that carefully structured educational programs may help in the development of social and communication skills:

> The mildly mentally retarded can also profit from systematic training in arts and crafts and arithmetic at the elementary education level. They are incapable of completing secondary school requirements although many can participate in a special class program located in a secondary school. (Stevens, 1964, p. 5)

A system of IQ classification similar to the above system has been used in educational circles. It includes the "custodial class" of retardates (IQ below 25), the trainable retardates (IQ between 25 and 50), and the educable retardates with IQs of 50 to about 75 (Kolburne, 1965).

Before dealing with language and speech, it would be relevant to consider first some of the characteristics of the mentally retarded that speech and language specialists see as being related to the problem of language-behavior development. Schlanger (1963) has listed the characteristics that he considers important in this regard. He notes that, besides being deficient in the linguistic functions of "generalizing, associating, discriminating and manipulating verbal concepts," the mentally retarded have the following characteristics.

1. Poor auditory retention span (auditory memory)
2. Short attention span developed through negative training and/or inherent in the biological mechanism
3. Linguistic ability deficiency as demonstrated by poor grammar and minimal content
4. Perseveration in oral expression
5. Inability to transfer meanings
6. Absence of self-criticism
7. Poor evaluation and organization of perceptual cues
8. Frustration in communication activities leading to withdrawal and lowered thresholds of frustration.

Any one of the above or their combination could result in delayed language-behavior development. As Schlanger views it, the multiple possibilities for "noise" in the expressive and receptive communication process alone in the mentally regarded can cause language problems, not to mention their "inner language" retardation as well.

THEORIES OF LEARNING IN THE MENTALLY RETARDED AND THEIR RELATION TO LANGUAGE AND SPEECH DELAY

Studies on the learning abilities of mentally retarded people can be divided into two major categories according to their corresponding theory of mental retardation. Zigler (1969) identifies the two viewpoints as the "developmental theory" and the "defect theory" (Ingalls, 1978). The developmental stages for retarded and nonretarded people are similar, except the retarded person proceeds through them at a much slower rate and does not reach the same final level. The defect theory, on the other hand, postulates that mental retardation is caused by a defect in one or more mental processes rather than by a slower rate of development.

Studies based on the development theory tend to utilize retarded and normal subjects of matched mental age (MA) and look for similarities in learning abilities for each stage. Studies conducted by defect theorists rely on samples of retardates and controls matched for chronological age (CA) to find learning similarities and samples matched for MA to find defects particular to the mentally retarded group.

Kolstoe (1970), a developmental theorist, suggests that a child with an IQ of 50 will have half the learning rate of nonretarded child. Work by researchers such as Zigler (1969) further supports the developmental theory by providing strong evidence that differences in performance between matched MA samples of retardates and normals are due to motivational or emotional differences rather than cognitive ones.

However, Luria (1961), a defect theorist, argues that retarded children are particularly deficient in using verbal mediation and inner language to structure thought and behavior. Work by Ellis (1963) further suggests that retardates have a particular deficit in their memory trace, while Spitz (1966) points to an inability to organize stimulus information. Heal and Johnson (1970) have noted retardates' difficulty with the inhibition of responses, and Brown (1973) points to a dearth of mediating strategies, such as rehearsal, to aid learning and memory.

It becomes clear that the learning behavior of mental retardates must be broken down into many components and that neither the developmental theory nor the defect theory can encompass all learning skills within their individual frameworks. Each theory can be appreciated for its pertinent insights and its complementary value to the other.

STUDIES OF LEARNING BEHAVIOR

Studies on the learning behavior of mental retardates have focused on areas such as classical conditioning, discrimination learning, verbal mediation, paired-associate learning, and memory stage. The following is a brief summary of learning studies with particular relevance for the understanding of retardate language behavior.

Classical Conditioning

Experiments by Baumeister, Beedle, and Urquart (1964) and Zeaman and House (1966) compared mentally retarded and nonretarded subjects on classical conditioning tasks and concluded that there was no difference in learning between subjects of low IQ and those of average intelligence (Ingalls, 1978, p. 196). Results such as these indicate that, on the basis of galvanic skin response and other sensory perceptions, there may be little or no difference between retarded and control populations for learning simple cues.

Discrimination Learning

Snyder and McLean (1976) suggest that the language delay of retardates is due to an information-gathering deficit. This contention is supported by studies of discrimination learning, which indicate that retarded subjects have difficulty attending to relevant dimensions in discriminating between objects. A typical study by Gruen and Berg (1973) tested mildly and moderately retarded adolescents on discrimination tasks involving objects with two and three irrelevant dimensions and compared their responses with a group of non-retarded children matched for MA. In order to choose the "correct" object, the subject had to distinguish which dimension (i.e., color, shape, size, position) was relevant for a given test, after a period of trial and error. Tests introducing a greater number of dimensions to discriminate among made the choice of a relevant dimension more difficult. Gruen and Berg (1973) found no difference between retardate and control learning performance on tests involving two irrelevant dimensions. The test involving three irrelevant dimensions was more difficult for both groups; however, the nonretarded children did significantly better than the retarded ones. Zeaman and House (1963) analyzed the shape of the learning curve for subjects tested on discrimination studies and concluded that the rate of learning for retardates was the same as that of nonretarded subjects once they attended to the relevant dimension. They suggest that the overall learning delay was due to the time spent by retardates attending to the wrong dimensions.

Ullman (1974) tested to see whether the number of dimensions a subject can simultaneously see might be a factor distinguishing retarded from non-retarded subjects on discrimination tests. Using groups of nonretarded, mildly retarded, and moderately retarded children matched for MA, Ullman showed each subject a series of single stimuli that could vary on five different dimensions. After each showing, the children were asked to pick out the stimulus they had seen from 32 others. Scores were assigned according to the number of correlating dimensions between the chosen stimuli and the previously seen one. Ullman found no difference in performance between the nonretarded and mildly retarded children but a significant difference with the moderately retarded children, even though the three groups were matched for MA.

Snyder and McLean's contention (1976) of a retardate information-gathering deficit is also supported by Piaget's (1970) developmental theory. According to Beveridge and Brinker (1980, p. 49), "From the Piagetian perspective, an object will not be represented by a name until that object has been differentiated from other objects on the basis of a specific set of actions." Work by Chatelariat, Henders, and Robinson (1974; cited in Beveridge & Brinker, 1980, p. 49) demonstrates that retarded children perform more actions with objects than nonretarded children; however, the actions of the retardates are simple schemes applied indiscriminately to all objects.

Beveridge and Mittler (1977) have shown that there may be considerable differences in the way retarded children relate their language to their actions. Three retarded children who performed equally on communication tasks exhibited wide discrepancies when asked for spontaneous verbalization to describe their actions.

Another study that does not fall under the rubric of discrimination learning but is of relevance to Snyder and McLean's theory is an experiment by Hermelin and O'Conner (1975) that indicates that nonretarded and retarded children encode information in different ways. A group of nonretarded, retarded, and deaf children were presented numbers that appeared sequentially in one of three windows and were then asked to repeat the sequence of numbers. The researchers made sure that the children could say the number sequences and that their digit span was sufficient. Hermelin and O'Conner found that most of the deaf children and a portion of the mentally retarded children repeated the digits in their spatial order from left to right rather than sequentially while the nonretarded children repeated the digits in their temporal order (Beveridge & Brinker, 1980, p. 48). The authors point out that the use of a temporal strategy for encoding information is "more appropriate for decoding spoken language since there is no eidetic array which can be stored in the spatial memory (Beveridge & Brinker, 1980, p. 48). Rossi (1963) and Stedman (1963) found that retardates cluster less in recall of verbal stimulus than normals. Spatial encoding strategies on the other hand are well suited to written language, which according to Beveridge and Brinker (1980) may account for the success of language systems such as nonslip, Premack's system, and Blissymbolics with retarded children (Deich & Hodges, 1977; McLean & McLean, 1974; Harris-Vanderhein, 1977, p. 48).

Verbal Mediation Studies

Luria (1961) is a major proponent of the view that retarded children suffer from a deficit of inner language compared with nonretarded children of matched MA (see also Luria & Yudovich, 1959). A study by Lobb and Childs (1973) supports this contention by providing evidence that when retardates are encouraged to verbalize about a task their discrimination learning behavior improves dramatically (Ingalls, 1978, p. 203): 85% of the retarded subjects asked to verbalize their choice reached criterion while only 15% of the retarded group left to its own devices did so. The effect of verbalization was similar for the nonretarded group, indicating that verbal mediation training was useful for both groups. A particular deficit of inner language in retardates is implicated by studies such as Klugh and Jansen (1966), in which retarded children were less able to verbalize the solution to a problem after they had solved it than were nonretarded children.

Paired-Associate Learning

Another inner-language strategy that is thought to facilitate learning is the linkage of two or more stimuli into a formal grammatical and/or semantic relation. Prelun's (1966) study of paired-associates learning with meaningful and nonsense verbal stimuli found public school retardates to be slower in acquisition than control. Jensen and Rowher (1963) tested to see whether association training could reduce the learning differential between controls and retardates. In a now-classic study, they used paired associates of ordinary household objects for a series of tests given to mildly retarded adults. Half the subjects were asked to form a sentence utilizing the stimulus and response object. The results indicated that subjects who had received verbal mediation training were able to learn the list of paired associates in 3.5 trials as opposed to the 16.3 trials required by the control group. A follow-up study by Milgram and

Reidel (1969) asked retarded and nonretarded subjects of matched MA to generate their own mediating sentences aloud. The responses were graded according to whether (1) the relation between the stimulus and response word was solely positioned and response word was solely positional (i.e., the TELEPHONE was in the BARN), (2) the sentence expressed a meaningful interaction (e.g., the CAT spilled the MILK), and (3) the relation was both innovative and optimally appropriate (e.g., the TELE-PHONE was in the BARN so that the cows could call other cows). The results indicated that the three age levels of mentally retarded children were considerably less able to generate appropriate and complex sentences as were nonretarded children matched for MA. Work by Martyn, Sheehan, and Slutz (1969) reports similar findings, suggesting that retardates are deficient in the use of verbal mediation strategies as compared with normals (Ingalls, 1978, p. 207).

MEMORY STORAGE

During the past several decades, the perception of memory as a passive process has given way to research evidence that information storage is facilitated or in some cases rendered possible by an individual's ability to use various encoding strategies. As a result, it has been suggested by defect theorists such as Ellis (1963, 1969, 1970) that short-term memory (STM) that relies heavily on encoding strategies would be particularly deficient in retardates. Ellis (1970) distinguishes between two types of STM: primary memory, which can retain only two or three items at best and only for a few seconds, and secondary memory, in which more items can be retained over a longer period if encoding strategies such as rehearsal are used.

In an experiment comparing retarded young adults with an IQ of 61 with college students of matching CA, Ellis (1970) found no difference between the two groups on tasks requiring primary memory and large differences on tasks involving secondary memory. Ellis attributes the difference to the failure of retardates to transfer information from primary to secondary memory by means of rehearsal strategies. Follow-up studies by Belmont (1966) and Butterfield, Wambold, and Belmont (1973) produced similar results. Lance (1966) and Vergason (1964) found that, with adequate overlearning, there was no appreciable short-term retention deficit in retardates as compared with nonretarded subjects.

Work by Shepard (1967), Martin (1970), and Brown (1973) on recognition memory, in which rehearsal strategies are not applicable, has shown that the performance of mental retardates is nearly as good as that of control subjects. When retarded people are shown hundreds of pictures and afterward asked to distinguish between seen and unpreviewed images, the recognition rate is more than 95% (Ingalls, 1978, p. 212). The small amount of work that has been done on long-term memory suggests that retarded people have the same capacity for long-term memory as do nonretarded people.

THE ASSESSMENT OF RETARDED LANGUAGE DEVELOPMENT

Schiefelbusch (1963) has defined delayed language and speech as a "marked deviation from the anticipated stages" of speech development. Perhaps a more comprehensive view is afforded by McCarthy's (1964) threefold categorization:

> three languages must be acquired by a minimally sophisticated language user: receptive language, inner language, and expressive language. Receptive linguistic ability can be defined as the facility with which linguistic symbols are comprehended. Inner linguistic ability can be defined as the facility with which ideas can be expressed by linguistic symbols. (p. 3)

The most objective way at present of diagnosing delayed speech and language is through available standardized tests that tap the three linguistic abilities from various angles. The Stanford-Binet IQ is, from this point of view, a composite score reflecting verbal comprehension (receptive linguistic ability), verbal problem-solving ability (inner linguistic ability), and fluency (expressive linguistic ability). The same is true of the WISC total score IQ, but the performance-scale subscore is probably more a test of receptive and inner linguistic ability than one of expressive ability. Both the Ammons Full-Range Picture Vocabulary Test and the Peabody Picture Vocabulary Test are fairly good measures of receptive and inner linguistic ability, as they require little expressive ability aside from pointing. Although only in experimental form, the Illinois Test of Psycholinguistic Ability (ITPA) measures the communication channels of auditory or visual stimuli and motor or vocal responses. The ITPA also tests inner linguistic ability by means of memory items.

Delayed speech and language can be operationally defined with reference to all the tests mentioned above. The least ambiguous of definitions would probably be in terms of the nonintelligence tests since they are most purely measures of linguistic ability. According to the Ammons, Peabody, or IPTA, language and speech delay would refer to total performance that, when converted to age norms, showed the individual to be deviating markedly from his age group. Nevertheless, a clinical judgment is necessary.

Etiology of Language Delay in Retardates

Lenneberg (Lenneberg, Nichols, & Rosenberger, 1964) is a prominent advocate of the developmental theory of language acquisition, postulating that language deficiencies of retardates are due to a slower rate of language acquisition rather than unique kinds of language disorders. He further suggests (Lenneberg, 1967) that language skills can be acquired until puberty, after which the preliminary acquisition of language is difficult, if not impossible.

Ingalls (1978) points out that "casual observation suggests that in general the developmental theory is an appropriate description of retarded language development. Since normal children have essentially mastered their native language by the time they are 5 or 6, it would be predicted that mildly retarded people who achieve mental ages of 8 to 11 years at adulthood, should have adequate language competence and in fact this is the case. . . . The majority of moderately retarded individuals also have a good deal of functional speech, although their group presents a great many more deviations from normal (Martyn et al., 1969). Even the most severely retarded have some functional language competence, and it is only among the profoundly retarded that one finds a high proportion of individuals with no functional language at all" (p. 231).

A theory of slow-motion language development implies that mentally retarded children will have linguistic codes that correspond to those of younger normal children. To test this assumption, Lachner (1968) wrote grammars for five mentally retarded children ranging in MA from 2 years, 3 months, to 9 years, 10 months, and five nonretarded children with CAs ranging from 2 years, 8 months, to 5 years, 9 months. Lachner compared the grammars of the two groups and concluded that the nonretarded and retarded children progress through similar linguistic stages (Schiefelbusch, 1980, p. 220).

Bloom (1968, 1970) notes that all the studies of emerging grammars confirm the speculation that children learn the syntax of a language before they learn the morphological inflections of grammatical forms. Mentally retarded children should therefore have particular difficulty with morphology because of their language delay. Studies by Newfield and Schlanger (1968), Spradlin and McLean (1967), and Lovell and Bradbury (1967) indicate that mentally retarded children and adolescents did not perform as well as preschool children and first graders on morphology tests. Furthermore, the mentally retarded children made little progress in school on inflecting either lexical or nonsense words as they grew older. Lovell and Bradbury (1967) attribute the general lack of generative uses for less familiar words and forms to the paucity of social interaction as well as a slower rate of linguistic development.

Various language tests have been used to measure the receptive, inner, and expressive language ability of mentally retarded subjects. Mueller and Weaver (1964) used the ITPA to test institutionalized and noninstitutionalized retardates with an average IQ of 42 and found that retarded subjects' language age was a year below that of their mental age. Mueller and Weaver concluded that the retarded group was particularly deficient in language skills beyond their overall cognitive deficit (Ingalls, 1978, p. 232). Similar results were noted by Bateman and Wetherell (1965; cited in Ingalls, 1978). Both of the above studies find that retarded subjects scored lowest on subtests requiring language skills and highest on those involving visual decoding and visual motor association.

Newfield and Schlanger (1968) used a technique developed by Berko (1958) to test whether retarded children have particular difficulty learning rules or grammatical inflection. A study group of 30 institutionalized patients with an average IQ of 60 was compared with normal kindergarten, first-grade, and second-grade children. Each group was asked to complete sentences such as "Here is a wog, and here are two _____?" or "This bird can zig. Here it is _____." Nonsense words were used as well as regular words to compensate for cases of memorization. The normal children made 90% correct responses to real words and 72% correct responses to imaginary words, as opposed to the retarded children's scores of 48% and 29% correct responses, respectively. Newfield and Schlanger (1968) noted, however, that the degree of difficulty for the various types of inflection was the same for nonretarded and retarded children, indicating that learning of grammatical rules took place in a similar fashion.

Papania (1954) tested retarded and nonretarded children of matched MA on vocabulary with the Stanford-Binet test. While the performance of the two groups was equal regarding the appropriateness of the definitions, the retarded children consistently replied with less abstract answers than did the nonretarded children. Ingalls (1978, p. 234) points out that these results are consistent with the finding that retardates are deficient in the more complex, abstract types of learning. Studies of receptive and expressive language ability have until recently been primarily concerned with sensory deficits, the bulk of the research being aimed at estimating the extent of hearing loss and speech defects in retarded populations. Tredgold (1947) found:

Defects of hearing are fairly common in the aments and include complete deafness, tonal deafness, and word deafness. Some of these conditions may be due to developmental anomalies or disease of the peripheral organ but others are of central origin. Even when no actual deafness is present, the acuity and range of auditory perception are usually below normal. (p. 13)

A study by Birch and Matthews (1951) concluded that more than 50% of a retardate sample group numbering 249 persons ranging from 10 to 39 years of age had hearing losses and 32.7% of the losses were severe enough to cause a significant handicap. Subsequent surveys reported similarly high incidences of hearing loss in retardate populations. Webb, Kinde, Weber, and Beedle (1964) have questioned these findings by pointing out that present auditory test procedures yield apocryphal results. He cites the variability of hearing-loss figures, which depend on the test used or level of retardation tested as evidence for the tests' unreliability. Schlanger (1963, pp. 82–83) attributes a large percentage of auditory deficits to the retarded subjects' incomprehension of what is required of them during testing. He suggests that a training program aimed at increasing the retarded subjects' understanding of auditory tests will yield improved hearing responses. Fulton and Lloyd (1969) have devised a comprehensive program of audiologic differential diagnosis that attempts to take these suggestions into account (Schiefelbusch, 1980, p. 217).

Similarly, a high prevalence of speech defects has been noted in retarded populations. Martyn et al. (1969) surveyed 364 institutionalized retardates and found a significant correlation between speech disorder and IQ: 60% of the mildly retarded had speech approximating normal, while less than 2% of the profoundly retarded did. Of the latter, more than 30% had no speech at all. Keane (1972) suggests that there is no unique configuration of speech or language disorders in retarded populations or subpopulations. He points out that speech difficulties are prevalent during the early developmental stages of nonretarded children and attributes a large percentage of retardate speech disorders to the retardates' arrestment in early stages of development (Ingalls, 1978, p. 229).

There has been a trend away from the treatment of retardate speech defects such as articulation to a more comprehensive therapy that includes discriminatory, associational, and rehearsal skills that facilitate language performance. The role of social/communicative environments in the inhibition or facilitation of retardate language has also drawn increasing research attention. Writers such as Rosenberg, Spradlin, and Mabel (1961) and McNeill (1965) feel that the paucity of social exposure and communicative opportunities characteristic of retardates' lives is a major hindrance to the acquisition and use of language. The impact of social deprivation is nowhere more apparent than in institutionalized retardates, among which the frequency of speech and language disorders is significantly higher than in other retarded populations. Rosenberg et al. (1961) point out that, the more retarded the child, the greater the social isolation and the less chances for language development. Children diagnosed as having a low IQ may not be placed in a learning environment designed to teach antecedent cognitive behavior (Schiefelbusch, 1980, p. 210). McNeill (1965, 1967) suggests that retardates' difficulty with semantic features such as inflectional rules and wh-questions can be partly attributed to less experience with interpersonal language (Schiefelbusch, 1980, p. 221). A study by Beveridge and Tatham (1976) supports McNeill's contention by showing that dyadic communication can improve between retarded subjects exposed to interactional language. A group of retarded adolescents who had passed tests on comprehension and production of basic language levels but could not use language to communicate were asked to listen to other children speaking among themselves in different communicative contexts. After such exposure, the adolescents began to interact verbally, and their ability to communicate about the referential items used improved considerably (Beveridge & Brinker, 1980, p. 59). The type of social communicative situation confronting a retardate may also play a critical role in either facilitating language or inhibiting it. Beveridge and Brinker (1980) point out that "communication is not just a combination of motivation and language, but also involves confidence derived from learned responses to particular communicative environments" (p. 57). There are various accounts of retarded people learning to use their verbal skills on overcoming inhibition in new or complex social situations. Although the literature on the subject is relatively recent and anecdotal, concern with the verbal environment of retarded subjects should produce fruitful results.

Treatment therapies increasingly incorporate environments in which the retarded person can gain verbal self-confidence in various interactive situations. Miller and Yoder (1970) have designed a teaching environment that helps children to learn and talk about their most relevant needs and interests (Schiefelbusch, 1980, p. 228). Spradlin, Baer, and Butterfield (1970) have developed a program for studying and modifying the language of retarded children to increase complex language. The prognosis for language acquisition and use by mentally retarded people has improved considerably in the last two decades and should spur the development of more sensitive experimental methods and comprehensive treatment therapies.

CONCLUSION

Research on language behavior in mental retardation has generally conformed to the "two-group distinction" (Sue, Sue, & Sue, 1986), according to which *cultural-familial retardation* is presumed to be produced by normal genetic processes, by adverse environmental factors (e.g., poor living conditions), or by some combination of the two. Individuals within this group make up the lower end of the normal spectrum of intelligence and do not exhibit any of the organic or physiological conditions associated with retardation. *Organic retardation*, which accounts for approximately 25% of all cases of mental deficiency, results from anatomical or physiological defects. Intellectual impairment within this group is more severe than is found within cultural-familial retardates, and many of these persons appear different from others in both physical appearance and behavior, for example, individuals exhibiting Down's syndrome.

Studies of language development have involved individuals of both categories and have differed in theoretical perspectives between investigators who subscribe to developmental theory and those who subscribe to defect theory. Developmental theorists view mental retardation as developmental lag, whereas defect theorists support the notion that *all* retardates—not only the organically retarded—suffer from specific cognitive or physiological defects. Despite the absence of physiological etiology in most mildly retarded persons, defect theorists emphasize the inferior cognitive performance of this group to sustain their position. Thus far, research has failed to provide conclusive support for either of these theoretical perspectives.

REFERENCES

Bateman, B., & Wetherell, J. L. (1965). Psycholinguistic aspects of mental retardation. *Mental Retardation, 3*, 8–13.

Baumeister, A., Beedle, R., & Urquart, D. (1964). GSR conditioning in normals and retardates. *American Journal of Mental Deficiency, 69*, 114–120.

Belmont, J. M. (1966). Long-term memory in mental retardation. In N. R. Ellis (Ed.), *International Review of Research in Mental Retardation* (Vol. 1, pp. 219–255). New York: Academic Press.

Berko, J. (1958). The child's learning of English morphology. *Word, 14*, 150–177.

Beveridge, M., & Brinker, R. (1980). An ecological-developmental approach to communication in retarded children. In M. F. Jones (Ed.), *Language disability in children* (pp. 5–69). Baltimore: University Park.

Beveridge, M. C., & Mittler, P. (1977). Feedback, language and listener performance in severely retarded children. *British Journal of Disorders of Communication, 12*, 149.

Beveridge, M. C., & Tatham, A. (1976). Communication in retarded adolescents: Utilization of known language skills. *American Journal of Mental Deficiency, 81*, 96.

Birch, J. W., & Matthews, J. (1951). The hearing of mental defectives: Its measurement and characteristics. *American Journal of Mental Deficiency, 55*, 384–393.

Bloom, L. (1968). *Language development: Form and function in emerging grammars*. Unpublished doctoral dissertation, Columbia University, New York.

Bloom, L. (1970, January). *Semantic features in language development*. Paper presented at the Conference on Language of the Mentally Retarded, University of Kansas, Lawrence, KS.

Brown, A. L. (1973). Conservation of number and continuous quantity in normal, bright, and retarded children. *Child Development, 44*, 376–379.

Butterfield, E. C., Wambold, C., & Belmont, J. M. (1973). On the theory and practice of improving short-term memory. *American Journal of Mental Deficiency, 77*, 654–669.

Deich, R. F., & Hodges, P. M. (1977). *Language without speech*. London: Souvenir Press.

Ellis, N. R. (1963). The stimulus trace and behavioral inadequacy. In N. R. Ellis (Ed.), *Handbook of mental deficiency* (pp. 134–158). New York: McGraw-Hill.

Ellis, N. R. (1969). A behavioral research strategy in mental retardation: Defense and critique. *American Journal of Mental Deficiency, 73*, 557–566.

Ellis, N. R. (1970). Memory processes in retardates and normals. In N. R. Ellis (Ed.), *International review of research in mental retardation* (Vol. 4, pp. 1–32). New York: Academic Press.

Fulton, R., & Lloyd, L. L. (1969). *Audiometry for the retarded*. Baltimore: Williams & Wilkins.

Gruen, G. E., & Berg, B. (1973). Visual discrimination learning in familially retarded and normal children. *American Journal of Mental Deficiency, 78*, 63–69.

Harris-Vanderheiden, D. (1977). Blissymbols and the mentally retarded. In S. C. Vanderheiden & K. Grilley (Eds.), *Non-vocal communication techniques and aids for the severely physically handicapped* (pp. 120–131). Baltimore: University Park.

Heal, L. W., & Johnson, J. T. (1970). Inhibition deficits in retardate learning and attention. In N. R. Ellis (Ed.), *International review of research in mental retardation* (Vol. 4, pp. 107–149). New York: Academic Press.

Heber, R. (Ed.). (1958). A manual on terminology and classification in mental retardation [monograph supplement]. *American Journal of Mental Deficiency, 64*, (2).

Hermelin, B., & O'Conner, N. (1975). Seeing, speaking and ordering language. In N. O'Conner (Ed.), *Language, cognitive deficits and retardation* (pp. 57–71). I.R.M.M.H. Study Group 7. London: Butterworth.

Ingalls, R. P. (1978). *Mental retardation: The changing outlook*. New York: Wiley.

Jensen, A. R., & Rohwer, W. D. (1963). The effect of verbal mediation on learning and retention of paired associates by retarded adults. *American Journal of Mental Deficiency, 68*, 80–84.

Keane, V. E. (1972). The incidence of speech and language problems in the mentally retarded. *Mental Retardation, 10*(2), 3–5.

Klugh, H. E., & Jansen, R. (1966). Discrimination learning by retardates and normals: Method of presentation and verbalization. *American Journal of Mental Deficiency, 70*, 903–906.

Kolburne, L. L. (1965). *Effective education for the mentally retarded child*. New York: Vantage.

Kolstoe, O. P. (1970). *Teaching educable mentally retarded children*. New York: Harper & Row.

Lachner, J. R. (1968). A developmental study of language behavior in retarded children. *Neuropsychologia, 6*, 301–320.

Lance, W. D. (1966). Effects of meaningfulness and overlearning on retention in normal and retarded adolescents. *American Journal of Mental Deficiency, 70*, 270–275.

Lenneberg, E. H. (1967). *Biological foundations of language*. New York: Wiley.

Lenneberg, E. H., Nichols, I. A., & Rosenberger, E. F. (1964). Primitive stages of language development in mongolism. *Proceedings of the Association for Research in Nervous and Mental Disease* (Vol. 42, pp. 119–137). Baltimore: Williams & Wilkins.

Lobb, H., & Childs, R. (1973). Verbal control and intradimensional transfer of discrimination learning in mentally retarded vs. intellectually average subjects. *American Journal of Mental Deficiency, 778*, 182–192.

Lovell, K., & Bradbury, B. (1967). The learning of English morphology in educationally subnormal special school children. *American Journal of Mental Deficiency, 71*, 609–615.

Luria, A. R. (1961). *The role of speech in the regulation of normal and abnormal behavior*. New York: Liveright.

Luria, A. R., & Yudovich, F. I. (1959). *Speech and the development of mental processes in the child*. London: Staples.

McCarthy, J. J. (1964). Research on the linguistic problems of the mentally retarded. *Mental Retardation Abstracts, 1*, 3–27.

McLean, L. P., & McLean, J. E. (1974). A language training programme for non-verbal autistic children. *Journal of Speech and Hearing Disorders*, *39*, 186.

McNeill, D. (1965). *A study of word association*. Unpublished paper. Harvard University, Center for Cognitive Studies, Cambridge, MA.

McNeill, D. (1967). The development of language. In H. L. Lane & E. M. Zale (Eds.), *Studies in language and language behavior* (Vol. 4, pp. 51–62). Ann Arbor, MI: Center for Research on Language and Language Behavior, University of Michigan.

Martin, A. S. (1970). *The effects of the novelty-familiarity dimension on discrimination learning by retardates*. Unpublished doctoral dissertation, University of Connecticut, Storrs, CT.

Martyn, M. M., Sheehan, J., & Slutz, K. (1969). Incidence of stuttering and other speech disorders among the retarded. *American Journal of Mental Deficiency*, *74*, 206–211.

Milgram, N. A., & Reidel, W. (1969). Verbal context and visual compound in paired associate learning of mental retardates. *American Journal of Mental Deficiency*, *73*, 755–761.

Miller, J. F., & Yoder, D. E. (1970, April). *A syntax teaching program (STP) circa 1970*. Paper presented at the Conference on Innovative Treatment Programs, University of Oregon Medical School, Portland, OR.

Mueller, M. W., & Weaver, S. J. (1964). Psycholinguistic abilities of institutionalized and non-institutionalized trainable mental retardates. *American Journal of Mental Deficiency*, *68*, 775–783.

Newfield, M. U., & Schlanger, B. B. (1968). The acquisition of English morphology by normals and educable mentally retarded children. *Journal of Speech and Hearing Research*, *11*, 693–706.

Papania, N. A. (1954). A qualitative analysis of the vocabulary responses of institutionalized mentally retarded children. *Journal of Clinical Psychology*, *10*, 361–365.

Piaget, J. (1970). Piaget's theory. In P. Mussen (Ed.), *Manual of child psychology* (Vol. 1, pp. 703–732). New York: Wiley.

Prelun, H. J. (1966). Associative learning in retarded and normal children as a function of task difficulty and meaningfulness. *American Journal of Mental Deficiency*, *70*, 860–865.

Rosenberg, S., Spradlin, J. E., & Mabel, S. (1961). Interaction among retarded children as a function of their relative language skills. *Journal of Abnormal and Social Psychology*, *63*, 402–410.

Rossi, E. L. (1963). Associative clustering in normal and retarded children. *American Journal of Mental Deficiency*, *67*, 691–699.

Schiefelbusch, R. L. (1963). The development of communication skills. In R. L. Schiefelbusch & J. O. Smith (Eds.), *Research planning conference in speech and hearing for mentally retarded children* (pp. 119–138). Lawrence: University of Kansas Press.

Schiefelbusch, R. L. (1980). Language disabilities of cognitively involved children. In J. V. Irwin & M. Marge (Eds.), *Principles of childhood language disabilities* (pp. 85–101). Englewood Cliffs, NJ: Prentice-Hall.

Schlanger, B. B. (1963). Issues for speech and language training of the mentally retarded. In R. L. Schiefelbusch & J. O. Smith (Eds.), *Research planning conference in speech and hearing for mentally retarded children* (pp. 6–20). Lawrence: University of Kansas Press.

Shepard, R. N. (1967). Recognition memory for word sentences and pictures. *Journal of Verbal Learning and Verbal Behavior*, *6*, 156–163.

Sloan, W. (1954). *Progress report of special committee on nomenclature of the American Association for Mental Deficiency* (Annual Report) *59*, 315–345.

Snyder, L. K., & McLean, J. E. (1976). Deficient acquisition strategies: A proposed conceptual framework for analyzing severe language deficiency. *American Journal of Mental Deficiency*, *81*, 338.

Spitz, H. H. (1966). The role of input organization in the learning and memory of mental retardates. In N. R. Ellis (Ed.), *International review of research in mental retardation* (Vol. 2, 29–56). New York: Academic Press.

Spradlin, J. E., & McLean, J. E. (1967). *Linguistics and retardation.* Unpublished manuscript, Bureau of Child Research, Parson, KS.

Spradlin, J. E., Baer, D. M., & Butterfield, E. (1970). *Communications research with retarded children* (HD 00870). Bureau of Child Research, University of Kansas: Lawrence.

Stedman, D. J. (1963). Associated clustering of semantic categories in normal and retarded subjects. *American Journal of Mental Deficiency, 67*, 700–704.

Stevens, H. A. (1964). Overview. In H. A. Stevens & Heber, R. (Eds.), *Mental retardation: A review of research* (pp. 1–15). Chicago: University of Chicago Press.

Sue, D., Sue, D., & Sue, S. (1986). *Understanding abnormal behavior.* Boston: Houghton Mifflin.

Tredgold, A. F. (1947). *A textbook of mental deficiency.* Baltimore: Williams & Wilkins.

Ullman, D. G. (1974). Breadth of attention and retention in mentally retarded and intellectually average children. *American Journal of Mental Deficiency, 78*, 640–648.

Vergason, G. A. (1964). Retention in retarded and normal subjects as a function of original training. *American Journal of Mental Deficiency, 68*, 623–629.

Webb, C., Kinde, S., Weber, B., & Beedle, R. (1964). *Procedures for evaluating the hearing of the mentally retarded* (Cooperative research project, U.S. Office of Education, No. 1731). Washington, DC: Government Printing Office.

Zeaman, D., & House, B. J. (1963). The role of attention in retardate discrimination learning. In N. R. Ellis (Ed.), *Handbook of mental deficiency* (pp. 159–223). New York: McGraw-Hill.

Zeaman, D., & House, B. J. (1966). The relation of I.Q. and learning. In R. M. Bagne (Ed.), *Learning and individual differences* (pp. 33–45). Columbus, OH: Merrill.

Zigler, E. F. (1969). Developmental vs. difference theories and the problem of motivation. *American Journal of Mental Deficiency, 73*, 536–555.

3

Language Pathology in Autism and Childhood Schizophrenia

In his review of the literature on childhood schizophrenia, Kanner (1973), the original diagnostician of autism, points out that, like adult schizophrenia, childhood schizophrenia does not exist as a unitary disease entity. The singularity of the term *schizophrenia* is misleading; it refers in fact to a group of disorders that share certain common factors. This position is shared by many others, such as Shapiro, who refer to this problem as a spectrum disorder.

CHILDHOOD SCHIZOPHRENIA: ETIOLOGIES

Berkowitz (1960) designates childhood schizophrenia as a form of emotional disturbance, distinguished from autism by an initial development of communication patterns. The source of difficulty is thought to stem from a mother-child relationship of such a degree of closeness that the two function as one. As Wood (1960) states, "It is as if the child has not yet been born" (p. 44).

There is no gradual increase of independence from one another. This relationship is disrupted as the child develops psychosexually and the enforced intimacy with the mother provokes a break that leaves the child on his/her own for the first time. The problem is that the child has not developed the ability to become independent and build up defenses for self-protection because the mother has done everything; anything the child has done has been for her. Consequently, the child cannot cope with the situation and reacts violently in one of two ways: (1) he or she panics and goes into periods of self-inflicted injury or (2) there is a revulsion toward the mother, with accompanying sadistic hostility that the mother cannot overcome. If she attempts to reestablish the relationship, the child becomes panicky, but if she does not try to reestablish the relationship, the child withdraws even more. Both of these reactions are accompanied by elective mutism. The play behavior of such children reveals the inability to alter the dependence on the mother, as the child imitates all that she does. Speech and language generally reappear at a later period, either gradually, when the child goes through the entire developmental sequence, or suddenly, when the child begins speaking at the level at which he or she ceased to speak.

Kanner (1973) warns against the repercussions of a movement begun in the 1940s that discredits hereditary and biological etiologies in favor of a psychogenic theory based on the mother-child relationship:

> A sizable group of workers . . . started out with interpretations in which the mother-child relationship was put on the pedestal as the only valid etiologic consideration. Thus arose a tendency to set up a pseudodiagnostic wastebasket into which an assortment of heterogeneous conditions were thrown indiscriminately. Infantile autism was stuffed into this basket along with everything else. Such looseness threw all curiosity about diagnostic criteria to the winds as irrelevant impediments on the road to therapy which was applied to all comers as if their problems were identical. By decree, mother-infant involvement was to be accepted as the sole key to everything that goes on within and around the neonate. (p. 131)

While not dismissing a psychogenic etiology based on the mother-infant relationship, Kanner (1973) as in favor of work that "lifts disorders out of the schizophrenic package" (p. 133). As examples, he mentions work by Mahler, Bergman and Escalona, Bender, Robinson and Vitale (cited in Kanner, 1973), and Goldfarb and Dorsen (1956), in which specific symptomatologies within childhood schizophrenia are isolated, indicating different disorders. For instance, the syndrome of symbiotic infantile psychosis was first coined by Mahler to describe a disorder characterized by a " 'desperate effort' on the part of a child to avert the catastrophic anxiety of separation from the mother" (Kanner, 1973, p. 133). Bergman and Escalona described children showing an unusual sensitivity to sensory stimulation, and Robinson and Vitale singled out children "with circumscribed interest patterns" (Kanner, 1973, p. 133). Other important attempts have been to classify childhood schizophrenia according to cases with or as (1) acute or insidious onset and (2) "organic and non-organic" (Goldfarb & Dorsen, 1956), and pseudodefective, pseudoneurotic, and pseudodelinquent types. Kanner is an advocate of the view, first formulated by Bender, of childhood schizophrenia as an integration of innate physiological and postnatal emotional factors rather than as either a functional or an organic group of disorders.

LANGUAGE STUDIES

Schizophrenia language studies have been conducted largely on adults or on mixed groups of psychotic children that include autistic children. Semantics has been the area in which most abnormalities have been found (see Tucker, 1975). One of the principal difficulties in language studies involving schizophrenic children and adolescents has been gauging and/or using an appropriate level of abstractness to correspond to development stages. Clusters of semantic trends toward certain cognitive-emotional concepts, for example, the self, power, and war and peace, have been identified in adults but have not yet been searched in younger schizophrenic patients. Adult schizophrenic language has been found to be more difficult to understand by others (viz. Salzinger, 1971). This may be due, however, to a combination of deviances in semantics and in desire to communicate with others. Seekers of deviant syntax (e.g., Chaika, 1974) have been disappointed, except when confronted with the acute schizophrenic patient in a decompensated "word salad" state and/or hallucinosis. Indeed, there is evidence in work of some investigators that the syntactic system may be *overdeveloped* and/or *rigidified* in schizophrenia (Carpenter, 1976; Rochester & Martin, 1979).

Studies of Maternal Speech

The speech of the mothers of schizophrenic children has failed to receive its share of systematic scrutiny. The potential importance of such study is readily apparent when one considers the mother's role as a primary model for imitative speech efforts in the child (McNeill, 1966). Also, a substantial body of psychiatric opinion supports the position that the incompetence of these mothers in communicating thought and feeling is a major pathogenic factor in the development of schizophrenic disorders (Bateson, Jackson, Haley, & Weakland, 1956).

Goldfarb, Goldfarb, and Scholl (1966) provided the first empirical study in what one hopes will continue to be a series of fruitful investigations of this hitherto largely speculative issue. As in Goldfarb, Braunstein, and Lorge (1956), Goldfarb et al. (1966) employed the services of a speech pathologist as judge/analyst in assessing such factors as volume, rate, pitch, phrasing, intonation, and the communication of mood and meaning. These aspects of speech and language were rated on a five-point scale: (1) very poor, (2) poor, (3) fair, (4) good, and (5) excellent. The material used in the ratings consisted of children's speech samples (normal and schizophrenic) obtained in a structured situation—reading and naming pictures in a story—and the last five minutes of an open-ended interview with the mothers (of normal and schizo-phrenic children) regarding their perception of the maternal role. According to the authors, identifying information was removed from the tapes and the material was presented to the speech pathologist in random fashion.

Goldfarb et al. (1966) report the results of their comparison between normal and schizophrenic children and the comparison between mothers of normal and of schizophrenic children with regard to general evaluations of speech quality. According to the conclusions of Goldfarb et al. (1966):

> The present study supports the hypothesis that one factor affecting the aberrant speech of schizophrenic children is the influence of poor speech and communicative capacity in one of their earliest objects available for emulation and as a source of reinforcement, namely, their mothers. (p. 1227)

Klein and Pollack (1966) have taken exception to this conclusion. Their argument is as follows:

> Laudably, systematic attention was paid to eliminating rater bias by blind-rating procedures. Not so laudably, very little attention was paid to the overriding question of matching the maternal samples for age, education, I.Q., social class, and special interests, since these factors have overwhelming importance for speech and language. We are told only that the schizophrenic children were age- and sex-matched with the normal children who were "in attendance in average classes at a public school which was selected because its population is culturally and economically comparable to that of the Ittleson Center population."
>
> There is no further information as to the mode of selection of these normal children and mothers. Obviously, unless proper sampling techniques were employed, it would be possible to inadvertently select 23 specially endowed mothers from a normal school sample. This would be likely if the selection of the "normal children" sample depended on the volunteering of cooperative, psychologically oriented parents. Such mismatched maternal samples would vitiate any comparisons.
>
> The authors' conclusion implies that there is a correlation between the degree of deviant speech and language in schizophrenic children and their mothers' speech deviations. Unfortunately, no correlation coefficients were presented, and thus we have no way of evaluating the strength of the relationship: i.e., did the mothers with the poorest speech have the children with the poorest speech? The same question should be asked of the relationship of the speech and language of normal children to their mothers! (p. 232)

Infantile Autism

Early infantile autism has until recently been diagnosed as a form of childhood schizophrenia. However, Kanner warned of the dangers of a lax, interchangeable diagnosis: "It is almost impossible to see how the phenome-nologically unduplicated autistic syndrome can be disregarded in favor of the bland subscription to the idea of an equality of all schizophrenia" (Rimland,

1964, p. 67). European researchers have opted to view autism as a unique disorder, while American counterparts such as Beaujard (1958) have classified it along with other forms of childhood schizophrenia. Rimland (1964) has argued that "the many differences appearing between the two diseases provide little excuse for confusing the two classes of disorder" (p. 68). Among the differences he cites are the following five characteristics.

(1a) Autistic aloneness, or a child's inability to establish interpersonal relationships, is a primary characteristic of infantile autism. The children have been described as aloof, unemotional, and completely indifferent to their environment. Whereas schizophrenic children are perceived to be anxiously rejecting a person or situation, autistic children given an impression of "independence and self-sufficiency." Schizophrenic children are· also known for their "pathologically invasive" need of contact (Ekstein, Bryant, & Friedman, 1958, p. 59).

(1b) In terms of physical responsiveness, autistic children show minimal responsiveness to the presence of adults, usually remaining stiff in the parents' arms, without adapting their bodies to the adult's form. Schizophrenic children, however, have a "strong tendency to mold to adults like plastic or dough" (Bender, 1956; Bruch, 1959; noted in Rimland, 1964).

(2) The inability to develop language is another important aspect of infantile autism. Certain children can parrot speech but are unable to use language for communicative purposes or self-expression. The language phenomenon of pronomial reversal common in verbal autistic children is unknown in. childhood schizophrenia. The autistic child lacks a concept of self and fails to differentiate between pronouns that address him/her and those that are used for self-expression. A mother who asks her child, "Do you want some milk?" will find her question repeated word for word by the child. She must then infer whether to interpret her child's reiteration as an affirmation of her question or not.

(3) It is generally accepted that the condition of autism can be diagnosed within the first two years of life and is thought to commence at birth. Childhood schizophrenia, on the other hand, has been established to be a latent psychosis that appears after an initial period of normal development.

(4) The autistic child's response to changes in his environment is one of acute trauma. The extreme intensity of the child's response to the slightest sign of change is unique to this childhood psychosis. No similar symptoms have been noted in schizophrenic children.

Finally, (5) Electroencephalography recordings (EEGs) of autistic children are usually normal (Bradley, 1943; Van Krevelen, 1960, 1965; Taterka & Katz, 1955).

As mentioned previously in this chapter, studies of language and other functions in childhood schizophrenia have concerned themselves with both organic and environmental factors. Kallman and Roth's work (1965) on the genetic inheritance of schizophrenia conclusively discloses a high rate of psychosis in the families of schizophrenics. Bender (1953) reports as much as 40% of her parent samples to be schizophrenic or otherwise mentally disturbed.

Autism, however, has primarily been considered to be a psychogenic disorder caused by a frigid, overintellectual home environment. The unusually high socioeconomic background of the families of patients has been one of the striking aspects of the disorder. Almost without exception, the parents of autistic children have been described as outstandingly intelligent, intellectual, and having important careers. Kanner (1954) found parents to be "indisputably intelligent, functioning in society with such distinction that they are often at the top of scientific, artistic, or commercial enterprises." Parents' personalities were generally found to be unemotional, reserved, and obsessive; the latter referring to the single-minded, fixated way in which many parents pursued their careers or activities. Researchers were also surprised by the strikingly low incidence of mental illness in the families of autistic children, lower than that of the general population. The lack of physical or neurological abnormalities found in autistic children has been used as further proof that autism is a form of withdrawal resulting from the use of parents' aloofness as a model or withdrawal from an emotionally unbearable situation.

Kanner was careful to point out evidence supporting biogenic causation that was, however, mostly disregarded in favor of a psychogenic interpretation. More recently, the hypothesis of environmental induction has been increasingly challenged. Writers such as Rimland (1964) and Eisenberg (1970) point out that the evidence used to support the hypothesis of psychogenic causation can support the biogenic hypothesis equally well. Who is to say, for instance, that the genetic predisposition that makes parents obsessive and aloof cannot be passed on their children? Also, opponents state that neurological examinations are limited in what they can reveal and may be overlooking localized forms of brain damage. For instance, there are ample cases in the literature in which brain damage in psychotic patients was discovered only after death. Rimland presents the following points in favor of a biogenic hypothesis:

1. Autistic children are behaviorally unusual "from the moment of birth."
2. With very few exceptions, the siblings of autistic children are normal.
3. Some clearly autistic children are born to parents who do not fit the autistic parent personality pattern.
4. There is a consistent ratio of three or four boys to one girl.

5. Autism can occur or be closely simulated in children with known organic brain damage.
6. The symptomatology is highly unique and specific.

Rutter (1971) and Campbell, Geller, Small, Petti, and Ferris (1978) have conducted studies that indicate a great incidence of language disorder among the siblings to autistic children.

LANGUAGE IN AUTISM

The inability of autistic children to develop language skills is one of the unique and most striking features of the autistic disorder. The enigmatic nature of the disease has elicited much study and controversy despite its rarity. The necessity of distinguishing between diagnostic practices (autism vs. childhood schizophrenia) and psychogenic versus biogenic hypotheses becomes relevant in studying the language dysfunction of the autistic child. Writers such as Rimland (1964) and Kanner (1973) feel that confusing childhood schizophrenia with autism will only render the diagnosis and study of language difficulties less specific than it should be and, therefore, more difficult to understand. Whether the dysfunction is viewed as an elective mutism or as an organic disorder over which the child has no control will depend on whether one favors the psychogenic or biogenic theory.

A review and investigation by Baker, Rutter, and Bartak (1976) elaborates a spectrum of language abnormalities (in syntax, semantics, and phonology as well as communicativeness) found in autistic children. This included echolalia, lack of questions, lack of proper use of personal pronouns, shorter sentences despite occasional employment of rotely performed automatic phrases, atypical/mechanical prosody, and metaphorical (personalized) language use. The authors found, in comparing a group of autistic children with a control group of aphasic children matched for language developmental stage and IQ, that the suggestion of Rutter (one of the authors) was supported: a set of "autistic language characteristics" of which different children may exhibit different subsets. Thus, there was no specific autistic language pattern, and the differences between the two groups was a quantitative one, with different subsets of features tending to be found in each group.

Shapiro's work in this area (Shapiro, Roberts, & Fish, 1970; Shapiro & Huebner, 1976; Shapiro & Lucy, 1977) focuses on (1) echoing and (2) communicativeness—more recently on the speech-act aspect of the latter. To him, diagnostic categorizations are less important than the age or stage at which deviant development began, that is, when normal development was blocked. (In contrast to Rimland (1964), Shapiro views schizophrenia simply as a later block of the developmental path—qualitatively no different from that in autism.) Within these two categories he formulates substages of development or pathology. Assessing patients in both frameworks gives a language level that can be well correlated with future development.

Shapiro's chronometric study of echoing (Shapiro & Lucy, 1977) confirmed his hypothesis that ending of the communicative sequence is the intention in exact echoing, which thus appears as an anticommunicative speech act.

Frank's work reveals, in yet a further dimension, the defect in the communication aspects of language in autistic children by exposing (in family settings) the lack of back-and-forth dialogue and its correlates. His work reviews prior work concerning parental linguistic influence on autistic children's language development and concludes, as did Frank, Allen, Stein, and Myers (1976) and Cantwell and Baker (1977), that the "language environment" of autistic children is, if anything, richer than that of children with other developmental abnormalities. A further finding confirms others' findings, including reports by Rutter (1971) and by Campbell et al. (1978) that siblings of autistic children have a greater incidence of language disorder. A speculation stemming from these and other data is that autism represents a final common path for early deviation in object relations with a closely associated deviation in language; both genetic predisposition and pre-, peri-, and/or postnatal physical trauma and/or infection seem to combine in many or most cases (see Table 3.1).

Differences between the Language Development of Autistic and Normal Infants

Marian K. DeMyer (1979) reports studies conducted on 155 autistic children at the Clinical Research Center for Early Childhood Schizophrenia, in which mothers were interviewed concerning prelinguistic and lingual characteristics of their autistic child's communication. Care was taken to match autistic children with normals of the same age, sex, and social background who were drawn from a sample of 700 normal children. Unlike many earlier studies, DeMyer specifically describes the diagnostic criteria used to define autism. Children were diagnosed as autistic if they met the following criteria: severe withdrawal from emotional contact, desire for preservation of sameness, failure to use language for communication, and lack of apparent neurological disorders. In the sample, 75% of the children were male, and the mean average age for the group was 5 years, 4 months.

TABLE 3.1.   Milestones in Normal Speech Development from 1 to 6 Years

Chronological age (months)	Expression	Comprehension
11	Uses 1–3 *meaningful* words	Comprehends "no"
18	Uses 10–15 words	Comprehends simple one-step commands ("Give me"; "Sit down")
24	Uses 100–200 words (25% intelligible); connected phrases of 2–3 words used for a purpose ("Go bye-bye"; "Want cookie"); verbalizes immediate experiences; pronouns appear; asks "what" questions	
36	Uses 300–500 words (50% intelligible); three words per speech attempt; carries on simple conversation and verbalizes past experiences; asks "where" and "who" questions	Comprehends prepositisions and two related commands
48	Uses 600–1,000 words (100% intelligible); Four words per speech attempt; Asks "why" and "how" questions	Comprehends three related commands with practice (54 months)
60	Articles appear; asks meaning of abstract words	Comprehends abstract dependent clauses introduced by "if," "because," "when," "why"
72	Uses 1,500–2,000 words; uses compound and complex sentences	

Prelingual Communication

A1. Crying: About 27% of the mothers reported that they could not interpret the sending cries of their autistic infant and that they felt at the time that their difficulty was not due to their inexperience. Also reported was the absence of body language accompanying crying that could help the mother identify the infant's needs.

A2. Echolalia: In the sample, 52% of the parents remembered their child's babbling as different from that of the child's siblings, as opposed to 9% of the mothers of normal children having that impression. However, more than half the parents could not clearly remember the prelingual vocal, imitative skills of their children. DeMyer mentions a study by Irene Stephens, who imitated the progressive stages of echolalia for mothers rather than ask them about their infants' early babbling. The mothers' recall was improved, and in all cases they reported that their autistic child had not babbled normally (DeMyer, 1979, p. 53). Ricks and Wing (1975) taped vocalizations of infants of seven sets of parents, each of whom spoke a different language. Care was taken to record responses to normal situations, such as "frustration, greeting, and pleased surprise." Parents were able to identify the sounds of children brought up in the other language households but could not understand autistic children's babble and vocal utterances.

Echoing the speech of others, as DeMyer (1979) notes, is a prominent feature of the speech of normal 18-month-old infants. The 21-month-old child repeats a single word said to him or her or the last word of a phrase addressed to him or her. At two to two and a half years of age, echolalia persists, but none of the child development specialists include echolalia as a normal feature of speech.

In autistic children, however, echolalia is often delayed and begins to increase after the third birthday, a time at which the normal child can use 300–500 words (with 50% intelligibility), say three-word sentences, carry on a simple conversation, ask where and who questions, and understand prepositions and related commands. DeMyer reports that 45% of the autistic children at 2.5 years old had never used a sentence in their lives and that those who did almost always used echolalic sentences.

MORE DIFFERENCES IN THE LANGUAGE DEVELOPMENT
OF YOUNG AUTISTIC AND NORMAL INFANTS

Cunningham and Dixon (1961) reported a study of the language behavior of a single autistic boy (age seven years) in a standard situation such as that employed by McCarthy (1930) and Sampson (1945) in their studies of language development in normal children. As Wolff and Chess (1965) have stated:

> Both Sampson and McCarthy found that quantitative and qualitative aspects of language were closely related. As children grow older they produce more words, more different words and longer utterances, and their language changes in quality such as the completeness of sentences and the parts of speech used. Adopting Piaget's (1969) functional classification of language into egocentric and socialized, McCarthy found that quantitative changes are closely related to functional changes. Both authors conclude that the total number of words uttered by a normal child in a standard situation is a good index of his general level of language development. It is interesting to note Sampson's observation that strong feeling often increased the motivation of normal children to communicate, and that this improved their standard of verbal expression. (p. 29)

Over a period of six months, Cunningham and Dixon collected observations of the language behavior of their autistic subject and conducted qualitative and quantitative analyses of the data in accordance with the functional classification schema of Piaget. The results presented and discussed in Cunningham and Dixon (1961) indicate a markedly lower level of development, despite the resemblance of the autistic child's language to that of a normal 24- to 30-month old child in certain quantitative respects (length of utterance, variety of words used, etc) and in many qualitative respects (monotony, frequency of incomplete sentences, frequency of use of nouns, rarity with which questions were asked or information given). Also, egocentric speech appeared much more frequently than is common in the speech of a normal 2.5–3-year-old child. The authors observed in conclusion that the autistic subject showed some progress during the six-month period of study, as gaged by McCarthy's and Sampson's criteria.

DeMyer divides the entire group into three sections between 3 and 6.5 years of age: (1) 64% had no useful speech at all; (2) about 25% used echolalia fairly regularly and in some instances used it communicatively; and (3) in 12% of the group echolalia was used more often as a communicative mode.

Word loss was frequent among 25% of the autistic children who had used words (noncommunicatively) between the ages of 11 months to 3 years. Of the 16 children who had stopped using words, only four (25%) had regained use of words and made some progress thereafter. There were 12 children who did not entirely cease using words, and nine of them had made some progress by interview time. Nearly all autistic children with enough speech to rate had one or more of the following abnormalities: reduced frequency of speech (about 90%), poor diction (about 80%), disorder in rhythm, tone, or stress ("dysprosody," about 75%), and too fast a rate of speech (about 13%).

In the introduction to his *Language of Autistic Children* (1978), Churchill notes that language depends on "precision skills" which "include the ability to make subtle sensory discriminations accurately and consistently, to associate certain stimuli with each other accurately and consistently and to transfer information 'bits' across various input and output channels. . . . The child's later ability to abstract, classify, and use these words metaphorically does not obviate these later requirements" (p. 9).

Descriptive studies of autistic language skills have been followed by attempts to pinpoint where language ability breaks down. Is the disease primarily a sensory disorder, an inability to integrate different sensory inputs into a meaningful whole, or a cognitive defect, a failure to interpret integrated sensory inputs and translate them into verbal symbols? Or is autism an elective mutism by which the child rebels against his parents? The early appearance of language difficulties reported in the descriptive studies mentioned previously tend to negate the latter hypothesis, as do studies such as Creak's (1972) who reported that "autistic children showed increased autistic withdrawal when they failed to understand a verbal request and increased compliance when they understood." She concludes that "much of the time, the autistic child is neither simply unwilling nor uninvolved but wholly at a loss" (DeMyer, 1979, p. 50).

One of the first sensory disorders suspected of causing autism is that of partial or complete deafness. Pronovost (1961) conducted a descriptive study of the speech and language comprehension of 12 autistic children who were observed over a period of two years in a residential setting. The author noted in his introduction a few of the problems encountered in dealing with autistic children: "The highly variable behavior of the autistic children precluded the use of formal testing procedures. In addition, no behavior rating scales that could appropriately describe the details of the behavior of autistic children were available" (Pronovost, 1961, p. 228). Finding it impossible to devise a situation that would dependently elicit speech from his autistic patients, Pronovost obtained speech samples from the tape recordings of regular therapy sessions, which were then subjected to analysis in order to obtain descriptions of the children's speech.

Among the five children on whom Pronovost reported briefly, where was a wide range of inter- and intrasubject variation in language behavior: babbling, echolalia, perseverative repetition of unidentifiable sounds, and rote repetition of number sequences, rhymes, or scraps of song. On the other hand, at least one of the children was able to produce complete sentences with well-articulated sound patterns but sentences that were totally irrelevant to the situation.

As part of his pilot study, Pronovost developed a rating scale to take the place of standard tests of linguistic comprehension that, for obvious reasons, could not be used with these children. According to the author, "The items of the scale are questions which may be answered by observation of the children and were designed to explore certain aspects of auditory discrimination of environmental sounds, response to gestures, and response to music, as well as to various aspects of spoken language" (Pronovost, 1961, p. 230). Observations were supplied by the three therapists who were in daily contact with the children.

On the basis of information supplied by the therapists using a rating scale (for details on the scale see Pronovost, 1961, pp. 228–233), Pronovost offers the following conclusions:

> The observed autistic children exhibited definite ability in certain aspects of language comprehension. They were able to discriminate environmental sounds and voices of adults. They were unable to recognize the names of people, objects and actions. However, comprehension of abstract or complex language was extremely limited, except in the case of one child who had developed the ability to read words by matching them with pictures. This child had limited response to environmental sounds and none to music. All other children exhibited considerable interest in and response to musical sounds. (Pronovost, 1961, pp. 231–232)

Pronovost identified his project as a pilot study, and there is no particular point in conducting a detailed criticism of its many shortcomings and weaknesses—the lack of adequate identifying information on his autistic patients, the absence of obvious controls, the failure to impose reliability checks on his raters, the lack of quantification, and so on. In these respects, Pronovost's study is typical of many descriptive studies in the clinical area that originate, one strongly suspects, in the ready and convenient access of the investigator to a particular group. Unfortunately, even when they are properly conceived and executed, they are often no better than suggestive; at worst, they can be definitely misleading.

Churchill conducted studies in which autistic children were systematically taught and tested on an experimental nine-word language (9WL) in order to screen for deficiencies in the child's linguistic ability. Children were tested individually, each acting as his own control so that assistance could be "both varied and subtle." A child started with simple tests requiring visual, auditory, and sensory discrimination between two objects or words, with new words being added to the tests according to the child's progress. Churchill's general conclusions are the following:

1. Autistic children can be systematically tested with the 9WL. There is no such thing as an untestable child. It is always possible to obtain consistent, predictable performance provided the tasks are made simple enough. Even the lowest functioning child in the series (Charles) displayed reliably measurable performance at the lowest level of testing for visual discrimination.

2. Children's responses on the 9WL showed all the properties of an operant, i.e., lawful relationships to discriminative and reinforcing stimuli which differed in no way from those relationships which are already well known. Some children already knew the basic nine words, and it remained only to rather quickly demonstrate the obvious (Jonathan, Leon, Edgar, Orson, Curtis, Steve). Where some or all of the basic nine words had to be learned, this was facilitated through the use of differential reinforcement, discriminative stimuli, temporary restriction of the stimulus array, and manipulation of reinforcement schedules (e.g., Charles, Carl, Edward, Manuel, Stan).

3. Lower functioning autistic children reached an impasse at some point on the 9WL grid. There appeared to be at least three types of impasses:

(a) Some children had channel specific deficits, i.e., they conditioned readily to auditory stimuli but not to visual (Carl, Stan) or vice versa (Andrew, Betsy, Leon);

(b) Other children appeared to reach an impasse in relation to particular parts of speech. For example, Stan was facile with nouns and adjectives but required extraordinary training to master verbs. Carl, mute but extremely dextrous and agile, mastered all three verbs in two sessions, while requiring 186 training sessions to reach criterion for nouns. Manuel and Steve, though, not color blind, showed no difficulty in learning either nouns or verbs but had great difficulty learning adjectives.

(c) A third type of impasse was seen even in the absence of channel deficits or difficulties with particular parts of speech. This type appeared to involve a *limited "capacity"* to deal with compounded stimuli. To illustrate, some children knew all nine words perfectly, but if two of these words were put together they would display surprising difficulty in responding correctly to two familiar elements simultaneously. Adding a third word made it worse (e.g., Manuel). This was in contrast to most children who, once they learned words singly, could combine them in 2- and 3-word combinations without extra training. Some of these impasses were surmountable with extraordinary additional training; more commonly, it was not possible to elicit "higher" performance beyond these impasses even using training measures which tested the limits of our imaginations. This was commonest with channel specific deficits.

4. Children who moved through the 9WL in minimum time and without impasses, when examined concerning higher language functioning, also displayed other impasses in such things as generalization and classification, cross-referencing and syntactic transformations.

5. Each child was unique. This cliche takes on meaning when it is seen that each child generated a profile of linguistic abilities and disabilities which were special to him. Through highlighting certain similarities between children, subgroups may be tentatively suggested. One way to subgroup children would be according to the type of impasses described above. A broader conceptualization would divide those children who displayed serious difficulty of whatever sort in their basic conditionability of precision skills as detected by the 9WL from those children who displayed no such difficulty on the 9WL but reached other impasses at higher levels of language functioning.

6. A child's responding was ordinarily found to be patterned and stable, given a suitable reinforcement schedule, regardless of whether the task at hand had been mastered or not. In other words, stable patterned responding was observed not only when a child had "learned" a task but also when he was "working at it" but still making many errors.

7. The most interesting information may be derived from a close scrutiny of stable error patterns. Thereby it often could be inferred that a child was operating according to a recognizable "strategy." His errors were not ordinarily random and chaotic. An autistic child, working comfortably within the confines of the 9WL, was not unpredictable and "out of contact." He was, as it were, experimenting with his world! And that can be observed on close

scrutiny of almost any portion of the children's work which is presented in the following chapter.

8. Errors became less patterned and more random or "diffuse" at times, and seemed to signal one or two happenings:

(a) increasing frustration, manifested by longer latencies, avoidance and tantrum behavior, and "giving up" (Orson, Manuel); or

(b) as a prelude to task mastery (Jonathan, Stan, Earl). The former occurrence was simply a matter of poor training technique. In the latter case, it was as if an old theory or strategy were being given up and a new one taking its place.

9. Two characteristics of error patterns were rather general across children:

(a) Given a compound stimulus, i.e., one which contained two or more parts of speech, there was evident a sequence effect. The last word was responded to correctly, while the first word was often missed. For example, a child might know all adjectives and nouns of the 9WL. Given the stimulus "red block," he would respond consistently to block but erratically to red. Changing the stimulus to "block red" would result in his responding with consistent correctness to red and missing block. This sequence effect was ordinarily independent of the part of speech involved unless the child had displayed particular difficulty with particular parts of speech.

(b) Introduction of new words (even within the same part of speech) to a recently-mastered stimulus array often resulted in a loss of "old skills." For example, a child demonstrating 100% accuracy with a stimulus array which was limited to two objects would, upon introduction of a third object, begin making errors with all three objects, old and new alike (e.g., Carl, Jonathan, Stan, Earl).

10. Learning usually occurred rather suddenly, as if in all-or-none fashion. Newly learned tasks were then performed consistently, with short latencies and with accuracy approaching 100%.

VOCAL PATTERNS OF AUTISTIC AND SCHIZOPHRENIC CHILDREN

The studies reviewed in the preceding section were primarily concerned with gross characteristics of language behavior in autistic children, abnormalities of syntax and semantic content. We now examine the findings of research on some nonlexical aspects of language behavior in schizophrenic children. The first of these studies represents one in a series of investigations on speech patterns in the schizophrenic conducted by Goldfarb and his associates.

In the introduction to Goldfarb et al. (1956), the authors expressed dissatisfaction with the instruments available at that time for the objective analysis of speech and voice production "except for specific articulatory deviations" and cited their justification for selecting instead a speech patholo-gist to serve as listener and recorder in their study: "In the last analysis, judgments regrading speech rest on a recognition of the hypothetical normal as a referent. It was presumed that the speech expert had had wide experience with normal speech and was capable of reacting to deviations from such normal speech" (p. 545).

Subjects included 12 schizophrenic children and six with "reactive behav-ior disorders." The median age in each group was slightly greater than eight years of age. Diagnostic criteria were not stated by the authors.

The primary data for the study consisted of tape recordings of spontaneous utterances, together with observations of the communication behavior of the children in various individual and group settings. Records were phonetically transcribed, then subjected to an intensive analysis by the speech pathologist for purposes of identifying patterns of articulation. It should be noted that the speech expert's examination was a "blind analysis," that is, one made without knowledge of the clinical status of the subject.

Comparison of the two groups indicates that the schizophrenic children surpassed the children with reactive behavior disorders in every category of speech deviation except voice quality. The authors noted that vocal qualities such as breathiness, hoarseness, nasality, throatiness, and so on do not appear to differentiate the two groups. However, they did note that "a kind of speech flatness" seems to characterize the schizophrenic children, whose voices were described as "dull and wooden."

Flatness of voice refers to the fact that the schizophrenic children were not effective in communicating feeling to the listener by means of voice qualities. According to the authors, "Flatness appears to be compounded of insufficiency of volume, pitch, rhythm, stress, and intonation" (Goldfarb et al., 1956, p. 550).

It is interesting to compare the above account with the "acoustic stereo-type" described as a "flat voice" by Ostwald (1963). The flat voice, according to Ostwald, "is the sound of patients who are listless, resigned, and depressed. No matter how convincingly such patients tell you (in words) that there is nothing wrong with them, their soundmaking says the opposite" (p. 67). Ostwald suggests that such a sound pattern seems to announce para-linguistically the patient's helplessness and dependency. In terms of the physi-cal description, Ostwald says:

> One might think of this configuration as acoustic energy which is smeared out rather evenly across a broad portion of the frequency spectrum. Flatness of the curse denoting this energy portion seems to be the distinguishing characteristic of the acoustic stereotype we are here dealing with. (p. 70)

The common factor identifying the six patients whose speech samples provided these curves is depression. The reason for this discrepancy between these two interpretations of what characterizes a "flat voice" seems to lie in the acoustic dimensions employed by the respective investigators. Ostwald's analysis plots sound intensity against frequency; Goldfarb employs, in addition to volume and pitch, the variables of rhythm, stress, and intonation. On a purely impressionistic basis, one is tempted to say that minimal variation in the latter three would tend to elicit judgments of flatness, even when peaks are noted in the middle of the spectrum of sound energy. Ostwald (1963) has provided a detailed description of an eight-year-old autistic boy named Bob.

> From a soundmaking point of view, the most remarkable thing about Bob is his very personal use of spoken language. When he speaks it is not with the sentence or word patterns one customarily hears in conversation. He does not ask questions, give replies, render descriptions, or make complaints. Instead, emission of speech sounds appears to be mainly a self-directed activity. Bob's soundmaking seems to be a kind of acoustic game, much like the babbling of babies which has little to do with the sort of communication aiming for outsider participation. Particularly with proper nouns, like the names of other persons, Bob does something very peculiar for a boy his age: he repeats, rhymes, and endlessly shuffles and reshuffles the component sounds (the phonemes and morphemes) of the words. In effect, in this boy's mouth, names lose all significance as labels for things and people.
>   Bob also tampers with other parts of speech. By incessantly distorting the rhythmicity, intensity, pitch, tone, speed, shape, and orderliness pattern of spoken language he makes it impossible for any listener to put the linguistic cues—phonemes, morphemes, and words—into any properly meaningful relationships. He seems to lack the capacity for adhering to those linguistic constraints which control verbal soundmaking, but instead produces sounds because they rhyme, resemble each other onomatopoeically, or are simply fun to mouth. (p. 129)

Ostwald rules out the possibility that Bob's speech abnormalities are a reflection of retarded language development. Bob shows at least a normal capacity to understand instructions or commands, and he even demonstrates verbal precocity in the playing of his favorite game, "alphabet." He mimics television advertising slogans and jingles ("I use pumolive rapinshave," "I use superblue blade"), but with a fine disregard for linguistic precision (e.g., the dropping of the plural phoneme /z/ in "blades") and complete indifference to the uncommunicative impact of such constructions on his auditor. As in the case of poets, the meter in Bob's discourse fights to displace the argument.

    In much the same manner as a skilled double-talk artist, Bob indulges in wordplay that comes close to pseudolanguage. As Ostwald puts it, "He strings a sequence of phonemes together in such a way that this resembles the sound of words but never actually comes close enough to known words to make sense" (Ostwald, 1963, p. 130). The effect of such pseudolanguage is to create an

almost intolerable conflict for others—an "ambivalent, double bind situation"—
in which Bob seems simultaneously to invite and reject communication with his
plausible sounding but meaningless utterances.

On the other hand, there are times when Bob seems to experience a sense
of frustration from his inability to use language normally. At such times he may
go through an insistent, repetitive pattern of sound making that involves, as
Ostwald calls it, "one of his typical phoneme-salads" (e.g., /aiskob-aiskob-
aiskob/), or engage in acoustic outbursts that suggest a desire to be relieved of
some intensely felt internal pressure. Ostwald provides the graph of a half-
octave band measurement of Bob's speech before and during one of these
outbursts, which partly resemble a baby's crying; he analyzes the pattern as
follows:

> A dashed curve denotes the linguistically comprehensible utterance "where is my
> doctor," uttered in a blunt, aggressive-sounding flat voice. Acoustically, this sound
> shows motant 1 rather broad and centered at 250 cps [cycles per second]; motant 2 is
> flat-topped in the center of the acoustic spectrum; motant 3 comes to a peak at 2,000
> cps. Compare this with the solid curve which denotes a robust cry-like outburst "I use a
> razor" that comes to a climax on the first syllable of "razor:" Motants 1 and 2 are fused
> into one large area of acoustic energy concentration centered at 500 cps which reaches a
> level of 67 decibels. There is a second very prominent area of energy concentration
> centered at 2,860 cps. The cry-like sound (8.3 sones) is 25 percent louder than the more
> normal sound (6.2 sones).
>   Half-octave band measurement of some of Bob's nonsense jargonizing shows even
> more clearly the resemblance between this patient's soundmaking and the cry-sound of
> young babies. The fragment denoted here is the sound /aiskob/. The first part, /ais/, is
> emitted in a scream-like manner that shows no clear differentiation of motants but
> simply a sharp peaking of acoustic energy at 715 cps. . . . The second part, /kob/, has
> more the acoustic characteristics of speech in that the fundamental tone is defined as
> motant 1 at 250 cps, while resonance energy is found in motant 2 centered at 715 cps.
> (Ostwald, 1963, pp. 131–133)

The importance of kinetic factors in the total behavioral picture of the
autistic child is apparent in the accounts of both Goldfarb and Ostwald.
Goldfarb, Braunstein, and Lorge (1956) reminds us that spoken language is
normally reinforced by facial and body gestures. With regard to the subjects in
his study, they state:

> Inadequate and unrelated language reinforcements characterize each of the 12 schizo-
> phrenic children and never characterize the six children with reactive behavior dis-
> orders. The schizophrenic children show what has ofttimes been called wooden features
> and, often, staring, unseeing eyes. Not only are the larger muscles of the face
> unmoving, but also the pupils usually are rigidly fixed in an almost pathognomonic and
> persistent dilatation. Facial and body gestures unrelated to the spoken word are evident
> in the inappropriate smile, bizarre mannerisms, giggling and "pogo-stick" jumping.
> (Goldfarb et al., 1956, p. 548)

Ostwald (1963) similarly talks of the grimacelike quality of his patient's facial expressions, his tendency to dart around the room or remain too long in an immobile posture, or his habit of moving his hands in a strange and repetitive way, "suggesting that he is engaged in doing something meaningful, but that he cannot get others to share this meaning by communicating it in a code they understand" (p. 129).

MODIFICATION OF LANGUAGE BEHAVIOR IN AUTISM

Autism and other forms of severe language retardation have long been resistant to treatment by traditional approaches. Several investigators, however, have reported initial success in the establishment of language behavior in autistic children through the use of operant conditioning procedures (Hewett, 1965; Lovaas, 1966; Lovaas, Freitag, & Kinder, 1966).

The procedures employed in these studies are similar to those used in animal research, which probably accounts for their effectiveness: We are dealing with children who behaviorally resemble the infrahuman subjects of the operant laboratory. The conditioning methods follow the operant experimental paradigm of successive approximations and include:

1. Determination of the reinforcer to be used (which is then empirically verified).

2. Magazine training, during which the positive reinforcer is paired with a highly discriminable stimulus (e.g., a buzzer) in order to produce an effective conditioned reinforcer.

3. Reinforcement of any verbalization. As soon as verbalizations begin to occur in increasing frequency, imitative verbal conditioning is initiated.

4. Reinforcement of imitative verbalizations. In this stage of the program, the psychologist says a word or utters a sound (depending on the known response repertoire of the child). Initially, any verbalization following the psychologist's utterance is reinforced. These verbalizations are gradually shaped so that the child is reinforced only for speech that is in direct imitation of that of the psychologist.

5. Reinforcement for imitative object identification. After imitative verbalization is brought under stimulus control, imitative verbal identification of simple objects is initiated. In this stage of the program, the psychologist presents a small toy object, such as a ball, to the child and names the object. The child is then reinforced for repeating the name of the object.

6. Reinforcement for spontaneous object identification. As soon as the subject is imitating the names of objects consistently, the objects are presented

to the child and the child is asked, "What is it?" The child is reinforced for correct identification. If the child does not name the object correctly, the psychologist identifies it for him/her. Then the child is asked again to name the object. These prompts by the psychologist are gradually faded out as the subject correctly identifies the objects.

7. Reinforcement for functional application of conditioned speech. After spontaneous object identification has been conditioned, the child is then reinforced for using speech functionally in sentences, for example, repeating "put the ball in (on, under) the box," and then following the instructions properly.

Lovaas et al. (1966) reported a study involving two autistic children who were both limited to echolalic behavior before the project and who exhibited the usual bizarre symptoms of autism. The work of Lovaas and his colleagues was done within a reinforcement paradigm, but they added a few unique modifications.

They instituted a rather intensive program. The children "worked" from 8:00 to 11:30 A.M., with three 10-minute recreation breaks, another rest period from 11:30 A.M. to 1 P.M., then another "working" period from 1:00 to 5:00 P.M., with four 10-minute breaks, for six days a week. The training was carried out in ward bedrooms that were familiar to the children. The adult and child were seated in chairs facing a table or in chairs facing one another.

In the first part of the program, the psychologist presented verbal or nonverbal stimuli, to which the child generally responded incorrectly if at all. The psychologist would then prompt the child to respond with the correct behavior, after which he would supply reinforcement. On successive trials, the prompting was faded out. Negative reinforcement in the form of loud yells and sometimes a slap were used primarily to suppress the child's inattention and self-stimulation, both of which were very high during the first week or two.

The original positive reinforcer was food. The child's meals were fed to him in small portions by the psychologist as reinforcement for correct responses during training. Each bite of food was accompanied by verbal approval and caressing the child. The ratio of primary (food) and secondary (approval) reinforcement was manipulated systematically until finally both children were receiving only social approval. With Rick, the 7-year-old boy, this was accomplished in 12 days; with Pam, the 9-year-old girl, it took almost 10 months before the food could be removed completely.

Within two months from the beginning of the program, the children's echolalia had been extinguished, they had learned the upper- and lower-case letters of the alphabet, they had learned to read one simple book, and they could verbalize descriptions of objects and actions seen in magazines and books.

In her *Parents and Children in Autism* (1979), DeMyer reports that

Creedon (1973) has taught simple sign language to autistic children between the ages of four and 10 years while simultaneously teaching them words. She used operant conditioning techniques of rewarding first partial and then correct performances with food, desired objects, and social approval. Parents were also taught the method. According to Creedon, "All children have used signs for their immediate needs and affective states. They have varied in acquisition rates and ability to combine words in sentence form." It is now generally accepted that if a child does not learn to use speech for communication by the age of six or seven years, it is unlikely that he will ever be able to do so. The results of these training experiments are an impressive demonstration of the efficacy of an approach which has recorded successes in an area where success is extremely rare. However, most researchers will agree with Churchill's statement that so far "those few autistic children who appear to progress further in language development do so by virtue of inherent developmental factors rather than training wizardry." (p. 129)

REFERENCES

Baker, L. D., Rutter, M., & Bartak, L. (1976). Language in autism. In S. Ritvo (Ed.), *Autism* (pp. 121–149). New York: Spectrum.

Bateson, G., Jackson, D. N., Haley, J., & Weakland, J. (1956). Toward a theory of schizophrenia. *Behavioral Science*, *1*, 251–264.

Beaujard, M. (1958). La schizophrenie infantile: Expose de quelques travaux americains contemporains. *Annales Medico-Psychologie*, *116*, 785–804.

Bender, L. (1953). Childhood schizophrenia. *Psychiatric Quarterly*, *27*, 663–681.

Bender, L. (1956). Schizophrenia in childhood: Its recognition, description and treatment. *American Journal of Orthopsychiatry*, *26*, 499–506.

Berkowitz, R. (1960). *The disturbed child*. New York: New York University Press.

Bradley, C. (1943). Biography of a schizophrenic child. *Nervous Child*, *1*, 141–171.

Bruch, H. (1959). Studies in schizophrenia: The various developments to childhood schizophrenia. Psychotherapy with schizophrenics. *Acta Psychiatricae Neurologica Scandinavica Supplementation* 34 (no. 130).

Campbell, M., Geller, B., Small, A. M., Petti, T. A., & Ferris, S. H. (1978). Minor physical anomalies in young psychotic children. *American Journal of Psychiatry*, *135*, 573–575.

Cantwell, D. P., & Baker, L. (1977). Psychiatric disorder in children with speech and language retardation. *Archives of General Psychiatry*, *34*, 583–591.

Carpenter, M. D. (1976). Sensitivity to syntactic structure: Good versus poor premorbid schizophrenics. *Journal of Abnormal Psychology*, *85*, 41–50.

Chaika, E. (1974). A linguist looks at "schizophrenic" language. *Brain and Language*, *1*, 257–276.

Churchill, D. W. (1978). *Language of autistic children*. New York: Halsted Press.

Creak, M. (1972). Reflections on communication and autistic children. *Journal of Autism and Childhood Schizophrenia*, *2*, 1–8.

Creedon, M. P. (1973). *Language development in nonverbal autistic children using a simultaneous communication system*. Chicago: Michael Reese Hospital. (ERIC Document Reproduction Service No. EDO 78624)

Cunningham, M. A., & Dixon, C. (1961). A study of the language of an autistic child. *Journal of Child Psychology and Psychiatry*, *2*, 193–202.

DeMyer, M. K. (1979). *Parents and children in autism*. Washington, DC: Winston.

Eisenberg, L. (1969). Child psychiatry: The past quarter century. *American Journal of Orthopsychiatry*, *41*, 371–379.

Ekstein, R., Bryant, K., & Friedman, S. W. (1958). Childhood schizophrenia and allied conditions. In L. Bellak & P. K. Benedict (Eds.), *Schizophrenia* (pp. 555–693). New York: Logos.

Frank, S., Allen, D., Stein, L., & Myers, B. (1976). Linguistic performance in vulnerable and autistic children and their mothers. *American Journal of Psychiatry*, *133*, 909–915.

Goldfarb, W., Braunstein, P., & Lorge, I. (1956). A study of speech patterns in a group of schizophrenic children. *American Journal of Orthopsychiatry*, *26*, 544–55.

Goldfarb, W., & Dorsen, M. M. (1956). *Annotated bibliography of childhood schizophrenia and related disorders as reported in the English language through 1954*. New York: Basic.

Goldfarb, W., Goldfarb, N., & Scholl, H. (1966). The speech of mothers of schizophrenic children. *American Journal of Psychiatry*, *122*, 1220–1227.

Hewett, P. M. (1965). Teaching speech to an autistic child through operant conditioning. *American Journal of Orthopsychiatry*, *35*, 927–936.

Kallman, F. J., & Roth, B. (1965). Genetic aspects of preadolescent schizophrenia. *American Journal of Psychiatry*, *112*, 599–606.

Kanner, L. (1954). To what extent is early infantile autism determined by constitutional inadequacies? *Proceedings of the Association for Research on Nervous and Mental Disease*, *33*, 378–385.

Kanner, L. (1973). *Childhood psychosis: Initial studies and new insights*. Washington, DC: Winston.

Klein, D. F., & Pollack, M. (1966). Schizophrenic children and maternal speech facility. *American Journal of Psychiatry*, *123*, 232.

Lovaas, O. I. (1966). A program for the establishment of speech in psychotic children. In J. K. Wing (Ed.), *Early childhood autism* (pp. 115–144). London: Pergamon.

Lovaas, O. I., Freitag, G., Kinder, M. I. (1966). Establishment of social reinforcers in two schizophrenic children on the basis of food. *Journal of Experimental Child Psychology*, *4*, 109–125.

McCarthy, D. A. (1930). *The language development of the pre-school child*. Minneapolis: University of Minnesota Press.

McNeill, D. (1966). Developmental psycholinguistics. In F. Smith & G. A. Miller (Eds.), *The genesis of language* (pp. 15–84). Cambridge, MA: MIT Press.

Ostwald, P. F. (1963). *Soundmaking*. Springfield, IL: Thomas.

Piaget, J. (1969). *The psychology of the child*. New York: Basic Books.

Pronovost, W. (1961). The speech behavior and language comprehension of autistic children. *Journal of Chronic Diseases*, *13*, 228–233.

Rimland, B. (1964). *Infantile autism: The syndrome and its implications for a neural theory of behavior*. New York: Century Psychology Series.

Rochester, S. R., & Martin, J. R. (1979). *Crazy talk: A study of the discourse of schizophrenic speakers*. New York: Plenum.

Rutter, M. (Ed.). (1971). *Infantile autism: Concepts, characteristics and treatments*. London: Churchill Livingstone.

Salzinger, K. (1971). An hypothesis about schizophrenic behavior. *American Journal of Psychotherapy*, *25*, 601–614.

Sampson, O. C. (1945). A study of speech development in children of 18–30 months. *British Journal of Educational Psychology*, *26*, 144–201.

Shapiro, T., & Huebner, H. F. (1976). Speech patterns of five psychotic children now in adolescence. *Journal of Child Psychology, Psychiatry, and Allied Disciplines, 15,* 278–293.

Shapiro, T., & Lucy, P. (1977). Echoing in autistic children: A chronometric study of semantic processing. *Journal of Child Psychology, Psychiatry, and Allied Sciences, 14,* 373–378.

Shapiro, T., Roberts, A., & Fish, B. (1970). Imitation and echoing in young schizophrenic children. *Journal of the American Academy of Psychiatry, 9,* 548–567.

Taterka, J. H., & Katz, J. (1955). Study of correlation between electroencephalographic and psychological patterns in emotionally disturbed children. *Psychosomatic Medicine, 17,* 62–72.

Tucker, G. (1975). Sensory motor disfunctions and cognitive disturbances in psychiatric patients. *American Journal of Psychiatry, 132,* 17–21.

Van Krevelen, D. A. (1960). Autismus infantum. *Acta Paedopsychiatrica, 27*(3), 97–107.

Van Krevelen, D. A. (1965). Autismus infantum and autistic personality: Two clinical syndromes. *Japanese Journal of Child Psychiatry, 6,* 29–41.

Wolff, S., & Chess, S. (1965). An analysis of the language of fourteen schizophrenic children. *Journal of Child Psychology and Psychiatry, 6,* 29–41.

Wood, N. E. (1960). Language development and language disorders: A compendium of lectures. *Monographs of the Society for Research and Child Development.*

4

The Language of the Psychopath

Personality abnormalities vary considerably in severity of symptoms and degree of maladjustment to society. But as Bromberg (1948) pointed out, "The group that supplies the most comprehensive and unmistakable illustrations of maladjustment to social life comprises those persons referred to as psychopathic personalities" (p. 54). Of all the recognized psychiatric syndromes, that of the antisocial personality, or psychopath, presents perhaps the greatest number of unsolved questions. Although it has long been recognized that each of us possesses an innate capacity for momentary dissociation vis-à-vis the accepted value systems of society and to such a degree is potentially psychopathic, true psychopaths, with their consistently antisocial behavior, present the average observer with a phenomenon so spectacularly alien that it seems almost incredible that such people can exist. And, granted that psychopaths do indeed exist, it is perplexing how they can manage to appear superficially sane, how they are able to wear, as one observer put it, the "mask of sanity." The true psychopath compels the psychiatric observer to ask the perplexing and largely unanswered question: "Why doesn't that person have the common decency to go crazy?"[1]

Given the mixture of awe, horror, and perplexity that the true psychopath evokes, it is perhaps not surprising that research into the etiology, course, and

---

[1]Since psychopaths have developed an extraordinary capacity to act as though they were perfectly sane, they must be skilled in a cunning manner to dissociate any real guilt that they might feel about their antisocial behavior. If they fail to dissociate, they would then be forced to face the guilt as most others would. In this sense, they lack the "common decency to go crazy," for that is what they would do if they really felt the guilt.

psychological mechanisms specific to this syndrome has lagged far behind that of other psychiatric classifications. When psychiatrists have such difficulty grasping the essentials of the picture that is presented, researchers can only have greater difficulty in finding an overall interpretive scheme around which to organize their research questions. Indeed, far too little is known about how the psychopathic character structure comes about, how it utilizes social experience to perpetuate its fundamentally antisocial outlook, and how it often manages to secure highly stable social niches in which both accomplices and subgroup prestige can be found.

TOWARD A DEFINITION

It seems feasible, for the first objective, to attempt a generalized picture of what the psychopathic personality entails. Lipton (1950) pictured the psychopath as "an individual who is ill equipped from birth to meet the demands of his environment. He may be looked upon as in a defective state with a constitutional lack of responsiveness to the social demands of honesty, truthfulness, decency and consideration for others. This is coupled with an inability to profit by experience." Coleman (1956) wrote, "This category applies to individuals who are not classifiable as mentally defective, neurotic or psychotic, but who manifest a marked lack of ethical or moral development and an inability to follow socially approved codes of behavior" (p. 337).

Probably the most complete definition has been constructed by Cleckley (1949), according to whom a psychopath is a person who may be described as follows:

1. He is free from the signs or symptoms generally associated with psychoses, neuroses, or mental deficiency. He knows the consequences of his antisocial behavior, but he gives the impression that he has little real inner feeling for that he verbalizes so rationally.
2. He is habitually unable to adjust his social relations satisfactorily.
3. The psychopath is undeterred by punishment; in fact, he desires it.
4. His conduct is often lacking in motivation, or if a motive can be inferred, it is inadequate as an explanation for the behavior.
5. He expresses normal affective responses but demonstrates a total lack of concern and callous indifference toward others.
6. He demonstrates poor judgment and an inability to learn by experience, which is seen in "pathological lying," repeated crime, delinquencies, and other antisocial acts. "Patients repeat apparently purposeless thefts, forgeries, bigamies, swindlings, distasteful or indecent acts in public, scores of times." (Cleckley, 1949, p. 415)

One main concern that disturbs some writers, and one that should be mentioned here, revolves around a conception that the psychopath may be neurotic. Pescor (1948), for instance, wrote that most psychiatrists concede that psychopaths are not neurotic, although some may develop a neurosis or even a psychosis at a later date. Some psychopaths, he said, add to the confusion by malingering insanity in order to escape punishment for their violations of the law. Yet other writers, such as Abrahamsen (1960), maintain that the psychopath definitely displays a neurotic "character disorder." Some will argue that many psychopaths commit crimes as a consequence of a strong feeling of guilt that they attempt to expiate through hoped-for punishment. To distinguish this type of "neurotic" from the ordinary neurotic, the term *neurotic character* has been proposed as a substitute for the psychopathic personality, but this has not really solved anything. Suffice it to say that the differences of opinions still exist and neither point of view can be completely ruled out at this point. Pescor (1948) attempted to resolve these differences in opinion by suggesting that "the psychopath vents his emotional tension on his environment, whereas the neurotic turns his emotional tension on himself. The one injures society, the other injuries himself" (p. 7).

McCord and McCord (1956), who also argued for a difference between the neurotic and the psychopath, explained the confusion by the fact that the psychopath is often confused with the "acting out" neurotic because their symptoms are so similar, that is, the behavioral symptoms of aggressiveness and asociality are common.

Psychopathic Types

Many authors have seen value and merit in categorizing different types of psychopaths. Given some of the formidable difficulties involved in understanding psychopathic behavior, it would seem advantageous to present a diagnostic classification of the psychopathic personality. For the most part, the following categories are those proposed by Bromberg (1948).

Paranoid Psychopath. Such individuals are characterized by the persistent feeling of being constantly discriminated against by everyone. They are tense in their manner and continually on the alert for adverse reaction toward themselves, and much of their energy is aimed at righting fancied wrongs or improving the unhappy situation in which they constantly imagine themselves. A distinction must be made between the psychotic individual whose judgment is so distorted by delusions of persecution as to be mentally ill and the psychopath whose feelings of being prevailed upon do not pass beyond a paranoid attitude. In both cases the criminal acts in which such individuals become involved are usually of an assaultive nature. However, the paranoid psychopath in whom persecutory attitudes are not channeled into delusions often becomes involved in crimes such as blackmail and extortion, which entail verbal rather than physical aggression. The psychology of the paranoid individual is marked primarily by a feeling of grandiosity and secondarily by a tendency to react aggressively toward others. They are basically quarrelsome and litigious but do not carry it to the point of actual delusions of persecutions.

Schizoid Psychopath. The schizoid personality encompasses many levels of psychopathology, varying from complete psychosis to attitudes of aloofness and introversion. Although the characteristics of schizophrenic psychosis are present, these individuals generally remain in contact with reality. They are the type of individuals who run away from situations, the shut-ins and the daydreamers. Contrary to what might be a natural conclusion, schizoid personalities do commit aggressive crimes. In contradistinction to other types of psychopathic offenders, schizoid personalities who commit crimes are likely to be more seriously affected in terms of intellectual and emotional disintegration. In murder, for example, the mental disorders can be traced to inner conflicts in the offender, which lead to delusional formations and become externalized on the victim. The victim becomes a symbolic representative of the murderer's self.

Aggressive Psychopath. These individuals are given to episodes of explosive anger, irritability, destructiveness, and the like. Their emotional equipment is insensitive, and their ethical standards are blunted to a degree that justifies their being included under the diagnosis of psychopathic personality. They are "enemies of society," displaying an attitude of social aggression beyond what is considered normal.

Psychopathic Swindler. These persons display marked asocial or amoral trends. Their antisocial activities begin at an early age. They lie, steal, cheat, and break promises repeatedly without the slightest compunction. Extremely selfish, they tend to think the world revolves around them and their desires. They are unresponsive to kindness. They are unwilling to accept blame and are totally irresponsible.

Sexual Psychopath. The sexual psychopath suffers from a serious distortion of sexual impulses, which produces the need for immediate gratification. Struggling with the restrictions of society, such individuals finally discard their inhibitions and succumb to their urges. Many of them may be well adjusted in all except the sexual sphere. They may have good educations, hold excellent jobs, and command the respect of their communities until their sex habits are disclosed. On the other hand, there are some, "like the sadists who commit sex murders, mutilate their victims and perpetrate other atrocious crimes, who are more dangerous to the public than a mad dog" (Pescor, 1948, p. 7).

One further point should be given a brief comment. Although it has not been included in the major divisions above, the "cyclothymic personality" should not be completely overlooked. These individuals are given to periods of depression alternating with periods of hyperactivity and elation, but not seriously enough to be recognized as manic-depressive psychotics.

Symptoms

On the whole, the psychopath is likable on first acquaintance. Although seemingly intelligent, these persons lack the depth, sincerity, and wisdom present in the truly intelligent person. Such individuals are often found living in a series of present moments without real consideration for past or future and with a callous disregard for the happiness of others. Coleman (1956) summarized the wide range of symptoms:

1. Inability to understand and accept ethical values, except on a verbal level, or to pursue socially accepted goals.
2. Marked discrepancy between level of intelligence and conscience development.
3. Egocentric impulsiveness, irresponsibility, lack of restraint, and poor judgment. Prone to thrill-seeking, deviant sexual patterns, and other unconventional behavior.
4. Inability to profit from mistakes and ordinary life experiences except by learning to exploit people and to escape punishment.
5. Inability to forego immediate pleasures for future gains and long-range goals. Hedonistic, lives in the present without consideration of past or future. Unable to withstand tedium and prone to nomad-like activities and frequent changing of jobs. External realities used for immediate personal gratification.
6. Ability to put up a good front to impress and exploit others. Often a charming, likeable personality with a disarming manner and ability to win the liking and friendship of others. Often good sense of humor and generally optimistic outlook. Prone to social climbing.
7. Defective interpersonal and general social relationships. Individual usually cynical, unsympathetic, ungrateful, and remorseless in his dealings with others. Usually shows a history of difficulties with educational and/or law-enforcement authorities. No close friends.
8. Rejection of constituted authority and discipline. Individual behaves as if social regulations did not apply to him and refuses except on a verbal level, to take any responsibility for his actions. Often shows considerable repressed hostility toward constituted authority or society in general, which may manifest itself in impulsive, hostile criminal acts. Many times drifts into criminal activities but is not typically a calculating professional criminal.
9. Quick ability to rationalize and project the blame for his socially disapproved

behavior. Lack of insight into his own behavior. Lies readily even though he
knows he may eventually be found out by friends and acquaintances
10. Irritating, disappointing, and distressing to others. Is frequently a great burden upon family and friends and creates a great deal of unhappiness for others.
Often promises to change but rarely does so permanently—incorrigible.
(Coleman, 1956, p. 338)[2]

It is interesting to note that these symptoms, Abrahamsen (1944) maintained, are most generally found in young people. More precisely, Abrahamsen
contended that the peak age for the psychopath is about 20 years of age, with the
age distribution varying from about 15 to 35 or 40. He explained that it has been
found that the psychopath frequently shows intelligent superiority that, to an
extent, has a bearing on a possible early sexual maturity. Emotional instability,
he says, is normal in the formative period of life. In a psychopathic person the
emotional instability is more pronounced. The individual reaches this instability earlier than the normal person and remains in such a condition long after
normal individuals have reached their state of normal mental and social
stability. This is why the psychopath is emotionally immature, impulsive, and
aggressive, resembling a spoiled, incorrigible child. This instability begins in
childhood, reaches a peak in young adulthood, and then dies down in the late
twenties and early thirties.

PSYCHOPATHY TODAY

For the purposes of this discussion, the term *psychopathy*, as opposed to
other synonymous terms such as *sociopath*, for example, is preferred precisely
because of its wide range of meanings in ordinary parlance. What we are at
present concerned with is a whole continuum of behavior ranging from what
might be called "normal psychopathy" or "pseudopsychopathy" to the horrific
extreme represented by the "antisocial personality," or the "true psychopath."
Cleckley pointed out as early as 1941, in his *Mask of Sanity*, that each of us
possesses in rudimentary degree the distinctively psychopathic capacity *not* to
respond to the salient moral or social requirements of a situation. A gang of
unruly 12-year-olds cutting up during a school outing to Carnegie Hall to hear
Mozart are behaving psychopathically, noted Cleckley, as are we all when we
momentarily break ranks with our conscience to laugh at what we otherwise
hold in highest reverence. Nor is such a capacity intrinsically bad. To paraphrase a point made by Cleckley, were it not for this ability to break ranks with

[2]Reprinted from *Abnormal Psychology and Modern Life* by James C. Coleman. © 1964 by Scott,
Foresman, and Company, Chicago.

our conscience occasionally, we would all be in danger of turning into pompous monsters of self-righteousness.

This said, it is important that we first acquaint ourselves with the extreme pole of the continuum occupied by the "true psychopath." This term indicates something more than a tendency to care about others only as a means to one's own self-centered aims; it indicates a *lack of capacity* to do otherwise. The true psychopath is lost to humanity, utterly incapable of human concern and involvement with others except at the most superficial and exploitative level.

It is important to distinguish the true psychopath from the career criminal, at least as an ideal type (there is clear overlap). Career criminals rely on superiority and cunning to gain wealth; they feed their ego on the fear they evoke and on their own ability to get things "done" outside the encumbrances of the law. Nonetheless, career criminals are quite capable of feeling empathy and concern for their immediate family and for their partners in crime. Moreover, they rely on the support of others and are capable of erecting and adhering to formal procedures for inclusion within the peer group. They are concerned with winning admiration and praise from their criminal partners, and they speak in derogatory and contemptuous terms of their victims. In short, they manifest salient characteristics of group identification and group loyalty. True psychopaths, by contrast, are typically a bust, even as members of an organized criminal ring; they cannot be relied on, they make unnecessary trouble, and although they may be useful for carrying out specific acts of a usually unseemly nature, there is no question of obtaining their long-term loyalty. When trouble arises, the psychopaths are the first to go, something that career criminals understand and for which they typically plan expeditious means. (New York City police are still investigating the murder in a midtown Manhattan restaurant of Irwin Schiff, wheeler-dealer and conman extraordinaire. The further the investigation proceeds into the incredible trail of extortion, bribery, and swindles that is Schiff's sole legacy, the harder it has become to fix a single motive for his death. Seemingly, everybody who ever knew him, including career criminals and ordinary businessmen, had something to gain by killing this man.)

Some progress in portraying the psychopath at a phenomenological, descriptive level has been made in the third edition of the *Diagnostic and Statistical Manual of Mental Disorders* (DSM-III) of the American Psychiatric Association. Among the criteria needed to merit a diagnosis of antisocial personality are the following: an inability to sustain consistent work; an inability to function as a responsible parent (evidenced by misconduct such as feeding children inadequately and failing to obtain medical care for a seriously sick child); a failure to respect the law (pimping, dealing drugs, fencing); an inability to maintain an enduring attachment to a sexual partner (desertion, promiscuity); a failure to honor financial obligations; a failure to plan ahead (impulsive traveling without prearranged job, destination, or time limit); aggressiveness (assault, wife beating, child abuse); a disregard for the truth (aliases, conning); and recklessness (drunk driving). It takes the presence of at least four of the nine criteria over a sustained period of time to merit the diagnosis, *plus* an onset before the age of 15 as manifested by a childhood history marked by such behavior as persistent lying, vandalism, theft, chronic fighting, truancy, repeated substance abuse, poor educational achievement, and so forth. (The behavior must not be due to mental retardation, schizophrenia, or manic episodes, a diagnostic point that need not concern us further.)

DSM-III declares that, although such antisocial individuals may present a stereotypically normal mental status, most frequently there are signs of person distress—including complaints of tension and depression, an inability to tolerate boredom, and the conviction of the hostility of others (which is of course a predictable consequence of their own behavior). The interpersonal difficulties these people experience and the discordant modes that they suffer persist far into midlife and beyond, even though their more flagrantly antisocial behavior, most especially assaultiveness, typically begins to diminish by the time they pass 45 or 50 years of age. Invariably there is a markedly impaired capacity to sustain any kind of lasting, close, normal relationship with family, friends, or sexual partners. Such individuals, in fact, generally cannot become independent, self-supporting adults without persistent criminal activity and outside the penal system. However, some who warrant this diagnosis are able to achieve a degree of political or economic success—the "adaptive psychopaths"— and to outward appearances, their day-to-day functioning is not characterized by the impulsivity, hostility, and general chaos that typify the general syndrome.

The problem of the adaptive psychopath is especially elusive, since such people come to psychiatric attention late and only after they have run seriously afoul of the law. (And an indeterminate number of them, an elite subgroup, have simply never been caught; thus, they have never been examined psychiatrically.) Accordingly, it is impossible to get a clear picture of how they functioned during their period of ostensibly normal adjustment. Apparently, whether by virtue of superior endowment or because their survival was facilitated by adopting an outwardly compliant facade, their educational development was substantially less hampered than is typically the case. Theodore Bundy, the notorious serial killer who was executed in Florida in 1988, had attended law school and become active in California politics. His truly horrifying career as one of the nation's most prolific serial murderers was incomprehensible to many who knew him during this phase of his life, though even then his temper was considered to be hair-trigger. Nonetheless, it should be observed that, although the enigma of the adaptive psychopath remains largely unsolved, such people are known to show certain hallmarks of the general syndrome, most especially the characteristic search for seeking thrills through dangerous behavior, an attitude of omnipotence typically expressed in a feeling that they will never get caught, and an innate dissociative capacity that among other things enables them to demarcate periods of frankly antisocial behavior from their "normal" periods.

We might note in passing how many of the points raised in previous diagnostic schemes are echoed in the contemporary diagnostic criteria. Thus, DSM-III subdivides the prodromal phase of a childhood "conduct disorder" into four subdivisions: unsocialized aggressive, socialized aggressive, unsocialized nonaggressive, and socialized nonaggressive. The first and third of these subgroups clearly invoke two of Henderson's subgroups, his aggressive and inadequate types. Then, too, the early onset of the syndrome—before age 15—coupled with the typical, though not invariable, lack of educational achievement, is suggestive of the heredity taint of older systems; this observed lack of achievement would superficially appear to be linked to a general incapacity in intellectual functioning. (The elusive adaptive psychopath, meanwhile, is reminiscent of the genius-criminal of Nordau's typology.) As well, though such a finding has no status in the contemporary diagnosis per se, Henderson's observation of frequent nonspecific brain abnormalities continues to be borne out with observations on a portion of this population. Finally, the overall lack of concern with others, manifested in every facet of life, coupled with the remarkable failure to learn from experience, is indeed suggestive of an intrinsic defect for which "moral imbecility" is an altogether-apt term. As for the implicit realization of the Royal Commission on the Feeble Minded that *all* treatment had proved ineffective, this too has been confirmed by subsequent clinicians. Harry Stack Sullivan (1953a) summed up his experience thus:

> I am afraid I cannot overcome my conviction that the real psychopathic personality is a very serious miscarriage of development in early life, so grave that it makes a very favorable outcome possible only with an almost infinite amount of effort, which in turn, I guess no one will ever be worth. By and large, I expect to find the psychopathic personality already clearly marked off, and expect it to continue without any great change except for a slow increase in the amount of hostility that it engenders in others and the bitterness and sometimes alcoholism, which it engenders in the person himself. (p. 360n)

THE MEPHISTO SYNDROME

In what follows, we attempt to identify the salient characteristics of the psychopathic syndrome with a view to establishing a taxonomy of psychopathic processes. Several points need to be made at the outset. We are far from believing that the underlying cognitive, conative, and emotional processes described below are unique to the psychopath; rather, we think in the first place that they represent gross exaggerations of tendencies found in everyone and in the second place that even in their pathologically exaggerated form they are present in other syndromes (e.g., the type and quality of dissociative processes exhibited by the psychopath can also be found in multiple-personality disorders). What is unique to the psychopath in our view is the combination of these processes, which discriminates true psychopathy from other syndromes. This said, it should also be noted that we are far from believing that ours will be the last word on the subject. Much research needs to be done, particularly in the areas of potentially predisposing neuropsychological factors and etiologically significant environmental variables. It is enough for our purposes if the following discussion captures some of the essence of psychopathy and does so in a way that allows meaningful generalization to what we term "the psychopathy of everyday life."

Let us begin at the level of discriminating characterological traits and then work our way down to the underlying processes. In our view, the following four salient characteristics—thrill seeking, pathological glibness, antisocial pursuit of power, and absence of guilt—distinguish the true psychopath.

Thrill Seeking

Psychopaths habitually rush in where angels fear to tread. The more dangerous an undertaking, the more irresistible it becomes. This behavior cannot be classified as merely impulsive, since it often entails planning and in a surprisingly large number of cases it includes the cooperation of an accomplice. But such planning as does occur does not mitigate the element of danger. There is some evidence to suggest that psychopaths have unusually high thresholds for perceptual stimulation. Certainly, their overt behavior suggests that only in situations of threat and danger do they feel truly alive. The world of predictable cause and effect, of instrumental acts and expectable rewards, has no emotional meaning to them; they grasp that this humdrum, predictable, and boring world exists, but they cannot relate to it. (Adaptive psychopaths have taken this to a paradoxical extreme: They can go about their routine duties precisely because they have turned them into a dangerous game of charades, of passing for normal, while in their off-hours they live an entirely different life.) Much of what Sullivan (1953a, 1953b) and other have observed of the psychopath's inability to learn from experience has to be related to this characteristic: Life would be less dangerous, and thus much less enjoyable for psychopaths, if they really allowed themselves to "learn" and thus "know" the altogether-likely consequences of their behavior. True psychopaths prefer an open-ended world: Whether they take off in their car cross-country with no planned destination or time of expected arrival or whether they merely say something shocking and outrageous in conversation, they are looking to create situations of ambiguity and potential danger.

We might pause here to distinguish psychopathic thrill seeking from the pursuit of excitement used by normal people to offset boredom. On a continuum of thrills, one might rate tennis relatively low and ice hockey, with its sanctioned violence, relatively high. But for true psychopaths, even ice hockey is boring, given the fact that there are too many rules. Psychopathic thrill seeking consists in breaking the rules, whatever they may be, or else in surreptitiously making up new rules. At a poker table, psychopaths do not want to win; they want to cheat and get away with it. That is, they want to turn the game into a new game, one in which they make the rules. Theirs is the "Mephisto Waltz" on the tightrope of danger.

Pathological Glibness

Psychopaths invariably speak well, colorfully, persuasively, and volubly about themselves and their past, although only minimally about their future. What is said, however, has no discernible relation to facts. There is a kind of "semantic dementia," as Cleckley (1976) has termed it, the point being that the ordinary emotional demands of a situation make no impression on psychopaths. Like rowdy schoolboys at a concert, they behave as though the accepted meanings of a situation were simply not present. But the same dissociation is also manifested in their speech; words have become detached from meaning and serve instead as means of placating a dangerous foe or of fleecing an unwary victim. By the same token, they do not allow themselves to be moved by words and concepts that others value.

Hare (quoted in Goleman, 1987) has conducted recent research using evoked brain potentials while the subject responds to words quickly flashing before his or her eyes. Hare interprets his results to mean that psychopaths have a shallower understanding of the meanings of words, particularly the meanings of word tokens having to do with emotional terms.

It is sometimes said that pathological glibness is to be found only in intelligent psychopaths. To the contrary, what distinguishes intelligent psychopaths is their greater productivity and their greater effort at maintaining consistency. The basic trait, however, can be found at all levels of intelligence within the syndrome. Hence the experience of one of the authors with an institutionalized, borderline-retarded psychopath: Having just raped a fellow patient, the psychopath promptly accosted the author at the door of the ward with a moving tale of woe about how the attendants were planning to gang up on him for no good reason. (We include further examples below in the section "The Manipulation of Meaning in the Communication of Deceit.")

Antisocial Pursuit of Power

Not only are psychopaths extremely sensitive to power relations and extremely interested in obtaining maximum power for themselves, but they also seem hell-bent on using power for destructive ends. Only in paranoid states and in the attitudes of career criminals can a comparable fusion of antisocial trends and the power drive be seen. It is as though, for psychopaths, power can be experienced only in the context of victimization: If they are to be strong, someone else must pay. There is no such thing, in the psychopathic universe, as the merely weak. Whoever is weak is also a sucker, that is, someone who demands to be exploited. Thus, when inmates seized control of the New Mexico State Penitentiary some years ago, they not only murdered but also mutilated selected victims. Afterward, one of the suspected ringleaders was interrogated at length. While being careful not to incriminate himself, he made it clear that the victims of the uprising "didn't understand morality." He also implied that he and his cronies ran the prison anyway and that, apart from the freedom to leave, they enjoyed every advantage they had maintained on the outside. The prisoners, given room to maneuver by legal reforms designed to safeguard their rights, had in effect created a psychopathic universe in which the strong preyed on the weak in the name of "morality." To be sure, the fusion of the power drive and antisocial trends in the psychopath need not always be so bloodthirsty (violence per se is not a distinguishing trait of the syndrome). Consider the young man who explained that he stole cars because it was the only thing he was good at—and everyone needs to be good at something.

Absence of Guilt

Psychopaths are aware that certain people at certain times will bring punitive sanctions to bear against them. Accordingly, they are skilled in evasion and rationalization. Some, gifted histrionically, can even feign remorse. But they do not feel guilt. The absence of guilt is essential to the syndrome for, as is immediately apparent on reflection, guilt, besides being a consequence of certain acts, is also a deterrent against committing those same acts in the future.

Psychopaths are undeterred; indeed, just those salient characteristics that to others would portend guilt as a consequence, to psychopaths promise the excitement of danger. And when psychopaths are caught, they are profoundly uncomprehending. Moreover, when one investigates the absence of guilt clinically, one discovers a general poverty of affective reactions. The young man who stole cars could distinguish only two feelings in himself, boredom and inadequacy. All other feelings were "for suckers."

If we combine these four characteristics—the absence of guilt, the antisocial pursuit of power, superficial glibness and thrill seeking—we have what might perhaps best be called the "Mephisto syndrome." Indeed, it is hard to resist the impression that the true psychopath is a personification of the demonic. Since time immemorial, humankind has outlined in figures of the demonic an inherently human capacity to fuse despair and drive discharge in an antisocial posture; the devil has always served as a personification of what as intrinsically social creatures human beings cannot afford to be. But it is precisely the inhibiting sense of being intrinsically social—Adler's capacity for social feeling—that psychopaths lack. They are not social, only superficially gregarious; not considerate, just polite; not self-respective, only vain; not loyal, only servile; and down deep, they are really quite shallow. In a word, they are fundamentally asocial beings. Hence the observed homologies with the figures of the demonic: The psychopath is free to be what ordinary humans dare not to be. For nonpsychopaths, the figure of the devil is always experienced as a projection, as something outside the ego. For the psychopath, the demonic is a way of life. Moreover, just as the devil has evolved through the centuries and has in the process of that evolution acquired a whole host of representations, ranging from the truly bestial all the way to the suave, silk-clad sophisticate of the comedy *Damn Yankees* and the philosophic troublemaker of George Burns's portrayal in *Oh God, You Devil*, so too can the presenting façade of the psychopath range from the grotesquely animallike all the way to the sweet-talking confidence man.

GROSS CHARACTERISTICS OF PSYCHOPATHIC LANGUAGE

As in the case of the specific syndromes we have already reviewed, there have been a number of attempts to discover relations between nonverbal behavior patterns and characteristics of language behavior in the psychopath. We examine one of these studies in some detail, then refer to the experimental literature that has accumulated within the past several years with regard to verbal learning and verbal-conditioning processes among psychopaths.

A study by Eichler (1965) was conducted at the Patuxent Institution for

Defective Delinquents. He used 25 inmates out of the total of 56; the group's mean age as 27.16 years and the mean IQ 106.08 on the Wechsler Adult Intelligence Scale. Among the group's members there was no history of crime in the family and no history of hospitalization for psychosis.

The author hypothesized that the speech habits of an individual reflect the characteristic coping mechanisms developed to handle anxiety. Previous findings (Weintraub & Aronson, 1962) showed that typical speech habits reflecting defense mechanisms could be measured objectively and that the speech patterns used by impulsive patients mirrored their typical behavior patterns.

The procedure used involved a 10-minute talk about any subject or subjects. The patient spoke into a tape recorder, and no questions were allowed once the experiment began.

The Weintraub and Aronson (1962) scoring method was used. Speech was divided into 12 categories:

1. The quantity of speech—all completed words
2. Long pauses and silences (more than five seconds)
3. The rate of speech—total words/nonsilence minutes
4. "Nonpersonal" references—A "personal" clause is one whose subject refers to a specific person or persons known to the speaker, including references to the volunteer himself
5. A shift to the past tense
6. Negators—"not," "no," "never," and so on
7. Qualifiers—"suppose," "more or less," "what one might call," and so on
8. Retractor—any word, phrase or clause that detracts from the statement preceding it. For example, "John is an honest person. Of course, he has been involved in some shady deals!"
9. Explaining or justifying—"because," "due to," "as a result of," and so on
10. Direct reference either to the experimenter or the physical surroundings
11. Expressions of feeling—this does not take into account the tone of voice, facial expression, and so on, which are lost in transcription
12. Evaluators that are value judgments.

Anything less than 200 words was not used, and there was a minimum of 600 words for negators and 800 words for shift to past tense.

According to Eichler's (1965) results, sociopaths were higher than control on negation, retraction, and evaluation. As compared with impulsives, sociopaths were higher on nonpersonal references.

The known behavior of the impulsive compares with his verbal responses as follows:

1. Cannot tolerate feelings of anxiety (*expressions of feelings*)
2. Attempts to deny feelings (*negators*)
3. Manipulates human environment (*direct reference*)
4. Arouses guilt (*evaluators*)
5. Tries to undo behavior (*retractors*).

The greater use of negators by the psychopaths seems broadly consistent with clinical interpretations of their tendency to protect themselves from awareness of conflict and guilt. Their more frequent use of qualifiers is not as clear; it might possibly correlate with their (often) apparent goallessness. With respect to evaluation, it seems possible that guilt feelings might lead an individual habitually to impose value judgments on external factors; hence, the psychopath is seen once again as protecting him- or herself from awareness.

The category retractors appears to be an important speech pattern. By an excessive use of retracting statements, the psychopathic individual is stating an incongruous belief. The difficulty arises from the individual's inability to perceive the contradiction in such statements as those that correlate honesty with "shady deals." The psychopath believes the first statement (about honesty) enough to place him- or herself in that position and thus justify his or her own "shady" behavior. It is almost in the nature of a syllogism that would read:

All people are honest
I am a person
Therefore, I am honest.

If one were unaware of the illogic in such a comparison, one would believe him- or herself to be honest regardless of particular dishonest actions. The psychopath frequently acts as though he or she had internalized this conception and therefore cannot understand why he or she becomes the target of blame and accusations.

Regarding nonpersonal reference, Weintraub and Aronson (1962) felt that the psychopath thereby proves him- or herself to be *not* impulsive. As the authors put it, "The impulsive act is often an explosive outburst of feeling." The psychopath takes time to plan, which means a delay in actions. The impulsive patient exceeds the psychopath in direct reference words.

VERBAL LEARNING AND RETENTION

The characteristic inability of the psychopath to profit from experience (Cleckley, 1976) suggests either a basic learning deficiency or perhaps an insensitivity to social rewards and/or punishments. Fairweather (1954) and

Kadlub (1956), using a rote serial-learning task, found no differences between psychopaths and normals under appropriate conditions of either concrete or social reward. Their results argue against the assertion that psychopathy is invariably accompanied by a basic deficiency in learning capacity or that psychopaths are insensitive to appropriate social rewards. The criterion for classifying subjects as psychopaths was, in both studies, a clinical diagnosis of "psychopathic personality." All subjects were institutionalized criminals.

Hetherington and Klinger (1964) cited evidence (from Lykken, 1957) of poor avoidance learning in psychopaths in support of the position that psychopaths are insensitive to punishment. The basic assumption, developed by Mowrer (1960), is that learning to make an avoidance response and learning to inhibit a punished response are both two-stage processes, the first stage of which is the classical conditioning of an emotional response, fear, to an originally neutral conditioned stimulus. Hetherington and Klinger hypothesized that psychopathy is inversely related to an underlying dimension of fear conditionability, which is applicable to nonpsychopathic individuals as well. As subject, they used female college students, classified on the Psychopathic Deviation (PD) scale of the Minnesota Multiphasic Personality Inventory (MMPI) as being above the mean (high PD) or below the mean (low PD). They predicted that high-PD subjects would be less affected by verbal punishment (critical, discouraging statements after each trial) than would be low-PD subjects and that the two groups would not differ under the verbal reward or no-reward conditions. These predictions were substantially confirmed for a rote serial-learning task. The performance of the low-PD subjects (trials to criterion) was significantly lowered by the verbal punishment; the scores of the other five experimental groups were almost identical.

A single study by Sherman (1957), using a retroactive interference design, provided empirical support for the clinical observation that psychopaths have excellent memories (Lindner, 1944; Pennington, 1954). The superior retention scores of psychopathic criminals, when compared with "model prisoners," was attributed to the relative absence of anxiety in the psychopathic group.

These studies must be considered merely suggestive of possible avenues of research in this area. Their generality, as well as their importance for psychopathic theory, is limited by the absence of a reliable, objective measure of psychopathy. What is the relation, for example, between "the men most difficult to manage" at a state penitentiary and college students with high-PD scores on the MMPI? Can we expect the same theory to explain the behavior of both groups? The absence of suitable control groups, particularly in studies using prisoners, is another methodological difficulty in this research. Non-institutionalized psychopaths are not easily detected, let alone induced into the psychological laboratory.

The theoretical difficulties in these studies concern primarily the problem of translating the language of clinical description into the operationally defined constructs of experimental psychology. The behavior seems to "lose something" in the translation, in addition to possibly being distorted. Hetherington and Klinger's (1964) experiment provided one example of this problem. The clinical observation was the frequent failure of punishment to modify the antisocial behavior of the psychopath. The confirming laboratory result was the failure of critical and discouraging remarks by the experimenter, between trials, to disrupt the performance of high-PD subjects on a rote verbal-learning task. The performance of the low-PD subjects was explained as follows: Since punishment follows the subject's verbal responses, a conditioned fear reaction develops, leading to partial suppression of those responses. The result is an increase in the number of trials to criterion in the serial-learning task. Since psychopaths, on the other hand, are presumably deficient in affective reactivity to social disapproval (Cleckley, 1976), the high-PD subjects show less inhibition of the punished responses. This line of reasoning stems from an attempt to apply uncritically a principle derived from animal conditioning studies to human subjects, namely, that punishment depresses all responding. It ignores the subject's awareness of the response-punishment relation: That the punishment is the result of a failure to respond, or of errors, is the most likely interpretation. This consideration makes the poor performance of the low-PD subjects the result in need of explanation. If the theoretical background of the study had been different, the authors might have concluded that low-PD subjects show a "neurotic" reaction to criticism and that—in college students at least—"a little PD" might be a good thing.

Verbal Conditioning

Quay and Hunt (1965) have reported a replication and extension of a previous study (Johns & Quay, 1962) in which psychopathic criminals were compared with neurotic offenders in a verbal-conditioning paradigm. The two groups were selected on the basis of their scores on the neurotic and psychopathic subscales of the Delinquency Scale, which was developed in earlier studies (Peterson, Quay, & Cameron, 1959; Peterson, Quay, & Tiffany, 1961; Quay & Peterson, 1958). The conditioning technique used was that reported by Taffel (1955), in which each subject is required to make up a sentence using a given verb and a choice of six personal pronouns. After 20 preliminary trials, during which no reinforcement is given, experimental subjects are told "good" in a "flat, unemotional tone" at the end of sentences in which they use the first-person pronouns *I* or *we*. This procedure is followed for an additional 60 trials.

The measure of conditioning is the increase in the use of the first-person pronouns in the last block of 20 trials when compared with the first (unreinforced) block.

In both studies, the experimental neurotics showed significant increases, whereas the experimental psychopaths and two unreinforced control groups did not. The investigators interpreted this result as providing support for Cleckley's (1976) concept of semantic dementia in psychopaths.

The original study was open to a number of methodological criticisms (Persons & Persons, 1965), some of which were met by the replication. What is of more concern, however, is the theoretical assumption that dictated the choice of the verbal-conditioning paradigm. The authors maintained that Kadlub's (1956) failure to find differences between psychopathic and normal criminals in serial learning was due to the psychopaths receiving self-administered rewards for being "correct." To eliminate such self-administered rewards, Johns and Quay (1962) selected a verbal-conditioning procedure, under the assumption that verbal conditioning occurs without awareness of the correct response.

Evidence (Spielberger, 1962, 1965) indicates that verbal conditioning does not occur without awareness of the response-reinforcement contingency. In fact, if the traditional learning-performance distinction of cognitive theory is maintained, so-called verbal conditioning is largely a matter of concept learning. Once subjects discover which responses produce reinforcement, their performance depends on their motive state and the appropriateness of the reinforcement. The conclusion to be drawn from the Johns and Quay study, then, is that the experimental neurotics, to the degree that they became aware of what the experimenter wanted *and* were willing to give him what he wanted, increased their use of the first-person pronouns. The fact that the experimental psychopaths did not "condition" could mean either that they did not become aware of the response-reinforcement relation or that they were indifferent to the problem of "translation" mentioned previously. The reaction of the psychopathic individual to social reinforcement, as mediated semantically through praise and blame, insults and threats, is an important part of the diagnostic and theoretical configuration of psychopathy. It is represented poorly by the "social reinforcement" of the present studies. The word *good*, pronounced in a "flat, unemotional tone" by a young graduate student, is hardly calculated to produce paroxysms of joy in hardened criminals.

The Manipulation of Meaning in the Communication of Deceit (beyond Semantic Dementia)

Consider the psychopath who was asked, out of the interviewer's exasperation, whether he had any compassion for his victims. "The only place you find compassion," the interviewer was told, "is in the dictionary between 'shit' and 'sucker.' " This example of semantic dementia has a shocking yet appealing and certainly humorous effect on the listener. As such, it manipulates the situation, warping reality, playing on words, creating a farce of values that have been accepted and upheld, for the most part, by society at large. Although we have used Cleckley's (1976) term *semantic dementia* to describe such language, we adhere to Cleckley's definition only in spirit rather than agree literally with what he meant by the concept. We take this term to imply a much richer and broader level of interpersonal communication, implying by "semantic dementia" something more along the lines of a manipulation of meaning in the communication of the psychopath, which amounts to a communication of deceit and deception. Unlike other examples of abnormal language that we have examined throughout this text, it is not the language itself that is deviant. Rather, the aberration lies in the deceptive quality of the language, a language that deceives not only the listener but also the speaker. Such a language is a tangible and analyzable trait showing the personality or the psychology keeping the psychopath from having the "common decency to go crazy." By warping reality to deceive others, the psychopath also deceives him- or herself and in so doing is actually dissociating any feeling of guilt about his or her antisocial behavior.

It is interesting to note the fascination that the psychopathic personality has held for mass entertainment, as evidenced by the myriad literary works, films, plays, and so forth portraying a psychopathic individual as the protagonist. Harry Lyme in the film version of Graham Greene's *The Third Man*, played by the young Orson Welles, is such a character. An American named Holly Martin arrives in post–World War II Vienna to meet up with his good friend who has offered him work, only to find that his friend has mysteriously passed away. The naive American begins to investigate the circumstances of his friend's possible murder, only to find that good ol' Harry was never dead, that instead he had found refuge from the police in the Russian sector. Lyme was involved in an underhanded racket consisting of selling bad penicillin at a profit. Holly catches up with Lyme at the Prater amusement park, where they both go on a ride on the Riesenrad, Vienna's giant Ferris Wheel. Harry rationalizes his actions with complete contempt for human values. "Remember what the fellow said," he tells Martin. "In Italy for thirty years under the Borgias they had warfare, terror, murder and bloodshed, but they produced Michelangelo, Leonardo da Vinci, and the Renaissance. In Switzerland they had brotherly love. They had five hundred years of democracy and peace, and what did that produce? The cuckoo clock."

Such semantically demented rationalizations are exemplary of the language of the psychopath. Consider further the comment in the film version of *The Great McGinty* after a band of cronies has ripped off the public. The female lead asks her partners in crime: "What's everybody so upset about? What you

rob, you spend, so the money goes back to the people anyway, doesn't it?"
Again, this rationalization of antisocial behavior stems from misled generalizations about accepted value codes, reinterpreting the meaning of moral behavior
to imply that it is not only naive but also absolutely unprofitable.

The character of Karl in the film version of *The Cloning of Joanna May*
provides his very own definition of a psychopath, which he has twisted to
exclude himself. The unscrupulous manipulator of the future, whose mistress
amounts to being a female version of himself, complains about the fact that
people have been calling him a psychopath: "Of course I'm not a psychopath.
I'm a man of principle. I've only killed people on the basis of principle." To this
she replies: "You've never killed anyone you really liked anyway. You can't be
a psychopath."

We now proceed to examine a further example that provides us with more
information about this exceptionally rich and unique feature of psychopathic
speech, based on the paradigm that Erving Goffman used in his "Cooling the
Mark Out" (1952). In this social critique, Goffman described a socially
patterned defect within our culture, "cooling the mark out," which is important in understanding our concept of the psychopath of everyday life. The term
mark refers to a person who is a potential victim of a "confidence game" type
of exploitation. The mark, or "sucker" in underworld parlance, is to be "taken
in." Often the mark is not prepared to accept the role as a victim and forget that
the incident ever happened. The mark may report it to the police or may tip
other people off. To avoid this occurrence, the conartist engineers the conclusion of the game, which is called "Cooling the mark out." A major participant
in the con takes the role of the cooler and thus performs the art of conciliation
with the mark. The objective is to make it easy for the mark to accept what has
happened, forget it, and quietly depart from the scene. One might say that the
mark, once "cooled," has been educated in accepting the situation as it is. In
effect, the mark becomes an individual who must accept this compromise in his
or her own eyes as well as in the eyes of others. The cooler must skillfully
protect himself or herself from any feelings of guilt by convincing the mark that
being taken is not really deprivational and that complaints are not an appropriate sign of injury or victimization. A major example used by Goffman is the role
of the psychotherapist in contemporary life. The victim needs a friend to cool
himself or herself. That is, psychotherapists take the responsibility for the
mark, because it is their business to offer a relationship to those who failed in
relationships with others. The practice is not confined, of course, to the mental
health professions but can be seen in the business world, in academic circles,
and in government, where it is the custom to allow a person to resign for
delicate reasons instead of firing him or her for indelicate reasons. In our
example, included in the Appendix to this chapter, of Ted Bundy's last words to

the public before his execution (Dobbs, 1989), one can find a perfect example of this process of cooling the mark out. We will interpret the protocol of this interview as if it were a "social dream" (Rieber, 1993).

It is important to point out that Bundy was one of the most infamous serial killers of the 1970s and 1980s. To many of his friends and enemies, nothing became his life more than departing from it. A California psychologist, James Dobbs, apparently arranged to interview Bundy the evening before his execution. Bundy was in the habit of exploiting the media, and the media were happy to make use of him as a commodity whenever possible.

In paragraph 1 (see Appendix), Bundy develops his con on the public by stressing his essential normality, as it were. He uses the term "all American boy" to describe himself, and then works his way into developing his presentation of himself as a victim. In paragraph 3, he claims he was a victim of pornography, which snatched the all-American boy out of him and ruined his wonderful Christian home. He turns the situation around in such a way as to make it look as though society is the perpetrator, to wit, the "influences that are loose in society, [that society tolerates]." All this he claims made him into the victim. The guilt that he should feel is turned around and given to the public. In a different interview, not reproduced here, Bundy elaborated on the question asked of him as to whether he felt any guilt for his crimes. He replied: "No, I don't feel guilt, but I do feel sorry for people who feel guilt about the things they did."

In the fourth and fifth paragraphs we see the first major cooling out of the mark when the interviewer sets Bundy up to make his next move by saying, "You feel this really deeply, don't you, Ted?" Then, in paragraph 7, Bundy, making a disclaimer about not being a social scientist, develops the rationalization of how pornography victimized him and other serial killers by referring to a study he claims to be authorized by the Federal Bureau of Investigation. Bundy attempts to prove that pornography is a common interest among serial killers. In paragraph 8 the interviewer reinforces the idea, that is, "cools it out," by saying, "That's true." Then, in paragraph 11, Bundy tries to argue that he would have been better off and maybe even normal had he not been victimized by pornography. In paragraphs 12 and 14 the interviewer sets him up to share his feelings about his victims. Then, in paragraph 18, the interviewer says, "Are you carrying that load, that weight? Is there remorse?" Bundy takes the bait in paragraph 19 and feigns guilt and remorse for his victims while calling attention to the love of God, among other things. Then, in paragraph 21, the interviewer unwittingly gives Bundy the opportunity to explain how this happened, by saying, "You had this compartmentalized." More appropriately, he should have said, "You dissociated this," which would have been an explanation of how Bundy avoided the guilt rather than feel compassion for his victims. Interestingly enough, Bundy, in paragraph 22, uses the phrase "it was like a black hole . . . a crack. And everything that fell into that crack just disappeared." Clearly, the use of these terms reveals the real process involved, namely, the dissociation of guilt.

Compassion is then played out in paragraph 29 when the interviewer sets up Bundy for his attitude toward execution, asking him whether he deserves punishment. Here Bundy, in the last few paragraphs, says he certainly does deserve extreme punishment, but then he invokes the victim role by saying, "There is no way in the world that killing me is going to restore . . . those beautiful children to their parents." In paragraph 35 the interviewer cools the mark out by suggesting that he has heard through a mutual friend that Bundy has accepted the forgiveness of Jesus Christ, thus making him a God-fearing man in the eyes of the public.

CONCLUSION

Most of the empirical studies reviewed above have attempted to validate in the laboratory clinically derived hypotheses concerning the psychopathic personality. While such attempts are important and useful for the development of psychopathic theory, they entail the constant risk of oversimplification. The behavioral patterns—verbal and nonverbal—that form the basic data that a theory of psychopathy must encompass are not easily translated into the unidimensional response measure of experimental psychology. In addition, a fuller understanding of the language of the psychopath, and of the psychopath's responses to the language of others, will probably require more extensive knowledge of the role of awareness in determining complex human behavior than we currently possess. We are fortunate in being able to record slow but steady progress toward the attainment of both objectives.

APPENDIX: PROTOCOL OF THE BUNDY INTERVIEW THE NIGHT BEFORE HIS EXECUTION TAKEN FROM NETWORK TELEVISION

1   BUNDY: Uh, I wasn't a pervert in the sense that you know, people look at somebody and say I know there's something wrong him, and they just tell. I mean, I, uh, I was essentially a normal person. I had good friends, I, I uh, I led a normal life. Except for this one small, but very potent, and very destructive segment of it that I kept very secret, very close to myself and didn't let, let anybody know about it. And part of the shock and horror from my dear friends and family when, years ago when I was first arrested was that they just, there

was no clue. They looked at me and they looked at the, you know, the, um, the all American boy. And I'm, I mean, I wasn't perfect but it's, it . . .

2   INTERVIEWER: They couldn't believe it.

3   BUNDY: I was okay. Okay, I was. The basic humanity and, and, and basic spirit that God gave me was intact but unfortunately it became overwhelmed at times. And I think people need to recognize that it's not some kind of, that, there are those of us who are, or have been, so much influenced by violence in the media, in particular pornographic violence, are not some kind of inherent monsters. We are your sons and we are your husbands. And we grew up in regular families and pornography can reach out and snatch a kid out of any house today. They snatched me out of my, it snatched me out of it, my home, twenty, thirty years ago. And as diligent as my parents were, uh, and they were diligent in protecting their children, and as good a Christian home as we had, and we had a wonderful Christian home, uh there is no protection against the kind that, against the kinds of influences that are loose in the society, that tolerates.

4   INTERVIEWER: You feel this really deeply, don't you, Ted? Outside these walls right now there are several hundred reporters that wanted to talk to you.

5   BUNDY: Yeah.

6   INTERVIEWER: And you asked me to come here from California because you had something you wanted to say. This hour that we have together, uh, is not just an interview with a man who's scheduled to die tomorrow morning. I'm here and you're here because of this message that you're talking about right here. You really feel that hard-core pornography, and the doorway to it, soft-core pornography, is doing untold damage to other people and causing other women to be abused and killed the way you did others.

7   BUNDY: Listen, I'm no social scientist and I haven't done a survey. I mean, I, I don't pretend that I know what John Q. Citizen thinks about this, but I've lived in prison for a long time now. And I've met a lot of men who were motivated to commit violence just like me. And without exception every one of them was deeply involved in pornography. Without question, without exception, deeply influenced and consumed by an addiction to pornography. There's no question about it. The FBI's own study on serial homicide shows that the most common interest among serial killers is pornography.

8   INTERVIEWER: That's true.

9   BUNDY: And it's, and it's real. It's true.

10 INTERVIEWER: Ted, what would your life have been like without that influence? (*Pause*) You can only speculate.

11 BUNDY: Yeah. Well I, I know it would have been far better. Not just for me, and, and its, excuse me for being so self-centered here. It would have been a lot better for me and lots of other, I know lots of other innocent people, victims and families. It would have been a lot better, there's no question about that, it would

have been a, a, a fuller life. Certainly a, a, a life that would not have involved, I'm absolutely certain, would not have involved this kind of violence that I, that I have committed. Uh . . .

12   INTERVIEWER: I'm sure Ted, if, ya know, if I were able to ask you the questions that are being asked out there . . .

13   BUNDY: Mm.

14   INTERVIEWER: . . . uh, one of the most important, as you come down to perhaps your final hours, are you thinking about all those victims out there and their families?

15   BUNDY: Well.

16   INTERVIEWER: . . . who are so wounded, ya know, years later, their lives have not returned to normal. They will never return to normal.

17   BUNDY: Absolutely.

18   INTERVIEWER: Are you carrying that load, that weight? Is the remorse there?

19   BUNDY: (Pause) I can't, I, I know that people will accuse me of being self-serving but we're beyond that now, I mean, I'm just telling you how I feel. But through God's help, I have been able to come to the point where I've, much too late, but better late than never, feel the hurt and the pain that I am responsible for. Yes, absolutely. In the past few days, myself and a number of investigators have been talking about unsolved cases, murders that I was involved in. And it's hard to, it's hard to talk about all these years later because it revives in me all those terrible feelings and those thoughts that I have steadfastly and, and diligently dealt with, I think successfully with the love of God. And yet it's reopened that and I've felt the pain and I've felt the horror again of all that. And I can only hope that those who I have harmed, those who I have caused so much grief, even if they don't believe my expression of sorrow and remorse, will believe what I'm saying now. That there is loose in their towns and their communities people like me today.

Each time I harmed someone, each time I killed someone, there'd be an enormous amount of, of, especially at first, an enormous amount of, of horror, guilt, remorse afterwards. But then that impulse to do it again would come back even stronger. Now, believe me, I didn't, the unique thing about how this worked, Dr. Dobbs, is that I still felt, in my regular life, the full range of, of guilt and uh, remorse about other things. Ah, regret, and . . .

20   INTERVIEWER: You had this compartmentalized . . .

21   BUNDY: . . . this compartmentalized, very well focused, uh, uh, uh, very sharply focused area where it was like a black hole, it was like a, ya know, like a crack. And everything that fell into that crack just disappeared. Does that make sense?

22   INTERVIEWER: Yeah, it does. Uh, one of the, the final uh, murders that you committed, of course uh, was apparently little Kimberly Leech, 12 years of

age. Ah, I think the, the public outcry is greater there because an innocent child was taken from a, from a playground. What did you feel after that? What was there? Were there the normal emotions three days later, where were you, Ted?

23   BUNDY: I . . . (*pause*) I can't really talk about that right now. That's . . .

24   INTERVIEWER: It's too painful.

25   BUNDY: I would like to, I would like to be able to convey to you what that, that uh, that experience is like. But I can't, I won't.

26   INTERVIEWER: Okay.

27   BUNDY: (*pause*) I can't begin to understand, well I can try, but I, I'm aware that I can't begin to understand the pain that the parents of these, of these children that I've, and these young women that I've harmed, feel. And I can't restore really much to them, if anything. I won't pretend to and I don't even expect them to forgive me and I'm not asking for it. That kind of forgiveness is of God and if they have it they have it and if they don't, well maybe they'll find it someday.

28   INTERVIEWER: Do you deserve the punishment the state has inflicted upon you?

29   BUNDY: That's a very good question and I'll answer it very, very honestly. I, I don't wanna die. I'm not gonna kid you, I kid you not. Um, I deserve certainly the most extreme punishment society has and I deserve, I think society deserves to be protected from me and from others like me, that's for sure. Um, I think what I, what I hope will come of our discussion is I think society deserves to be protected from itself. Because, because as we've been talking there are, there are forces at loose in, in this country, particularly again uh, this kind of violent pornography, uh, where on the one hand, well-meaning, decent people will condemn behavior of a Ted Bundy while they're walking past a, a magazine rack full of the very kinds of things that send young kids down the road to be Ted Bundys. That's the irony. We're talking here not just about moral, we're talking, I'm, what I'm talking about is going beyond retribution, which is what people want with me. Going beyond retribution and punishment. Because there is no way in the world that killing me is going to restore uh, those beautiful children to their parents and, and, and correct and, and, and soothe the pain. But I'll tell you there are lots of other kids playing on streets around this country today who, who are gonna be dead tomorrow or the next day, and next day and next month because other young people are reading the kinds of things and seeing the kinds of things that are available in the media today.

30   INTERVIEWER: Ted, as you would imagine, there is tremendous cynicism about you on the outside and I suppose for good reason.

31   BUNDY: Mm-hm.

32   INTERVIEWER: I'm not sure that there's anything that you could say that people would uh, would believe, some people would believe.

33 BUNDY: Yeah.

34 INTERVIEWER: And uh, and yet, you told me last night, and I have heard this through our mutual friend John Tanner, that you have uh, accepted the forgiveness of Jesus Christ and are a follower and a believer in him. Do you draw strength from that as you approach these final hours?

35 BUNDY: I do. I can't say that uh . . .

36 INTERVIEWER: . . . it's gonna be easy.

37 BUNDY: Even though the valley of the shadow of death is, is something that I've become all that accustomed to. And that I'm, ya know, that I'm strong and that uh, nothing's bothering me. Uh, listen, it's no fun.

REFERENCES

Abrahamsen, D. (1944). *Crime and the human mind*. New York: Columbia University Press.

Abrahamsen, D. (1960). *The psychology of crime*. New York: Columbia University Press.

Bromberg, W. (1948). *Crime and mind*. Philadelphia: Lippincott.

Cleckley, H. (1949). Psychopathic personality. In *Encyclopedia of criminology*. New York: Philosophical Library.

Cleckley, H. (1976). *The mask of sanity*. St. Louis: Mosby.

Coleman, J. C. (1956). *Abnormal psychology and modern life*. Chicago: Scott, Foresman.

Dobbs, J. M. (January 23, 1989). National Broadcasting Corporation Interview with Ted Bundy the night before his execution.

Eichler, M. (1965). The application of verbal behavior analysis to the study of psychological defense mechanisms: Speech patterns associated with sociopathic behavior. *Journal of Nervous and Mental Disease*, *141*, 658–663.

Fairweather, G. W. (1954). The effect of selected incentive conditions on the performance of psychopathic, neurotic and normal criminals in a serial rote learning situation. *Dissertation Abstracts*, *14*, 394–395.

Goffman, E. (1952). On cooling the mark out: Some aspects of adaptation to failure. *Psychiatry*, *15*, 451–464.

Goleman, D. (1987, July 7). Brain deficit tied to utter amorality of the psychopath. *New York Times*, p. C1–C2.

Hetherington, E. M., & Klinger, E. (1964). Psychopathy and punishment. *Journal of Abnormal and Social Psychology*, *69*, 113–115.

Johns, J. H., & Quay, H. C. (1962). The effect of social reward on verbal conditioning in psychopathic and neurotic military offenders. *Journal of Consulting Psychology*, *26*, 217–220.

Kadlub, K. J. (1956). *The effects of two types of reinforcement on the performance of psychopathic and normal individuals*. Unpublished doctoral dissertation. University of Illinois, Urbana.

Lindner, R. M. (1944). *Rebel without a cause*. New York: Grune & Stratton.

Lipton, H. (1950). The psychopath. *Journal of Crime, Law and Criminality*, *60*, 584–600.

Lykken, D. T. (1957). A study of anxiety in the sociopathic personality. *Journal of Abnormal and Social Psychology*, *55*, 6–10.

McCord, W. & McCord, J. (1956). *Psychopathy and delinquency*. New York: Grune & Stratton.

Mowrer, O. H. (1960). *Learning theory and behavior*. New York: Wiley.

Pennington, L. A. (1954). Criminal and psychopathic behavior. In L. A. Pennington & I. A. Berg (Eds.), *An introduction to clinical psychology* (pp. 421–447). New York: Ronald.

Persons, R. W., & Persons, C. E. (1965). Some experimental support for psychopathic theory: A critique. *Psychological Reports, 16*, 745–749.

Pescor, M. (1948). Abnormal personality types among offenders. *Federal Probation, 12*, 3–8.

Peterson, D. R., Quay, H. C., & Cameron, G. R. (1959). Personality and background factors in juvenile delinquency as inferred from questionnaire responses. *Journal of Consulting Psychology, 23*, 395–399.

Peterson, D. R., Quay, H. C., & Tiffany, T. L. (1961). Personality factors related to juvenile delinquency. *Child Development, 32*, 355–372.

Quay, H. C., & Hunt, W. A. (1965). Psychopathy, neuroticism, and verbal conditioning: A relication and extension. *Journal of Consulting Psychology, 29*, 283.

Quay, H. C., & Peterson, D. R. (1958). A brief scale for juvenile delinquency. *Journal of Clinical Psychology, 14*, 139.

Rieber, R. W. (1993). *Manufacturing stress: Psychopathy in everyday life*. Unpublished manuscript.

Sherman, L. J. (1957). Retention in psychopathic, neurotic, and normal subjects. *Journal of Personality, 25*, 721–729.

Spielberger, C. D. (1962). The role of awareness in verbal conditioning. In C. W. Eriksen (Ed.), *Behavior and awareness* (pp. 175–183). Durham, NC: Duke University Press.

Spielberger, C. D. (1965). Theoretical and epistemological issues in verbal conditioning. In S. D. Rosenberg (Ed.), *Directions in psycholinguistics* (pp. 49–62). New York: Macmillan.

Sullivan, H. S. (1953a). *Interpersonal theory of psychiatry*. New York: Norton.

Sullivan, H. S. (1953b). *Conceptions of modern psychiatry*. New York: Norton.

Taffel, C. (1955). Anxiety and the conditioning of verbal behavior. *Journal of Abnormal and Social Psychology, 51*, 496–501.

Weintraub, W., & Aronson, H. (1962). The application of verbal behavior analysis to the study of psychological defense mechanisms. *Journal of Nervous and Mental Disease, 134*, 169–181.

5

Language and Cognition
in the Affective Disorders

Kraepelin (1896) introduced the term *manic-depressive psychosis* to designate a series of attacks of elation and depression with intervals of relative normality and a generally favorable prognosis. He regarded manic-depressive psychosis as an organic illness, which he distinguished from the less severe disturbances of mood that were later identified as neurotic, a distinction that traditionally rested on the factor of reality contact. What was called "neurotic depression" could be characterized as deep dysphoria, but the individual retained awareness of the surroundings and did not lose the capacity to carry on some semblance of normal daily activities. Psychotic depression, on the other hand, featured hallucinatory and delusional experiences and extreme withdrawal to the point of immobilization.

Opposed to this position were a number of theorists (e.g., Beck, 1967) who held that psychotic depression, neurotic depression, and what are commonly known as "the blues" in the typical individual are points on a continuum. According to this *continuity hypothesis*, the distinction between neurotic and psychotic depression is quantitative rather than qualitative. In addition, proponents of the continuity hypothesis tended to believe that all depression is psychogenic in origin, while those who adhered to the Kraepelinian interpretation maintained that neurotic depression is psychogenic and psychotic depression is biogenic.

Psychiatric tradition sided with the Kraepelinian tradition: DSM-II contained separate diagnostic categories for neurotic and psychotic depression.

However, DSM-III abandoned this distinction, at least in terms of diagnostic categories. Clinicians are still expected to note whether a person's behavior is psychotic; nevertheless, all *severe* affective disorders, regardless of whether they exhibit psychotic or neurotic features, are classified under the heading of *major affective disorders*. Less severe or incapacitating disorders are categorized as (1) *dysthymic disorders* if they involve depression alone or (2) *cyclothymic disorders* if the disturbance has both manic and depressive phases. Both of these syndromes are by definition nonpsychotic. If depression occurs as a consequence of an identifiable life event and is expected to disappear within a reasonable time after the conclusion of the event, it is then classified as an *adjustment disorder with depressed mood*.

Within the category of major affective disorders, a distinction is made between unipolar and bipolar disorders. An individual who has undergone one or more major depressive episodes with no intervening manic episodes is said to exhibit a unipolar disorder. If the disorder exhibits both manic and depressive disturbances, the diagnosis is a bipolar disorder. Bootzin (1980) notes that the presence of manic episodes is not the only feature that distinguishes unipolar and bipolar disorders:

> The two syndromes differ in many respects. First, bipolar disorder is much less common than major depression, affecting an estimated .4 to 1.2 percent of the adult population. . . . Second, whereas major depression can occur at any time of life, bipolar disorder usually has its onset before age thirty. Third, unlike major depression, bipolar disorder occurs in both sexes with equal frequency. Fourth, bipolar disorder is more likely to run in families than major depression. Fifth, the course of the two disorders is somewhat different: in bipolar disorder, episodes are generally briefer and more frequent than in major depression. (p. 303)

Keller (1987) discusses the further distinction between what are identified as Bipolar I and Bipolar II disorders. The DSM-III criteria for bipolar disorder require an episode of mania with or without a history of depression. Bipolar II patients are those who exhibit brief hypomanic (nonpsychotic) episodes and episodes of major depression.

Focal to the clinical picture in manic-depressive reactions is the prevailing mood of the patient—elation or depression. "The severely depressed individual views the world with extreme pessimism and is deeply convinced that he and others are evil. The euphoric individual is unrealistically optimistic, feels that he and others are wonderful, and elatedly anticipates a rosy future" (Rosen & Gregory, 1965, p. 283). It is now widely recognized that more typical feelings of happiness, joy, and pleasure are rarely present during full-blown manic or hypomanic syndromes (Keller, 1987, p. 11).

Against the background provided by this conspicuous deviation from normal mood there may occur various secondary disturbances of cognitive functioning, perception, and overt behavior that are consistent with the predominant emotional tone. In manic reactions there is often a delusional overvaluation of intelligence, sexual attractiveness, power, wealth, and so on and the possible accompaniment of hallucinatory experiences. Depressive patients typically develop delusions of sin and guilt, self-accusation, worthlessness, and hopelessness. Older depressed patients may also develop bizarre hypochondriacal delusions or delusions of nihilism.

Manic-depressive reactions may vary from a few hours to many years. The shorter the attack, the greater is the likelihood that the patient will be free of marked personality disorganization. Rosen and Gregory (1965) state that untreated depressions last an average of 1.5 years, as compared with 4–6 months for untreated manic attacks. Although many patients show spontaneous recovery from manic and depressive episodes, there is a high rate of readmission to mental hospitals. Age is an important variable: Older patients, particularly manic patients, tend toward longer attacks, briefer periods of remission, and increasing personality deterioration.

CLINICAL OBSERVATIONS AND EARLY STUDIES

Despite the comparative lack of research on language behavior in affective disorders, aberrant speech has figured prominently in the diagnostic picture of manic reactions. The classic "triad of mania" consists of euphoria, hyperactivity, and a flight of ideas or push of speech. The term *flight of ideas* was introduced by Kraepelin in 1899 and refers to a rapid digression from one idea to another with tenuous connections in the train of thought. According to Kraepelin (1921):

> The easily stimulated ideas of the movements of speech gain too great an influence over the flow of the train of thought while the relations of the contents of the ideas pass more into the background. In the higher grades . . . combinations of words, corresponding sounds and rhymes, usurp more and more the place of the substantive connections of ideas. (p. 31)

Push of speech was interpreted by clinicians to mean an increase in the rate of speech and a pressure to keep talking, with a resulting resistance to being interrupted. As we will see, both flight of ideas and push of speech have assumed importance in research on language behavior in manic disorders.

Cumulative clinical impressions have supported the view that the speech of the manic is symptomatic of the behavior in general and of the individual's disordered thinking. As Sherman (1938) stated, "The manic is easily distracted and therefore cannot convey his ideas clearly. There is no actual distortion of language except for the type of reaction which represents ideas of grandeur. And this is probably not a true language distortion" (p. 637).

Eisenson, Auer, and Irwin (1963) provide us with the following characterization of language behavior in manic patients on the basis of clinical observations:

> He is likely to talk incessantly and rapidly, incorporating many marginal or tangential
> ideas into his stream of speech. The rapid tempo often results in slurring and in the
> production of word fragments. When these are run together they may suggest either
> neologisms or "word salads." The style of the manic's utterances tends to be tele-
> graphic; many connecting words, participles, relative pronouns and prepositions are
> likely to be omitted. Because the flow of ideas is not checked, the content of the patient's
> speech is highly diversified and is frequently far in excess of the listener's rate of
> absorption. The manic's speech is at first fascinating, but ultimately wearying. Little if
> any attention is paid to the auditor; the manic speaks to express his own emotional and
> mental state. The presence of an auditor serves as a stimulant for speaking rather than as
> a stimulant for communicative utterance. (p. 374)

It is interesting to note that this description of manic language behavior
contains several features that have also been ascribed to schizophrenic language
behavior. Indeed, the issue of whether manic and schizophrenic language
exhibit fundamental similarities is one that has interested—and continues to
interest—several investigators. We will return to this point.

In contrast to the euphoria, excitement, hyperactivity, and logorrhea of the
manic, the depressed patient exhibits dejection, psychomotor retardation, and
severe restriction in intellectual activity. In addition, the patient may perseve-
rate on a single, fixed idea; obsessive thoughts, particularly of suicide or death,
may predominate. Like the manic patient, the depressive's language behavior is
symptomatic of his disturbance. According to Eisenson et al. (1963):

> The patient speaks slowly, often verbalizing the same thoughts over and over again.
> This is frequently a loss of insight or judgment as to the significance of the thoughts
> that are presented; the consequential and the inconsequential, from the listener's point
> of view, are offered as if they were of equal importance. Diversification of utterance is
> extremely low, so that the auditor becomes quickly bored and seeks an escape. His
> efforts to change the direction of discourse are generally futile. The depressive pa-
> tient speaks to express himself, rather than to elicit responses from his auditor.
> (p. 376)

In acute depression, the patient may become completely mute and inaccessible
to verbal communication of any kind.

One of the earliest studies of spoken language in the affective disorders
was conducted in 1938 by Stanley Newman, a language specialist, and Vera
Mather, a psychiatrist. Their study dealt with phonograph recordings of spoken
language, including both spontaneous speech and verbal material elicited by
questions from the psychiatrist. The list of descriptive criteria used in the
eventual analysis of speech was built up over the course of replayings of the
records. The 40 subjects for this study were drawn from four groups that were

characterized by the authors as *classical depression*; *states of dissatisfaction, self-pity, and gloom*; *manic syndromes*; and *mixed affective states*. Newman and Mather (1938) examined the speech of their patients with reference to such variables as pitch, tempo, syntax, and latency of response. It must be emphasized that their findings (Newman & Mather, 1938) are largely descriptive and provide no quantitative data.

Lorenz and Cobb (1952) compared the speech of manics to control by using more rigorous quantitative methods, such as determining the distribution of parts of speech or the number of words spoken per minute. They reported a relative increase in the use of pronouns and verbs, a relative decrease in the use of adjectives and prepositions, and a high verb-adjective quotient (i.e., the proportion of adjectives is decreased) in the speech of manic patients. The authors conclude: "If the assumption of a correlation between emotional states and verb-adjective quotient is correct, the manic patient's speech gives objective evidence of a heightened degree of anxiety" (Lorenz & Cobb, 1952; p. 428).

Before turning to later studies of language behavior in affective disorders, it seems appropriate briefly to review and attempt to summarize what can be gleaned from the clinical literature as well as the findings of the earliest studies. It would appear that a fairly well delineated portrait of the manic patient emerges from the study of his language behavior. The content of the patient's utterances is circumstantial and anecdotal—like a diary account of the day's events and activities. There is little personal qualification or evaluation; the speaker is "outside" the things that are narrated, a spectator rather than a participant. The patient's speech is discursive and verbose, neither directed toward some specific objective nor used in the service of rational argument. Marginal ideas continually intrude, and transient stimuli are a constant source of distraction.

Certainly one of the most striking characteristics of the manic's language behavior is this tendency for the content of speech to be determined by associates. The automatic filtering process that selects and rejects verbal material and orders semantic content in the nonmanic person according to a complex encoding process is greatly diminished in the manic patient, though each stimulus and each response serve to summon up another. What results seems to be the concatenation of thought and language aberrations that has been called flight of ideas. Arieti (1959) states:

Actually, this type of verbal behavior has a goal—that of maintaining this superficial effervescent euphoria and of escaping from intruding thoughts which may bring about depression. In not-too-pronounced cases the patient realizes that he unduly allows details to interfere with the original goal of his conversation and tries to go back to it, but again he is lost in many details. (p. 427)

Both the clinical literature and the earliest few studies show little evidence of gross pathology or disorganization at the level of structural elements in the speech of either manic or depressive patients. Most of the phenomena observed in these patients appear to reflect either psychomotor acceleration or retardation. The defect, Arieti (1959) suggested, occurs at higher integrative levels of language formulation.

SPEECH IN MANIA: SYNTACTIC ASPECTS

Durbin and Martin (1977) undertook a study involving six subjects (two males and four females), ranging in age from 19 to 74, who had been admitted to an inpatient psychiatric hospital. All the subjects exhibited marked euphoria or irritability and three of the following symptoms: (1) hyperactivity, (2) grandiosity, (3) decreased sleep, and (4) distractibility. Subjects were interviewed initially within 72 hours of admission. The interview was structured in two parts—an analytic section and a discourse section. In the analytic section, a protocol was followed that explored systematically the subject's linguistic competence. This portion took approximately 30 minutes. In the discourse section, subjects were asked to speak on anything they wished or to comment on basic matters such as experiences since coming to the hospital.

Basic linguistic competence was assessed by means of a brief vocabulary test and by asking subjects to supply meanings to sentences and to identify and correct ungrammatical sentences.

Durbin and Martin report that, in both the analytic and discourse situations, the speech of the subjects was phonologically intact. No lexical impairment was present, and subjects were able to retrieve lexical items without difficulty. With regard to rate of speech, subjects varied from a slow, deliberate style to one that seemed accelerated. However, the authors note that the speech of a subject who appeared to be speaking rapidly showed a word count of 104 words per minute, a rate that was not accelerated (Lorenz & Cobb, 1952, p. 307). The results of the vocabulary test indicated that subjects were capable of defining words and providing antonyms within the limits of their intellectual and educational levels.

In the discourse section, considerably more disruption of syntactic capability was observed than in the analytic section. Specifically, this disruption occurred in the proper utilization of *ellipsis.* According to the authors, ellipsis deletes lexical strings and leaves syntactic markers (e.g., *"and," "but," "or," "as," "although"*) to indicate that the deletion has taken place. Ellipsis provides rules for the recovery of information. When ellipsis errors occur in the output of the speaker, the inability of the auditor to recover deleted information makes it difficult or even impossible to maintain a meaningful progression of thought in discourse.

Fromkin (1975) has pointed out that all speakers make ellipsis errors. Durbin and Martin (1977) identify two differences between nonmanic and the manic subjects in their study. First, while such errors are sporadic in nonmanic speakers, they occurred pervasively in the manic patients. Second, nonmanic speakers often correct themselves, but the manic subjects never corrected themselves.

In noting that violations occurred among their subjects even in the absence of an increased rate of speech, Durbin and Martin (1977) suggest that such deletion errors may "play an important part in the long-reported *flight of ideas* and other abnormalities manifest in the speech of manics" (p. 217).

DISORDERED SPEECH: MANICS AND SCHIZOPHRENICS

There has been a considerable amount of controversy over whether or not the same aberrant language phenomena appear in both mania and schizophrenia. Mania and schizophrenia are considered functional psychoses, meaning that they do not present identifiable organic pathology. In such psychoses, as Durbin and Martin (1977) point out, "the basic functions of the central nervous system, i.e., motor control, memory, orientation, and basic intellectual capacities, are generally preserved" (p. 209). In the absence of specific organic impairments such as the ones that characterize those who have sustained brain damage, the nature of the "thought disorder" or thought disturbance that is presumed to be systematically related to disordered language behavior in either schizophrenia or mania becomes a matter of focal importance.

Andreasen (1979a) notes that the concept of thought disorder was given preeminence by Bleuler (1911) in his conceptualization of schizophrenia and points out the lack of common ground on the definition of thought disorder: "Clinicians do not have available any standard and uniformly agreed-upon definitions of most terms commonly used to characterize thought disorder, and consequently there is great variation in the use of terminology across the country" (p. 1315). She attempted to provide a consistent set of definitions capable of being used with high reliability.

Thought disorder in a clinical setting is generally inferred from observation of the patient's speech and language behavior. Thus, as Andreasen (1979a) points out, the definitions in this study were written "to describe speech and language behaviors commonly seen in psychiatric patients without any attempt to characterize the underlying cognitive processes unless they were reported by the patient" (p. 1316). For example, the definition of *blocking* is based on the observation of a break in the patient's train of speech—and on the patient's statement that he somehow lost track of what he meant to say. The author states that this strictly empirical approach was selected because it was considered likely to improve reliability.

The set of definitions includes the following:

1. Poverty of speech (poverty of thought, laconic speech)
2. Poverty of content of speech (poverty of thought, empty speech, alogia, verbigeration, negative formal thought disorder)
3. Pressure of speech
4. Distractible speech
5. Tangentiality
6. Derailment (loose associations, flight of ideas)
7. Incoherence (word salad, jargon aphasia, schizophasia, paragrammatism)
8. Illogicality
9. Clanging
10. Neologisms
11. Word approximations (paraphasia, metonyms)
12. Circumstantiality
13. Loss of goal
14. Perseveration
15. Echolalia
16. Blocking
17. Stilted speech
18. Self-reference.

In addition to the above, two language disorders that occur in aphasia— semantic and phonemic paraphasia—were also defined in order to encourage clinicians to include aphasia in their differential diagnosis.

The reliability of these definitions was assessed in a pilot study using both tape-recorded interviews with a series of 44 patients with diagnoses of mania (*n* = 13), depression (*n* = 16), and schizophrenia (*n* = 15). Two raters listened to these tape-recorded interviews and recorded their ratings for each. In the second phase of development, the definitions and rating scale were used to evaluate the speech of 69 patients during a standardized interview. These patients were drawn from three diagnostic groups: mania (*n* = 19), depression (*n* = 20), and schizophrenia (*n* = 30). Data from the pilot study were pooled with those from the final study. Interrater reliability for most of the definitions was very good. Only six of the 18 definitions have weighted kappa values below .6, the figure often considered an appropriate cutoff point for good reliability.

These six definitions were tangentiality, clanging, echolalia, self-reference, neologisms, and self-reference.

Andreasen (1979b) comments, "Some subtypes of thought disorder that have traditionally been given great significance are in fact relatively uncommon, so uncommon that they are of little use for either clinical or research purposes" (p. 1329). These uncommon subtypes include clanging, blocking, echolalia, neologisms, and word approximations. She identifies the most common subtypes as poverty of content of speech, pressure of speech, tangentiality, derailment, loss of goal, and perseveration. Andreasen adds that poverty of speech, incoherence, circumstantiality, and distractible speech, while they occur less frequently, are important for clinical and research purposes because they have some diagnostic significance. She emphasizes that incoherence tends to be associated with severe psychopathology. The author concludes that her data "indicate quite clearly that the concept of thought disorder as pathognomonic for schizophrenia is incorrect" (p. 1329). It should be noted that these definitions were subsequently incorporated in the glossary of DSM-III (1980).

Wykes and Leff (1982) acknowledge the difficulty in differentiating the speech of manics and schizophrenics cross-sectionally but suggest that speech may be differentiated longitudinally: "The 'thought disorder' in schizophrenia is found even with normal mood, whereas, in mania, the 'thought disorder' generally remits with normal mood"(p. 118). They point out that, despite studies such as that conducted by Andreasen in which direct comparisons are made between manic and schizophrenic speech, the intuition of many clinicians is that the disturbed speech of manics is easier to understand. To investigate this intuition, Wykes and Leff (1982) employed a method of discourse analysis developed by Halliday and Hasan (1976) that measures one aspect of the coherence of speech, the way in which patients relate their sentences together to make a coherent communication. The system involves the measurement of different kinds of links in the text known as "cohesive ties," "the means whereby elements that are structurally unrelated in the text are linked together" (Halliday & Hasan, 1976, p. 27). Table 5.1 provides an explication of the several different categories of cohesion provided by Rochester and Martin (1979).

Transcriptions were made of samples of discourse collected from a eight schizophrenic and four manic patients who exhibited incoherence of speech. The following examples of "disordered speech" are supplied in the appendix to Wykes and Leff (1982) without comment:

Example I
Where did all this start could it possibly have started the possibility operates some of the time having the same decision as you and possibility that I must now reflect or wash out

TABLE 5.1.   Categories of Cohesion

Category	Subcategory	Example[a]
Reference	1. Pronominal	We met <u>Joy Adamson</u> and had dinner with <u>her</u> in Nairobi.
	2. Demonstrative	We went to a <u>hostel</u> and oh <u>that</u> was a dreadful place.
	3. Comparative	<u>Six guys</u> approached me. The <u>last</u> guy pulled a knife on me in the park.
Substitution	1. Nominal	The oldest <u>girl</u> is 25 and the next <u>one's</u> 22.
	2. Verbal	Eastern people <u>take it seriously</u>, at <u>least</u> some of them <u>do</u>.
	3. Clausal	I'm <u>making it worse for myself</u>. I would think <u>so</u>.
Ellipsis	1. Nominal	He's got <u>energy</u> too. He's got a lot more Ø than I do.[b]
	2. Verbal	<u>I could</u> go to the university all my life. Ø keep going to school.
	3. Clausal	Have you ever <u>been to Israel?</u>—No. My brother has Ø.
Conjunction	1. Additive	I read a book in the past few days <u>and</u> I like it.
	2. Adversative	They started out in England <u>but</u> got captured on the way.
	3. Clausal	It was a beautiful tree <u>so</u> I left it alone.
	4. Temporal	My mother was in Ireland. <u>Then</u> she came over here.
	5. Continuative	What kind of degree?—<u>Well, in</u> one of the professions.
Lexical	1. Same root	Mother needed <u>independence</u>. She was always <u>dependent</u> on my father.
	2. Synonym	I got <u>angry</u> at M. But I don't often get <u>mad</u>.
	3. Superordinate	I love catching <u>fish</u>. I caught a <u>bass</u> last time.
	4. General items	The <u>plane</u> hit some air pockets and the <u>bloody thing</u> went up and down.

[a]The cohesive item is double underscored; the presumed item has single underscoring.
[b]Null set (Ø) indicates missing information.
Source: Rochester & Martin (1979).

any doubts that that's bothering me and one instant what's bothering me in the whole thing must stop immediately otherwise that is damned if that is damned that's no use and if I don't tell the truth that's bothering me an awful lot in my wisdom the truth is I've got the truth to tell you with mine signing here and as I am as God made me and understand my position and you'll listen with intelligence your intelligence works lit again and is recorded in my head.

Example II
Yeah well somebody stole gold from their plate so as to prove it in the plate you know sort of a click click like the candid camera and it did just prove that because it proved the hells angels in america with a dentists mirror because he wanted to make his name as the squire but not as E squire or A squire as well but clickety click clap clap and then clapping himself and getting pins and needles while he was clapping himself it aroused

him from that situation too and I went to see Dr. Hellycar all about it and he told his
father all about it. (Wykes & Leff, 1982, pp. 123–124)

Speech samples were divided into sentence units, each of which consisted of a
verb and at least one other noun. According to Wykes and Leff, "Embedded
sentences, relative clause sentences, and other subordinate constructions (e.g.,
John saw Jane while she was in town) were counted as one unit, but two clauses
joined by a conjunction such as 'and,' 'though,' 'but,' etc. were considered as
two units" (Wykes & Leff, 1982, p. 120). Each sentence unit in a transcript was
scanned for links with previous ones, and when a link was found, it was coded
into one of the five cohesion categories.

In their results, Wykes and Leff note that two of the cohesion categories—
substitution and ellipsis—occurred so rarely that they were included under the
category "lexical cohesion." The total number of cohesive ties for each speech
sample was calculated. The authors conclude, "The speech of all the patients in
the group studied here was difficult to understand. However, the manic patients
provided the listener with more ties to relate his sentences together than the
schizophrenic did" (Wykes & Leff, 1982, p. 123). They suggest that the
difference might be potentially useful for diagnostic purposes and as a way to
investigate cognitive functioning in manic and schizophrenic patients.

CRITICAL REVIEW

An attempt to assess the current status of knowledge and inquiry with
regard to language behavior in the affective disorders might begin with a
commonplace observation about the nature of psychiatric diagnosis. While the
symptoms of psychosis involve both nonverbal and verbal behavior, the latter is
more important by far. Andreasen (1976) puts it this way:

> Psychiatrists frequently speak about their patients' content of thought, stream of
> thought, or thought disorder. Too often we forget that our only way of learning about a
> patient's thoughts is through his speech and language, either spoken or written. Spoken
> or written language may not be an accurate or reliable index of thought, even when it is
> supposed to approximate it closely as in free association, *but it is the only index* we have
> available. Given this fact, it is something of an oddity that so much has been written by
> psychologists and psychiatrists about thought and so little about language. (p. 1361;
> italics ours)

As we have seen, Bleuler's conceptualization of schizophrenia assigned preeminence to "thought disorder," a characteristic disturbance that was presumed to be expressed symptomatically as "associative loosening." Thus,
disordered thought equals disordered speech in schizophrenia.

With respect to affective disorders, disordered speech in mania and severe depression attracted the interest of psychiatrists and psychologists in the hope that careful study of the speech would provide some insight into the disorders themselves. As of the 1930s, there was general agreement that the linguistic phenomena loosely identified as "flight of ideas" or "push of speech" are present in manic disorders, although their definitions were neither explicit nor linguistically formulated. In addition, the picture of disordered speech or "thought disorder" in severe depression was even less clear than in manic reactions.

In subsequent research, progress was made in efforts to identify more precisely the language behavior observed in manic disorders. Beginning with the pioneering study by Newman and Mather (1938), a number of findings by investigators have helped to establish some empirical generalizations concerning the "disordered speech" of manics.

(1) Basic speech capacities are preserved, including the ability of comprehend and generate grammatical sentences and to utilize highly complex linguistic transformations. A disruption in the ability to utilize properly ellipsis and semantic (discourse) anaphora may, however, be present, such that manics do not maintain a meaningful progression of thought in discourse (Durbin & Martin, 1977).

(2) "Thought disorder," as it has traditionally been conceptualized, occurs with high frequency in manic patients. Phenomena identified as tangentiality, derailment, incoherence, and illogicality occur with nearly equal frequency in both mania and schizophrenia (Andreasen, 1979b).

(3) The concept of "associative loosening" is of little value in the differential diagnosis between mania and schizophrenia (Andreasen, 1979b).

(4) While there is some evidence that the disordered speech found in mania and schizophrenia is similar, the speech of manic patients is easier to understand (Wykes & Leff, 1982).

With regard to depression, there is conflicting evidence concerning traditional thought disorder. While some evidence for its presence has been reported (Ianzito, Cadoret, & Pugh, 1974), Andreasen (1976) was led by the data in her study to conclude that it is absent:

> Although a few (depressed patients) display tangentiality and derailment, none show incoherence or illogicality. Poverty of speech, poverty of content of speech, circumstantiality, and loss of goal occur occasionally, but the presence of these subtypes is probably related to affective symptomatology. (p. 1329)

It seems obvious that this is an area requiring additional study.

Both schizophrenia and mania manifest aberrations of thought and speech that are often difficult to differentiate cross-sectionally, that is, at a given point in time. Following the course of these illnesses longitudinally, however, the thought disorder in schizophrenia is found even with typical mood, whereas, in mania, the thought disorder generally remits with typical mood. Andreasen and Powers (1974) suggested that overinclusive thinking, often referred to as a hallmark of schizophrenic thought, exists in mania as well. Stressing a longitudinal perspective, Carlson and Goodwin (1972) argued that course and prognosis may be a more valid method of distinguishing mania from schizophrenia than any particular disturbance in cognition, mood, or speech. Mania generally has an episodic course with relatively symptom-free intervals between ill periods, whereas schizophrenia generally has a more persistent, often declining course. If mania can be differentiated from schizophrenia on the basis of speech, either cross-sectionally or longitudinally, such a differentiation will first demand more adequate delineation of speech in each condition.

Research methods in linguistic and psycholinguistic research have grown considerably more sophisticated since the crude techniques such as word counts and type/token ratios found in earlier studies. Newer methods that are amenable to quantitative analysis can help provide the kind of data base required to establish empirical underpinnings for further research and theoretical development.

Investigators in this area have continually emphasized the restrictions imposed on the validity and generality of findings by the lack of normative data and by the small samples involved in most research. Given the kinds of problems involved in attempting to conduct systematic studies in clinical situations, these restrictions are probably not susceptible to extensive change in the foreseeable future. But it is necessary to point out the limitations that such problems impose on the interpretation of research findings.

REFERENCES

Andreasen, N. J. C. (1976). Do depressed patients show thought disorder? *Journal of Nervous and Mental Disease*, *163*, 186–192.
Andreasen, N. J. C. (1979a). Thought, language and communication disorder: I. Clinical assessment, definition of terms, and evaluation of their reliability. *Archives of General Psychiatry*, *36*, 1315–1321.
Andreasen, N. J. C. (1979b). Thought, language and communication: II. Diagnostic significance. *Archives of General Psychiatry*, *36*, 1325–1330.
Andreasen, N. J. C., & Powers, P. S. (1974). Over-inclusive thinking in mania and schizophrenia. *British Journal of Psychiatry*, *125*, 452–456.
Arieti, S. (1959). Manic-depressive psychosis. In S. Arieti (Ed.), *American handbook of psychiatry* (Vol. 1, pp. 419–454). New York: Basic.
Beck, A. T. (1967). *Depression: Causes and treatment*. Philadelphia: University of Pennsylvania Press.
Bleuler, E. (1911). *Dementia Praecox oder Gruppe der Schizophrenien*. Leipzig: Deuticke.

Bootzin, R. R. (1980). *Abnormal psychology: Current perspectives* (3d ed.). New York: Random House.

Carlson, G. A., & Goodwin, F. (1972). The stages of mania: A longitudinal analysis of the manic episode. *Archives of General Psychiatry, 28*, 221–228.

Durbin, M., & Martin, R. L. (1977). Speech in mania: Syntactic aspects. *Brain and Language, 4*, 208–218.

Eisenson, J., Auer, J. J., & Irwin, J. V. (1963). *The psychology of communication*. New York: Appleton-Century-Crofts.

Fromkin, V. A. (1975). A linguist looks at "A Linguist looks at language." *Brain and Language, 2*, 498–503.

Halliday, M. A. K., & Hasan, R. (1976). *Cohesion in English*. London: Longman.

Ianzito, B., Cadoret, R., & Pugh, D. (1974). Thought disorder in depression. *American Journal of Psychiatry, 131*, 703–707.

Keller, M. B. (1987). Differential diagnosis, natural course, and epidemiology of bipolar disorder. In R. E. Hales & A. J. Frances (Eds.), *Psychiatry update, American Psychiatric Association annual review* (Vol. 6, pp. 10–31). Washington, DC: American Psychiatric Association.

Kraepelin, E. (1896). *Psychiatrie: Ein Lehrbuch für Studierende und Ärtzte*. Leipzig: Barth.

Kraepelin, E. (1921). *Manic-depressive insanity and paranoia*. Edinburgh: Livingstone.

Lorenz, M., & Cobb, S. (1952). Language behavior in manic patients. *Archives of Neurology and Psychiatry, 69*, 763–770.

Newman, S., & Mather, V. G. (1938). Analysis of spoken language of patients with affective disorders. *American Journal of Psychiatry, 94*, 913–942.

Rochester, S., & Martin, J. R. (1979). *Crazy talk: A study of the discourse of schizophrenic speakers*. New York: Plenum.

Rosen, E., & Gregory, I. (1965). *Abnormal psychology*. Philadelphia: Lippincott.

Sherman, M. (1938). Verbalization and language symbols in personality adjustment. *American Journal of Psychiatry, 95*, 621–640.

Wykes, T., & Leff, J. (1982). Disordered speech: Differences between manics and schizophrenics. *Brain and Language, 15*, 117–124.

6

Language Behavior in Schizophrenia

One of the major difficulties confronting any attempt to analyze the behavioral phenomena that characterize schizophrenia is the problem of dealing with such a broad range of complex behaviors as though they were similar. We must begin by recognizing that the term *schizophrenia* refers to a group of disorders with common features but a wide range of behavioral differences rather than to a single disease entity with a well-defined series of symptoms. There is even some justification for questioning whether the numerous and varied manifestations currently labeled schizophrenia in the aggregate should not be considered distinct syndromes.

It must also be noted that, in addition to intraindividual variations in symptomatology, schizophrenic reactions show intraindividual variations over time. If one were to conceive of "mental health" as a continuum, schizophrenia would have to be depicted in terms of a range rather than a point. The limitations of neurogenic interpretations are hardly discussed and the need to parse schizophrenia and reduce heterogeneity must be recognized through a neurobehavioral approach to resolving the problem. Heinrichs (1993) is, to our knowledge, the best discussion of major issues in theory and research in schizophrenia and neuropsychology.

Among the most frequent behavioral manifestations of schizophrenia, we might list the following:

1. Withdrawal from, and retraction of interest in, the environment.

2. Disturbances of thought expressed in blocking, symbolization, incoherence, perseveration, and condensation.

3. Increased daydreaming and autistic behavior in general.

4. Alteration of overt behavior with a tendency toward excess, either in a marked increase of activity or in a marked decrease, in the direction of immobility; motor behavior tends toward perseveration and stereotypy.

5. Distortion or inappropriateness of affect, especially with regard to the thoughts of the individual and the meaning of the situation; divergence between thinking and feeling (e.g., dysphoric thoughts are accompanied by grins, smiles, or laughter) is one of the most general characteristics of schizophrenic behavior.

Within the broad scope of schizophrenic behavior, linguistic phenomena were among the first to attract attention, because of their striking and often bizarre qualities. As Gottschalk, Gleser, Magliocco, and D'Zmura (1961) have noted:

> the content of the patient's communications has been found difficult to understand or quite unintelligible. The language has been seen as ambiguous, with a tendency to diffusion or generalization. The words, themselves, have been noted to be used inexactly, and frequently there is frank incoherence of disjunction. Elliptical statements may occur. The sentences may have frequent self-contradictions and euphemisms, and they may contain many self-references and impersonal construction. (p. 101)

Roger Brown (1973), on the other hand, denies the existence of any such phenomenon as "schizophrenic language." Reminiscing about a three-week period of "total immersion in schizophrenia" at several hospitals in the vicinity of Harvard University, during which he attended at least one meeting of the Cambridge chapter of Schizophrenics Anonymous, Brown stated that he had found "plenty of schizophrenic thought" but nothing that qualified as "schizophrenic speech." If this conclusion raises the eyebrows of those who have spent much longer than three weeks observing and studying people who have been labeled schizophrenic, the explanation might lie in Brown's definition of "schizophrenic speech." He equates such speech with regressed speech, which suggests childlike speech, and he tells us:

> While I fairly often heard patients spoken to with what I call nursery school intonation, a kind of exaggerated prosody that most adults use with children, I have to report that in my three weeks I never heard anything childlike from a patient nor indeed anything I would want to set apart as schizophrenic speech. (Brown, 1973, p. 397)

More specifically, "childlike" refers to several characteristics of speech development in preschool children, which Brown has designated as "State I."

1. Sentences start short and only very gradually get longer.

2. Consonant clusters, an aspect of phonotactics are reduced or simplified in various ways.

3. Functional morphemes, like inflections for person and number, case endings, articles, prepositions, and so forth are almost always omitted, even in contexts in which they are obligatory in the adult language.

4. Semantically, Stage I speech is limited almost entirely to the sensorimotor world; it concerns objects, actors, actions, locations, nominations, recurrence, disappearance, attribution, and a few other things. Notably lacking is talk about emotions, personalities, personal relationships, religion, and all of the things schizophrenics talk about (Brown, 1973, p. 398).

His failure to find any of these characteristics in the speech of the schizophrenic persons he met convinced Brown that "Schizophrenic speech" is a myth.

The concept of schizophrenia as a "regression psychosis" has been popular with theorists from a psychoanalytic background. Among psychopathologists whose orientation is behavioral rather than psychodynamic, the concept has largely been discredited. As Maher (1966) has noted, the mere demonstration of a superficial resemblance between some feature of schizophrenic behavior and that of child behavior does not bring us appreciably closer to an understanding of psychotic behavior. He concluded that the concept of schizophrenia as a psychosis of regression has not been demonstrated with respect to language and expressed doubt as to the potential usefulness of such demonstrations in psychopathological investigations.

If schizophrenic speech is neither childlike nor regressed, what are its salient characteristics? Lorenz (1968) provides some extracts from recorded interviews with schizophrenic patients:

"Am I a good cook? It depends on whose house I'm cooking. No, I haven't had any dreams. They took the *Ladies Home Journal* out of my room and I haven't had any dreams. . . . Do you know the census population of the made world? I seem to have become so to speak the property of other people."

"I started with a sense that justice was next to the nebulous thing which no one can describe, but which dissolves all other relationships in its vapor, so that one notices other influences only insofar as they may help this nebulous aim, but without feeling of judgment otherwise."

"My teeth are killing me by expert dentistry of Dr. Brown the dentist and must be pulled as soon as possible as I will not live as I am."

Written productions as well as the spoken utterances of schizophrenics have engaged the attention of investigators. The specimens given below, representing extracts from documents written by schizophrenic patients, were reported by Maher (1966). Italicized words are those identified as neologisms.

"I am St. Michael the Archangel and the Red Horse of the Apocalypse. Some may say I have delusions of grandeur, but like Jesus Christ, I glorify myself for my Father's sake. For additional proof, I refer you to metaphysicians and Jehovah's Witnesses. I am in disguise and one might say a blessing in disguise. . . . I am for Goals for Americans, Strategy of Peace, Medical Care for the Aged, the Common Market, Peaceful Co-existence, and Self-Preservation not survival of the fittest, and also for freedom of religion."

"If things turn by rotation of agriculture or levels in regards and 'timed' to everything; I am referring to a previous document when I made some remarks that were facts also tested and there is another that concerns my daughter she has a lobed bottom right ear, her name being Mary Lou. . . . Much of abstraction has been left unsaid and undone in this product/milk syrup, and others due to economies, differentials, subsidies, bank-ruptcy, tools, buildings, bonds, national stocks, foundation craps, weather, trades, government in levels of breakages and fuses in electronic too all formerly 'stated' not necessarily *factuated.*"

"The players and boundaries have been of different colors in terms of black and white and I do not intend that the futuramas of supersonic fixtures will ever be in my life again because I believe that all known factors that would have its effect on me even the chemical reaction of ameno [*sic*] acids as they are in the process of *combustronability* are known to me." (p. 395)

Lorenz (1968) cautioned against the tendency to assume a schizophrenic language from limited samples of language behavior observed in schizophrenic individuals: "When we have a name for something, we tend automatically to assume the existence of a corresponding reality. Language, as used by schizo-phrenic patients, becomes identified by the term 'schizophrenic language.' This term suggests an entity with distinct features, a language differing from ordinary language" (p. 95). Says Forrest (1968), with regard to investigators' failures to establish a "schizophrenic dictionary" for use by the friends and relatives of patients, "Their question—Is there a schizophrenic language?— is as fruitless as the older quest for a poetic language. If one may search in vain for *a* schizophrenic language, one may on the other hand easily find schizo-phrenic language" (p. 1).

No professional training is required to recognize the deviant character of schizophrenic speech when it is unintelligible or incoherent. But the difficulty, for both lay persons and professionals, has been to pinpoint what makes schizophrenic language so different. Bleuler helped coin the term *schizo-phrenia* (Bleuler, 1911) when he described himself as a listener confused by incoherent talk. The disordered nature of the patient's language productions was interpreted by him as a "splitting" of psychic functions, the "schizo" of schizophrenia.

In the case of language disturbances such as stuttering, cluttering, and aphasia, we assume that the speaker's cognitive processes are essentially intact and that he or she desires to communicate in normal terms. In the case of the schizophrenic, the cognitive processes frequently appear to be distorted, and there is often good reason to doubt that the patient wishes to communicate in the normal sense. Indeed, there is a likely and perennial debate over whether the phenomena that have been identified as "schizophrenic language" are actually the symptoms of "schizophrenic thought." These two issues—the relation between disordered thought and disordered language and the peculiarities of schizophrenic communication—have dominated a good deal of the research and theory on schizophrenic language.

LANGUAGE DISORDER OR THOUGHT DISORDER?

Clinicians have tended to regard speech as a direct reflection of thought. Thus, schizophrenic patients whose speech is disrupted to the point of incoherence and unintelligibility are identified as demonstrating the symptoms of "formal thought disorder." Attention has been drawn by Chaika (1974), LeCours and Vanier-Clement (1976), and others to some of the problems created by treating speech and thought as isomorphic. But Rochester and Martin (1979) emphasize that the issue is further complicated by this "inferential tradition":

> To say that a speaker is incoherent is only to say that one cannot understand that speaker. So to make a statement about incoherent discourse is really to make a statement about one's own confusion. It is therefore just as appropriate to study what it is about the listener which makes him or her "confusable" as it is to study what it is about the speaker which makes him or her "confusing." The focus of study simply depends on the direction of attribution. (p. 3)

One of the consequences of the inferential tradition is that the assessment of "thought disorder" in both clinical and experimental contexts has been based on speech not thought. As the figure from Rochester and Martin (1979; Fig. 6.1) suggests, thought disorder and incoherent talk constitute parts of a tautology. A second consequence is that "talk failures" are inferences based on the listener's own experience of confusion. We will return to this interesting notion when we take up the crucial topic of schizophrenic communication.

PSYCHOGENIC AND DESCRIPTIVE THEORIES OF THOUGHT DISORDER IN SCHIZOPHRENIA

Arieti (1955) suggested that the language of the schizophrenic may be studied in two ways, the dynamic and the formal. The dynamic approach studies language from a predominantly motivational point of view, that is, the schizophrenic is motivated to change his speech purposively, possibly as a defense against threats posed by stressful interpersonal relationships. The

Figure 1. Imaginary conversation between student and textbook writer. (From S. Rochester and J. R. Martin *Crazy talk*. New York: Plenum Press, 1979. Reproduced by permission of the authors and publisher.)

motivation is maintained by a chain of psychogenic causes and effects that originate early in the development of each individual. Arieti takes the position that the removal of anxiety through dissociation from society permits the schizophrenic to feel safer and less disturbed. In rejecting society, he creates his own individuality and language. In this attempt to be unique, the schizophrenic resorts to archaic ways of expressing thoughts and feelings, ways that were long ago discarded in the course of evolution. The schizophrenic goes through what Arieti terms "teleologic regression." The schizophrenic uses material (words and symbols) from the environment but remolds them by his or her own archaic psychological processes. This attempt to be unique thus fails to a certain extent because the schizophrenic resorts to methods that are not individualistic but may be classified and analyzed in structural categories. What was a dynamic, historical process becomes crystallized in formal mechanisms. Any attempt to study the formal mechanisms of schizophrenia must be conscious of these dynamic qualities, of this fleeting mutability.

Arieti feels that the pathology of language as it appears in schizophrenia has three major headings: (1) impairment of the ability to abstract, (2) impairment of the ability to symbolize, and (3) impairment of the ability to socialize or to integrate into society. These three impairments overlap and are possibly different expressions of the same phenomena.

Goldstein (1944) indicates that expressions of abnormal concreteness are characteristic of schizophrenic behavior. He defines the concrete attitude as passive and the abstract attitude as active. The concrete attitude is realistic, given over and bound to the immediate experience of a given thing or situation in its particular uniqueness—thinking and acting are directed by the immediate claims made by one particular aspect of the object or situation in the environment. The abstract attitude, in being active, transgresses the immediately given specific aspect or sense impression and abstracts from particular properties. It is oriented by the conceptual viewpoint and is necessary for the individual to assume a voluntary mental set, to shift voluntarily from one aspect of a situation to another, to keep in mind various aspects at once, to grasp essentials of a given whole, to break up a whole into parts, to generalize, to abstract common properties, to plan ahead, to think symbolically, and to detach the ego from the outer world.

"Concrete," as used to characterize behavior and activity, indicates we are governed to an abnormal degree by external stimuli and the images, ideas, and thoughts that act on us at the moment. Goldstein suggests that the schizophrenic experiences only those objects to which he can react in a concrete way. He does not consider the object as part of an ordered world separated from himself as the nonschizophrenic person does.

The strange utterances of the schizophrenic can be better understood when considered in relation to the concrete situation that the patient experiences at a given moment and wants to express in words. The rare occurrence of general terms indicating categories or classes in schizophrenic speech samples supports the contention that patients have difficulty making generalizations. Goldstein suggests an origin in a disturbed function of the frontal lobes and the subcortical ganglia, which suggests also that the concreteness of the schizophrenic might be considered as a way out of the organism's unbearable conflict—a protection against the danger of severe catastrophe.

In using blocks of different sizes, shapes, and colors, Ach (1921) reported witnessing endless hesitancy and vacillation on the part of patients organizing the blocks, as if they were simultaneously considering all possibilities. Subjects put heterogenous blocks together, insisting, for example, that they were "all policemen," and appeared to classify objects according to the physiognomic aspects of the material. The researchers postulated that schizophrenics think largely in more concrete, realistic, matter-of-fact terms in which things have a personal rather than a symbolic value. They refuse to use the classification system of nonschizophrenic observers when it is explained to them and seem unable to grasp certain general principles.

The schizophrenic's inability to think abstractly or detach his/her ego from the outer world sheds some light on the undue importance patients attach to coincidental happenings. For instance, a schizophrenic lighting a cigarette and hearing a telephone ringing in the same instant will immediately assume a cause-and-effect relationship. He views the telephone ringing as a result of his lighting his cigarette. Schizophrenics often report observing conversations between people unknown to them and being convinced that the people are discussing them. The notion that objects and people have a purpose or life of their own and can exist outside the individual's sphere of direct experience requires abstract-thinking skills. Schizophrenic perception seems to transform abstract-thinking skills and to change abstract events into intensely personal ones, thereby "concreticizing" them.

Von Domarus (1944) indicates that a nonschizophrenic person ("logician") accepts identity only on the basis of identical subjects, whereas the schizophrenic ("paralogician") accepts identity on the basis of identical predicates. In the sample, "Socrates is a man—all men are mortal—Socrates is mortal," the schizophrenic would come to the conclusion, "Socrates is a man—I am a man—I am Socrates." Von Domarus gives as an additional example a schizophrenic patient in the asylum of the University of Bonn who believed that Jesus, cigar boxes, and sex were identical. On investigation, it was found the connection was one of being encircled: Jesus is a saint with a halo encircling his head, a package of cigars is encircled by a tax band, and a woman is encircled by the sexual glance of a man. Von Domarus suggests that the logic a schizophrenic uses are atavistic or that of higher animals. Arieti feels that such things as the identification between the symbol and its referent, the confusion of part and whole, the bizarre composition of different objects such as are seen in schizophrenic drawings and neologisms can all be interpreted as applications of Von Domarus's principle.

In the impairment of ability to symbolize (Arieti, 1955), four categories of increasing complexity are listed:

1. Signs (presence of certain things)
2. Images (visual, auditory, etc.; perceptions of external objects or objects themselves)
3. Paleosymbols (symbols created by the individual when a part or a predicate is selected to represent the objects he/she wants to symbolize)
4. Common or social symbols (paleosymbols accepted socially, eliciting the same reaction in another person).

According to Arieti, the schizophrenic abandons the common symbols and reverts to signs, images, and paleosymbols. When the schizophrenic loses the use of social symbols he/she also desocializes—thereby living in isolation. As the schizophrenic becomes more desocialized, the understanding of his/her language becomes more difficult, reaching a peak in the "word salad," which consists of speech composed of words that seem unrelated, such as "the house burnt the cow horrendously always."

Arieti maintains that the schizophrenic's impairment of language, since it is functional, is not permanent. In the absence of anxiety, the schizophrenic has the potential to regain the use of communicative language.

Critique

The views of Von Domarus and Arieti have not gone unchallenged. Nor has Goldstein's abstract/concrete dichotomy escaped criticism. Said Brown (1958):

> Research workers believe in the psychological unity of children, in the mind of primitive man, in the animal mind. They believe in disease entities called schizophrenia and aphasia. And so they are disposed to unify each category through the use of a common descriptive term. All of these categories are fallen away from the healthy, civilized, human adult. Each category lacks one attribute of the category to which the researcher himself belongs. There is a beautiful simplicity in the notion that all departures from ourselves are basically the same kind of departure. *Abstract* is the word that has been chosen to name the special quality of mind and *concrete* the word for all

other minds. The words have been used so as to maintain this master preconception rather than with referential consistency. The result is that *concrete* and *abstract* name all sorts of behaviors having no clear common properties. These unwitting shifts in reference are responsible for the general agreement that all kinds of subhuman mind are concrete as opposed to the abstract mind of the healthy, civilized adult. (p. 297)

Brown reviewed several experimental studies that reported performances for schizophrenic subjects that were more concrete than the performances of normal subjects. These included the findings of De la Garza and Worchel (1956) that schizophrenics were less oriented in time and space than control and Moran's (1953) report that schizophrenics were less able to deal with abstract analogies and less likely to give abstract definitions for words than control. Brown (1958) observes:

> It is the general rule with these studies to find a statistically significant group difference but also to find that the two distributions have a large area of overlap. This means that these characteristics are not reliably diagnostic. Some of the performances of the schizophrenic clearly involve a preference for narrow categories (e.g., a failure to define a term by its superordinate) but many do not and it is often difficult to figure out the general definition of concreteness under which the performance is subsumed. Furthermore, there are some schizophrenic performances which must be judged abstract by our definition. Morgan, for instance, found that schizophrenics would accept an abnormally large number of synonyms for words. They gave to words an exceptionally wide range of meanings. (pp. 294–295)

As an example of the latter, Brown refers to a study in which the investigator found that schizophrenics would accept an unusually large number of synonyms for words. Not only is it clear that giving a large range of meanings to words is an exercise in abstraction, but in more or less typical examples of what is described as a penchant for dealing concretely with questions there may be a clear awareness of conceptual categories of kind and type, as Maria Lorenz (1968) observed after citing the following example:

> Patient is asked to define certain terms:
> Q. Book.
> A. It depends what book you are referring to.
> Q. Table.
> A. What kind of table? A wooden table, a porcelain table, a surgical table, or a table you want to have a meal on?
> Q. House.
> A. There are all kinds of houses, nice houses, nice private houses.
> Q. Life.
> A. I have to know what life you happen to be referring to. *Life Magazine* or to the sweetheart who can make another individual happy. (Lorenz, 1968, p. 36)

Another haunting example is a letter addressed to Arieti by one of his patients in which the writer examines the varied meanings of the word passion.

Dear Dr. Arieti,
  It Is Because I Am So Passionate
That They Brought Me Here.
  Doctor Webster Asked Me Why I
Was Brought Here and I Couldn't Answer Without
A Certain Hesitation, But Now I Know, I Know Now:
  I'm Too Passionate!
  That's Why I Can't Get A Job.
You Had The Wrong Diagnosis
Take This For Instance
Look Up: The Word Passions in The
Encyclopedia (A Masterpiece of A Word)
And In The Dictionaries. Don't Get
Cerebral Meningitis In Your Studies.
But You Will Find That There Is A
Difference Between the Passions of Jesus of
Bethlehem and the Passions of Bluebeard.
Between the Passion of Misplaced Sympathies
And the Passions of Suicidal Thoughts.
Are You Passionately In Sympathy With
Your Great Poet Dante, Doctor Arieti?
And I Am In Passionate Admiration of the
Works of Moliere, The French Troubadour.
And There Is the Passion Flower
And The Passion Plays of Oberammergau. (Arieti, 1974)

Cameron (1963) has also been critical of the kinds of evidence advanced to support the regression hypothesis. He maintains that schizophrenic thought does not simply involve concreteness, that there are difficulties that are peculiar to schizophrenia, with tests such as the Vigotsky Blocks. For example, a schizophrenic patient may group the examiner's arm with the red blocks because the blood in the examiner's arms is also red.

Perhaps it is not the schizophrenic's capacity for abstract thinking that should be questioned, since there is also a tendency to overgeneralize. As Von Domarus points out, schizophrenics seem to disregard the individual traits of entities in order to equate things or people on the basis of insubstantial similarities. Taken to the extreme, this precocity for generalization indiscriminately lumps all things into one category, thereby giving an appearance of concreteness. Maher (1966) has objected to the variations introduced by Arieti in Von Domarus's original formulations. First, Maher denies that the formal laws of logic are representative of how nonschizophrenics think in commonplace situations. Second, he contends that Arieti's substitution of "paleologician" for "paralogician" (i.e., the schizophrenic) adds the connotation of regression to paralogic—a connotation that Von Domarus did not intend. In any case, Maher suggests that the elaborate set of assumptions involved in such theorizing is hardly justified when it is possible to explain instances of paleologic much more parsimoniously on the basis of simple generalization:

> When we say that patient accepts two dissimilar things as being identical, we mean that he behaves toward both of them in the same way—that he does not discriminate between them either in his verbal responses or in his other behavior in relation to Them. Insofar as he is responding to the attribute that the predicate describes his behavior is appropriate. It is when he is responding to attributes not covered by the predicate that his lack of discrimination becomes pathological. Even here, the behavior is only pathological when it is applied to one of the subjects; it may be quite appropriate when applied to the other.
>
> Let us consider a hypothetical example. A patient reasons as follows: "General Eisenhower is a veteran. My therapist is a veteran. Therefore my therapist is General Eisenhower." He then addresses his therapist as "General," salutes him whenever they meet, stands to attention in his office, and so forth. All of this is inappropriate behavior in relation to the therapist. Should be happen to meet General Eisenhower, the same behavior would be appropriate. Thus the behavioral consequences of paleological reasoning are exactly the same as the behavioral consequences of extended stimulus generalization.
>
> Behavior which is appropriate to one set of stimulus conditions is elicited by a stimulus of minimal (but some) similarity. What makes this generalization pathological is that it is being elicited by a degree of similarity that would be too small to elicit it in the normal subject. Looked at in this way, the problem of paleological reasoning is not that it is assuming identity on the basis of similar predicates. The problem is that the patient assumes identity on the basis of the similarity of very *limited* predicates. Where the range of attributes covered by a predicate is comparatively broad, the absence of discrimination between the subjects of those predicates is not at all unusual.
>
> Consider now a normal example. A person who has been ill-treated by someone with a foreign accent avoids the next person he meets who has a foreign accent. We should say that this is an example of simple avoidance learning generalizing to the stimulus of the foreign accent. Regarding the same events as the outcome of "reasoning," we might argue that the person was thinking paleologically in the following way: "The man who injured me had a foreign accent. This man has a foreign accent. Therefore this is the man who injured me." The avoidance behavior would then be seen as the outcome of a serious error in logic! (pp. 426–427)

Maher goes on to point out that, when verbal intelligence is controlled and emotionally provocative stimuli are avoided, hospitalized schizophrenics and nonschizophrenic subjects give comparable performances on logical reasoning tests.

"Verbal Behavior" Studies in Schizophrenia

Much of the early and even relatively recent history of language study in schizophrenia was addressed to the search for formal characteristics of schizophrenic language. Tabulations of word-count frequency, type/token and verb/adjective ratios, and detailed analyses of theme and content constituted the bulk of systematic inquiry. Said Maher (1966):

Many investigations have been directed toward the discovery of formal differences between schizophrenic language and other kinds of language without regard to the testing of hypotheses. Other studies have attempted to find similarities between schizophrenic language and that of other specific groups in the hope of adding to the probability that schizophrenia may be subsumed under some more general category or process. Generally speaking, we may regard these studies of formal characteristics as having two possible values. First, they attempt to discover simple differences per se, and as such they might provide empirical bases for the development of hypotheses about the processes involved in schizophrenic language. However, their second value lies in their relevance for existing hypotheses. (p. 398)

The Hypothesis of Overinclusion

Cameron (1938, 1963) suggests that a special characteristic of schizophrenic language is its extremely loose organization; the substitution of an approximate but related term or phrase for a more precise definitive term is characteristic. The loose structure of schizophrenic thinking permits the presence at the same time of potentially contradictory elements, simply because the actual contradiction that would arise in the process of the functional organization of concept formation does not come to pass. The schizophrenic's understanding of word meanings will be different from that of the control subjects in that it will be characterized to a greater extent by substitution of approximate but imprecise terms.

According to Cameron, the schizophrenic does not have the ability to "select and eliminate" words. Schizophrenics will be less able than control subjects to maintain adequate boundaries in their concepts and will tend toward "overinclusion" in their understanding of word meanings.

Cameron's contentions that the schizophrenic's language impairment is in part due to a distorted understanding and usage of individual words have been investigated in more than 100 studies, beginning with the work of Weckowitz and Blewett (1959) and extending to the investigations of Chapman and Chapman (1973). Through multiple-test formats, these studies have compared schizophrenic and nonschizophrenic interpretations of vocabulary words appearing in differing contexts. A typical study (Chapman, Chapman, & Daut, 1976) required patients to discriminate between principal and tangential meanings of a word, with the following format:

Mark the statement or statements which tell what a book is often like.
(a) You read it. ("strong meaning response")
(b) It has a back. ("weak meaning response")
(c) It's edible. ("irrelevant alternative")
(d) None of the above. (Chapman et al., 1976, p. 36)

The results supported findings by past experiments that "chronic patients chose the 'strong meaning response' whether it was appropriate or not, while normal subjects chose that response only when it fit the sentence frame" (Rochester & Martin, 1979, p. 12). However, the scores of schizophrenics on standard vocabulary tests were equal to those of nonschizophrenics. These findings suggest that, while schizophrenics can define words in the same way as nonschizophrenics, they are less able to infer word meanings from a given context. This has some interesting implications when one considers the schizophrenic's rejection of, or alienation from, society. The schizophrenic's inability to grasp the connotative or culturally conditioned meanings of words greatly impoverishes the communicative value of his/her speech.

The "verbal behavior" studies just described have been criticized for testing skills that bear limited resemblance to language processes. According to McGhie (1970), the patient's language difficulties stem "not from an inability to perceive the individual words comprising a connected discourse, but from an inability to perceive the words in meaningful relationship to each other as part of an organized pattern" (p. 12). A study by McGhie, Chapman, and Lawson (1964) narrating subjective reports from 26 schizophrenic patients strongly indicated that patients were unable to make use of "the organization inherent in language." One patient recounted:

> When people talk to me now it's like a different kind of language. It's too much to hold at once. My head is overloaded and I can't understand what they say. It makes you forget what you've just heard because you can't get hearing it long enough. It's all in different bits which you have to put together again in your head—just words in the air unless you can figure it out from their faces. (McGhie & Chapman, 1961, p. 375)

As a result of such narratives, researchers turned to devising studies that tested the extent of the schizophrenic's reliance on language structure. Gerver (1967) drew on tests formulated by Miller and Selfridge (1950) in which normal subjects were asked to recall sentences bearing various approximations to English. Results indicated that normal subjects "could remember more and more words as the order of approximation to English increased from 0 to about 5." (After 5 there was approximately no increase.) Gerver compared schizophrenic and control subjects' ability to recall phrases including normal sentences (e.g., "Trains carry passengers around the country"), syntactically admissible but semantically anomalous sentences (e.g., "Trains steal elephants around the highways") and random strings (e.g., "On trains live elephants simplify"). Unexpectedly, the rate of improvement in recall for acute and chronic schizophrenics, psychiatric control patients, and nonpsychiatric control subjects proved to be the same, though schizophrenic subjects recalled fewer words than did control subjects.

Variations on Gerver's studies were carried out by Truscott (1970) and

Rochester, Harris, and Seeman (1973), all producing similar results. Carpenter (1976) had subjects recall narrative passages that were frequently interrupted and found that schizophrenic listeners, like normal adults and 11-year-old children, recalled adjacent clauses better if the clauses belonged to the same sentence than if they belonged to different sentences.

The General Inquirer

Descriptions of schizophrenic language and thought by early investigators tended to be rather subjective and metaphorical. Cameron (1938) referred to thinking that "tends to stick to everything it touches"; Storch (1924) wrote of "an onion coming unpeeled"; and Kraepelin (1919) likened schizophrenic thought to a train that becomes derailed. The elusive nature of such descriptions over the years spurred the search for an objective and systematized approach to linguistic description that led to the development of the General Inquiry System by Stone, Bales, Namenworth, and Ogilvie (1962) and Stone, Dunphy, Smith, and Ogilvie (1966). The sentence was chosen as the unit of analysis and words are classified according to grammatical categories (e.g., subject, subject modifier, verb, verb modifier) and thematic categories (e.g., natural-world, legal, political). Though human intuition is infinitely more sensitive to the multifold patterns and content of language, the General Inquirer System ensures a quantitative, objective approach to language analysis.

Maher, McKean, and McLaughlin (1966) used the General Inquirer System to analyze written samples from more than 100 hospitalized schizophrenic patients. Unlike most studies, the hypotheses Maher and his workers propose concerning information processing and attentional behavior are supported by quantitative, language-based data. Among other conclusions, Maher's workers propose that (1) "the attentional mechanisms that are necessary to the maintenance of coherent language are weaker at the end of the sentence than elsewhere" and (2) "where high ratios exist (schizophrenic patients) are likely to be judged thought-disordered, but the absolute probability that (such ratios) will be found in a randomly selected document from a schizophrenic patient is not high" (Maher et al., 1966, p. 497). Maher's findings must be considered conservative because of the limited sensitivity of the General Inquirer System.

In their survey of literature on schizophrenic language studies, Rochester and Martin (1979) report work by Tucker and Rosenberg (1975) using the General Inquirer System:

In a pilot study, they took 600-word samples from acute schizophrenic patients and form two control groups of patients and normal subjects. The patients' samples were taken from 15-min interviews collected during their first week in hospital; the normals' samples were taken after they had experienced 10 min of REM sleep and were awakened and asked to describe their dreams. An adaptation of the Harvard III Psychological Dictionary was used to sort words from the samples into 84 categories which had been "specifically selected for their psychological and sociological relevance" (Tucker and Rosenberg, 1975, p. 612). They found that 14 out of 84 categories differentiated schizophrenic from nonschizophrenic subjects.

In a replication (Rosenberg and Tucker, 1976), the authors studied larger samples (which included subjects from the original samples) and refined their procedures. The results of the replication, once gender differences were controlled, were that 3 out of 31 categories differentiated schizophrenic from nonschizophrenic patients. Thus, when the technique was refined and the sample size increased, the replication was no more promising as a discriminative procedure. The categories that discriminated the larger sample of schizophrenic patients were "Not" (schizophrenics used more words denoting negation), and two categories that schizophrenic underused relative to nonschizophrenic patients. (p. 37)

A survey of language-based studies ranging from verbal behavior to General Inquirer Studies supports the position that schizophrenicity among patients varies widely and that schizophrenia can be considered a range of disorders rather than a single disease. Marked distinctions occur, for instance, between chronic and acute schizophrenics, with the latter having consistently higher verbal IQs than the former.

PSYCHOLINGUISTIC STUDIES OF SCHIZOPHRENIC LANGUAGE

In 1974, linguist Elaine Chaika reported the results of an analysis of a taped interview with a 37-year-old female schizophrenic patient who was under medication with thorazine—a major tranquilizer—at the time of the recording. The patient's record indicated that she spoke in a normal fashion for periods ranging up to several weeks but that her deviant language coincided with "psychotic episodes," some excerpts of which (in Chaika, 1974) are described as "virtually a monologue": The patient's intonation did not allow intrusions, and she often seemed to be talking to herself. Chaika (1974) notes that several items pronounced by the patient are gibberish, but except for these, "the phonology of each utterance seems to be entirely normal. It strikes the listener as being in no way deviant" (p. 261).

On the basis of her analysis of his corpus of utterances and of samples of schizophrenic speech reported in the literature, Chaika identified six characteristics of such language:

  5. Sporadic disruption in the ability to match semantic features with sound strings comprising actual lexical items in the language . . .;
  6. Preoccupation with too many of the semantic features of a word in discourse . . .;
  7. Inappropriate noting of phonological features of words in discourse . . .;

8. Production of sentences according to phonological and semantic features of previously uttered words, rather than according to a topic . . .;
9. Disruption in the ability to apply rules of syntax and discourse . . .;
10. Failure to self-monitor, e.g., not noting errors when they occur. (Chaika, 1974; p. 275)

Chaika maintains that all of these characteristics "suggest a disruption in the ability to apply those rules which organize linguistic elements, such as phonemes, words, and sentences, into corresponding meaningful structures, namely words, sentences, and discourse" (Chaika, 1974, p. 275). She raised the possibility that speech judged "schizophrenic" by researchers results from an intermittent cyclical aphasia.

Linguist Victoria Fromkin (1975) questioned Chaika's conclusions on the grounds that all of the phenomena identified as characteristics of schizophrenic speech, with the exception of disruption of discourse, can be found in normal speech performance. As evidence she cites some excerpts from *The White House Transcripts* (Gold, 1974) to show that normal productions "are filled with incorrect deletions, repetitions, syntactic rule misapplications" and other deviant properties (p. 501).

In her rebuttal to Fromkin, Chaika (1977) contrasts the samples from *The White House Transcripts* with a specimen of schizophrenic "word salad" reported by Lorenz (1968): "The honest bring-back-to-life doctors agents must take John Black out through making up design meaning straight neutral underworld shadow tunnel." The structure of the syntactic errors in this passage cannot be easily identified, while the deviance in the White House passages is "caused by piling sentence upon sentence, often failing to embed subsequent sentences into the matrix, or to finish the matrix" (Chaika, 1977, p. 466). But within each utterance, the phrases and sentences are understandable and, for the most part, syntactically correct.

The possibility raised by Chaika that schizophrenic speech may reflect an intermittent aphasia has been of interest and concern to aphasiologists, as indicated by the attention this issue has received in the professional literature (Benson, 1973; Gerson, Benson, & Frazier, 1977). LeCours and Vanier-Clement (1976) have contributed to this discussion with their review of "schizophasia" and its relation to jargonaphasia. They identify four characteristics of schizophasia:

1. a normal or greater than normal speech flow;
2. a normal arthric and prosodic realization (i.e., normal use of intonation and pronunciation);
3. a production, in various amounts and combinations, of paraphasias and/or telescopages and/or neologisms;
4. a more or less apparent component of glossomania (LeCours & Vanier-Clement, 1976, p. 524).

Paraphasia refers to deviant-language segments. Phonemic paraphasias are operations such as deletion, displacement, or addition of phonemic units, resulting in a deviant word ("inaktif"—"inaktik"). Morphemic paraphasias are those in which deviant segments are used as single words that do not conform to any of the speaker's community's word inventories (final + primitive → finitive). Verbal paraphasias are those in which word deletion, displacement, or addition occurs ("a scent of cadaver" instead of "a scent of caviar"). Syntactic paraphasias involve those in which one word or phrase is replaced by another with the same syntactic function ("My sister worked in a doctor" instead of "My sister worked for a doctor"). Telescopages involve deviant segments taking the form of a single phrase and are produced by borrowing verbal elements from several conceptually and/or formally related phrases ("transformation" instead of "transmission of information"). Formal glossomania is linguistic behavior characterized by production of sentences, the verbal components of which are chosen mainly on the basis of phonological kinship to one another (alliteration, assonance, homophony, etc.), as illustrated by a word string such as "I was a glass bowl and I don't mean grass in hole." Semantic glossomania, in the case of sentences, the verbal components of which are chosen mainly on the basis of conceptual associations apparently unrelated to the conversational topic, is illustrated by a quotation from Chaika's (1974) patient: "My mother's name was Bill (pause) and coo? St. Valentine's Day is the official startin' of the breedin' season of the birds. All buzzards can coo. I like to see it pronounced buzzards rightly. They work hard. So do parakeets" (p. 260). Neologisms are deviant segments used as single words (reserved for items that cannot be identified by other categories). Finally, glossolalia is deviant linguistic behavior characterized by the production of long stretches of neologistic segments. LeCours and Vanier-Clement (1976) observe that glossolalia occurs in both schizophrenics and aphasics, as well as among people who are involved in Pentecostal (charismatic) religious movements.

Schizophrenic Communication

It is possible to account for discourse failures among schizophrenics by positing some pathological process within the central nervous system that disrupts information processing and thus operates to produce the kinds of language behavior that Rochester and Martin have described as distinguishing thought-disordered speakers from nonthought-disordered speakers. This, in fact, has been the traditional way to approach schizophrenic thought and language disruption. We feel, however, that this approach is unduly restrictive in the emphasis it places on the individual schizophrenic person and its tendency to minimize or totally ignore an important alternative approach. People can talk to pets, small children, inanimate objects, or to themselves, but most human speech takes place within the context of linguistic interaction with other adults, that is, in the context of communication. Failure to relate speech to the communicative context can result in some extremely questionable interpretations of schizophrenic speech production. Let us refer once again to Lorenz's sample, cited earlier, of the patient who was asked to define a series of words. The interaction went as follows:

> Q. Book.
> A. It depends on what book you are referring to.
> Q. Table.
> A. What kind of table? A wooden table, a porcelain table, a surgical table, or a table you want to have a meal on?
> Q. House.
> A. There are all kinds of houses, nice houses, nice private houses.
> Q. Life.
> A. I have to know what life you happen to be referring to. *Life Magazine* or to the sweetheart who can make another individual happy. (Lorenz, 1968, p. 36)

Linguistically, of course, there is no difficulty. The problem is, in part, one of differing assumptions about the nature or purpose of the communicative act. The questioner expects an abstract, dictionary-type definition to cover the general case, while the subject rejects that expectation. Compare the apparent perversity of the speech of the schizophrenic in the above exchange with one of the examples reported by Garfinkel (1967): The victim waved his hand cheerily.

> (S) How are you?
> (E) How am I in regard to what? My health, my finances, my schoolwork, my peace of mind, my . . .?
> (S) (Red in the face and suddenly out of control.) Look! I was just trying to be polite. Frankly, I don't give a damn how you are. (p. 44)

Garfinkel's experimenter (E) was not schizophrenic: he was dramatizing the fact that assumptions or common understandings that underlie interaction lack properties of strict rational discourse as these are idealized in rules that define an adequate logical proof:

> For the purposes of conducting their everyday affairs persons refuse to permit each other to understand "what they are really talking about" in this way. The anticipation that persons will understand, the occasionality of expressions, the specific vagueness of references, the retrospective-prospective sense of a present occurrence, waiting for something later in order to see what was meant before, are sanctioned properties of common discourse. (Garfinkel, 1967, p. 41)

If Garfinkel is correct, a good deal of our daily interaction depends on ambiguous or vague communication that seems designed to bind two parties while actually ensuring their separation. The particular example quoted from Garfinkel illustrates what Malinowski called "phatic communion," in which it is the mere fact of exchanging utterances that is important and the content of the utterances is almost irrelevant. By insisting on a literal interpretation of the greeting, the experimenter was behaving in a way that was perceived as hostile. In other examples, the experimenters were seen as ill or in a "bad mood."

Many clinicians would probably subscribe to Ferreira's (1960) notion that the schizophrenic manipulates or disguises his or her language, in order to conceal thoughts known to be dangerous and forbidden: "In the privacy of his language, the schizophrenic finds the much looked-after opportunity to say a piece of his mind about a relationship the nature of which he could not state publicly" (p. 136).

Bateson, Jackson, Haley, and Weakland (1956, 1963) have advanced the theory that schizophrenia originates in the "double bind" in which a youngster finds himself when a parent consistently conveys simultaneous but incongruent messages. That is, the mother says words to the effect, "Come here, I love you," but at the same time communicates rejection by her tone of voice, gestures, and other subtle cues. If the child discriminates accurately between the messages, he or she will be punished by the realization that his mother does not really love him or her, but if the child does not discriminate accurately between them and takes the verbal message at face value, then he or she will approach her. When the child approaches she will become hostile, so the child will withdraw; then she will rebuke him for withdrawing, because the withdrawal signified she was not a loving mother. Either way the child loses and is thus in a double bind.

We will examine the double-bind concept at greater length in Chapter 7, below. It is sufficient at this point to note that, if Bateson and his associates are correct, it may be more than a coincidence that schizophrenic verbalizations are frequently ambiguous, difficult, or impossible to interpret. That is, the schizophrenic frequently offers difficult messages to those with whom he appears to be interacting.

The schizophrenic's apparent flatness of affect, inappropriate expression of affect combined with withdrawal, or loss of interest in the social and physical environment is probably the most widely cited characteristic of the disorder. It is typically withdrawal that seems to be expressed in schizophrenic speech. Tangential responses and the pursuing of irrelevant details are easily interpreted as an avoidance of direct communication.

The omission of transitional expressions and joining of disparate ideas (called scattering) is less readily interpreted in the same way, although the effect is still poor communication. The following written example of scattering (from Maher, 1966) seems almost like a third or fourth approximation of English:

> If things turn by rotation of agriculture or levels in regards and "timed" to everything; I am re-ferring to a previous document when I made some remarks that were facts also tested and there is another that concerns my daughter she has a lobed bottom right ear, her name being Mary Lou. . . . Much of abstraction has been left unsaid and undone in this product/milk syrup, and others due to economics, differentials, subsidies, bankruptcy, tools, buildings, bonds, national stocks, foundation craps, weather, trades, government in levels of breakages and fuses in electronic too all formerly "stated" not necessarily factuated. (p. 395)

The idea that the schizophrenic employs language so as not to communicate is intriguing, but a contrary school of thought that also finds considerable support. Ullmann and Krasner (1969), for example, argue that in a sense the deficiency is located in the listener rather than in the patient. If the listener were able to fill in the gaps, he or she would "understand" the patient. These researchers seem to suggest that seemingly unintelligible material may actually make some sort of sense. Of course, the patient and the listener are not observing the same interactional rules, but, according to this view, the desire to communicate in the normal sense of the word may actually be present.

Schizophasia speech, as Rochester and Martin have emphasized, is episodic in nature, that is, it varies from situation to situation. It may well be that the clue to this variation lies in some underlying pathological condition within the brain of the schizophrenic that produces distortions in language processing. This explanation does not rule out the possibility that certain features of communicative contexts may provide severe stress and anxiety for the schizophrenic individual—and that it is these varying demands, rather than some internal source of cognitive disturbance, that result in the kinds of distortion in communication that typify thought-disordered and nonthought-disordered schizophrenic speakers.

ROCHESTER'S ANALYSIS OF SCHIZOPHRENIC DISCOURSE

In reviewing descriptive analyses such as that by LeCours and Vanier-Clement (1976), Rochester and Martin (1979) observe that we can learn (1) not every schizophrenic patient is schizophasic and (2) not every schizophasic patient is schizophasic all of the time. According to the authors:

> These facts have been responsible for great confusion in experimental investigations. Experimenters have behaved as if schizophasia could be sampled at random from unselected schizophrenic patients. It is no wonder that there have been so many failures to replicate even the simplest 'verbal behavior' studies. (Rochester & Martin, 1979, p. 43)

They conclude that, if schizophasia is episodic, then investigators must seek to capture such episodes and describe them. A further requirement is that more precise descriptions must be given of patient characteristics in order to determine "whether some sorts of patients are more likely than others to, say, show discourse failures other than 'verbal paraphasias'; whether 'phonemic telescopages' can occur without other manifestations of schizophasia; whether phonemic aberrations always occur with aberrations at the verbal level and at the level of discourse; or whether chronic patients are more likely to show some of these behaviors and acute patients to show others" (Rochester & Martin, 1979, p. 43).

The research project reported by Rochester and Martin incorporated these considerations in an intensive study of schizophrenic patients who were selected on the basis of clinical judgments of whether their speech samples indicated the presence or absence of thought disorder. The experimental groups consisted of 10 thought-disordered schizophrenic speakers and 10 nonthought-disordered schizophrenic speakers, who were interviewed during their first month of hospitalization. These 20 patients were matched with a control group with comprised both volunteers and nonpsychiatric hospital patients. The age range over all subjects was 18 to 48 years, with a mean of 26.7 years.

Subjects participated in what Rochester and Martin call three "speech contexts": (1) an unstructured interview lasting about a half hour; (2) a brief narrative, which was read to the subject at the end of the interview and retold in the subject's own words; and (3) a cartoon task adapted from Goldman-Eisler (1968), in which the subject described and interpreted 10 cartoon pictures, as shown in Figure 6.2.

The findings of this study are difficult to summarize in a manner that does justice to the sophistication of the research design and the issues explored. As Rochester and Martin (1979) put it, "There is a clear problem in the use of language" (p. 173) for the patients studied here, but it is not a simple problem. For one thing, no instances were found of the severe agrammatism that has sometimes been identified in previous investigations of schizophrenic language. The distinction between thought-disordered speakers and other speakers is at a highly developed level of language use, not at the level of word salads, neologisms, or speech blocking. This finding may have something to do with the sample of thought-disordered speakers used in the study: young, relatively intact persons. Much of the literature dealing with schizophrenic language and speech, especially the older clinical reports, features language samples from chronic schizophrenics—the kind of people who have traditionally been referred to as "backward patients." The speech or language samples collected from such patients are usually presented with little or no accompanying diagnostic or life-history data, leaving considerable room for the possibility that both thought and language have suffered the ill effects of prolonged institutional confinement. There is also the distinct possibility that older patients may be suffering the adverse consequences of organic brain damage.

Two aspects of discourse failure that distinguished thought-disordered speakers from other speakers in the Rochester and Martin study were (1) a strong dependency on the lexical meanings of words to achieve cohesion between clauses and sentences and (2) a tendency to rely on the prosodic features of clauses and words to link these clauses to the prior context. These findings confirm previously reported results of a similar kind. They appear to be closely related to a third feature of thought-disordered discourse noted by Rochester and Martin: the difficulties posed for the listener in comprehending the thought-disordered speaker as a consequence of the tendency for the latter to rely on high proportions of implicit reference in which the referents are frequently obscure to the point of inaccessibility.

Rochester and Martin (1979) have sought to interpret their findings within the theoretical/analytical framework provided by Halliday (1978; Halliday & Hasan, 1976) on "phoricity systems." These systems structure utterances on the basis of what speakers assume their listeners know; thus, the study of phoricity systems supplies an analytical approach to reference and referential processes. On the basis of Halliday's work, Rochester and Martin (1979) "assume that the speaker processes meanings into expressions by making choices within a number of language systems" (p. 177): phonological/written expressions, lexicogrammatical forms, and semantic meanings within text. It is assumed that the fully competent adult speaker can produce coherent texts by making appropriate decisions at each of the three levels or strata mentioned above.

If the speaker is subjected to fatigue, stress, or some other factor or factors that result in the reduction of control over language processing, he or she begins to fail to produce coherent discourse in certain orderly, predictable ways:

> The first failures occur at the level of sentence-to-sentence links and may be seen in a lack of topic direction, in failures to establish major and minor role actors and clear event lines, and in a lack of certain kinds of cohesion between clauses. Later failures would include the earlier ones and, in addition, involve mistakes at the lexicogrammatical stratum of language use. In this case, one would see the use of neologisms, inadequate grammatical forms, and the use of inappropriate wordings of various kinds. However, the intonation patterns and pausing and other prosodic features of normal speech would be more or less intact. Finally, a complete breakdown in language operations would be signaled by the speaker's inability to match intonation patterns or select rhyming words when asked. (Rochester & Martin, 1979, pp. 177–178)

Rochester and Martin (1979) use the concept of "stratal slips" to summarize this interpretation of discourse failures at the various successive levels of linguistic functioning. Stratal slips can occur within text (when cohesion based

Figure 2. Cartoon task for eliciting discourse samples in the Rochester and Martin study of schizophrenic speech. (Adapted from R. Goldman-Eisler, *Psycholinguistics: Experiments in spontaneous speech*. New York: Academic Press, 1968. Reproduced by permission of the author and publisher.)

FIGURE 2. (*Continued*)

on semantic linkage is replaced by cohesion based on lexicogrammatical forms or prosodic features) or outside text (when connections within the text are reduced and connections between the text and the verbal or nonverbal aspects of the situational context are increased).

The significance of the Rochester and Martin analysis is that it directs attention toward the process or processes that adversely affect the control of language operations. The "depth of processing" formulation the authors have adopted is not restricted to dealing narrowly with linguistic functions but is concerned with a much broader range of cognitive activities. As Rochester and Martin (1979) have stated, it seems essential "to add onto studies of language processing simultaneous studies of other aspects of cognitive and perceptual functioning so that one can assess the extent to which incoherent discourse occurs with disrupted functioning in other domains" (p. 186).

Harvey (1983) replicated the findings of Rochester and Martin and found that reference failures were specific to the actual sections of discourse that met clinical criteria for thought disorder, suggesting that these failures contribute to the impression that thought processes are impaired in schizophrenic patients. In addition, reference failures were also found to be present in children of schizophrenics (Harvey, Weintraub, & Neale, 1982) and schizophrenic patients in clinical remission (Docherty, Schmur, & Harvey, 1988). These findings would appear to support the possibility that speech disorders characterize aspects of vulnerability to schizophrenia, as well as correlating with the severity of clinical measured speech disorder. They also suggest a possible impairment among schizophrenic patients in terms of determining shared knowledge, since the subject refers to nonexistent objects in a way that presumes commonality. Interestingly enough, some investigators have found evidence that young children tend to communicate as though the listener possessed privately held information (Anderson, Clark, & Mullin, 1991; Glucksberg, Krauss, & Weisberg, 1966; Piaget, 1926, 1955).

Chaika (1990) reports a list of linguistic errors produced by schizophrenics and nonschizophrenics while completing a narrative task. Only schizophrenics generated word rhyming, neologisms, misordered events, and intrusions of personal memories—and most of these were disruptive and seemingly accidental. She noted errors at almost every level of speech with particular difficulties in organizing and ordering the narratives. In contrast, nonschizophrenics were able to organize their narratives tightly and never introduced personal memories or subjective comments.

VOCAL ACOUSTIC STUDIES OF SCHIZOPHRENIC SPEECH

Alpert, Merewether, Homel, Martz, and Lomask (1986) and Welkowitz, Bond, and Zelano (1990) have developed computer-based voice-analysis systems ("Voxcom" and "Welmar," respectively) for analyzing various speech characteristics that reliably assess the physical properties of speech. Alpert and his colleagues devised a measurement for the study of the negative syndrome of schizophrenia with internally consistent scales. The subject's voice is analyzed through a hybrid analog-digital microcomputer system that locates silences and speech. The program identifies syllables and for each peak notes the amplitude (loudness) and fundamental frequency (pitch) and the duration of utterances, silences, and peaks. The software groups the acoustic measures into the categories of expressiveness, rate, dyadic interaction, and productivity. For example, productivity measures utterance-based productivity, pause-based productivity, and percentage of time spent talking from the time available. Expressiveness measures the amplitude and frequency of utterances. Dyadic interactions measures durations of interactional turns and duration of switching pauses. Interactive measures are assessed with the Welmar software (Welkowitz et al., 1990), which identifies a number of dyadic measures that include response latency (a measure of transition time from one speaker to the other), simultaneous speech, interruptive speech, pause, and turn durations, providing interactional objective acoustic measures of speech.

Alpert and his colleagues report that acoustic measures of vocal expressiveness and productivity are attenuated in schizophrenic patients with flat affect and increased in patients with positive symptoms. Schizophrenics with flat affect tend to vary their amplitude and frequency less when compared with normal subjects (Andreasen, Alpert, & Martz, 1981) and when compared with schizophrenics without flat affect (Alpert, Rosen, Welkowitz, Sobin, & Borod, 1989). Flattening of affect, a constriction in the range of content-appropriate expression of feelings, is the most clinically observed disturbance of affect. In schizophrenics, flat affect is a powerful predictor of treatment outcome. Similar behaviors are typical in progressive Parkinson's disease, where patients show affective constriction and a high incidence of depression (Alpert et al., 1989). In one study, Alpert et al. (1990) examined the vocal acoustics and interactional patterns of a group of patients with Parkinson's disease and mild to moderate dementia. These objective measures of vocal acoustic communications correlated with independent clinical ratings by a neurologist. The more impaired subjects had shorter conversational turns with brief utterances and longer pauses than did the least impaired subjects. These lengthier pauses interfered with the normal turn-taking pattern of communication, leaving the listener unsure of where his conversational turn was expected, and produced increased response latency from the interviewer. On the other hand, the least impaired subjects spoke for longer periods of time and made lengthier and more complex utterances. According to the authors, these findings suggest that objective computer analyses of speech patterns indicate the differing interactional style of patients with dementia and the way that dementia affects communication (see also Alpert, Clark, & Pouget, in press).

Certain neurological conditions also produce evidence of affective blunting, as evidenced through multiple behavioral channels, including speech. The types of lesions that produce affective impairments (i.e., lesions of the anterior frontal cortex and of the right hemisphere) are detected with neuropsychological assessment on which schizophrenics are themselves deficient. A clinical challenge is to assess flat affect and depression in patients who show an admixture of both signs.

Neuroleptic drugs, which are used universally to treat schizophrenic patients, may also influence behavior in ways that mimic flat affect. Demoralization, frequently seen in chronic schizophrenic patients, may also be difficult to distinguish from flat affect. Finally, retarded depressed patients may also show reduced expressiveness in face and gesture and be rated as showing flat affect. It is important to distinguish retarded depression, for example, from flat affect because of the difference in etiology and treatment response for these clinically similar presentations.

In one study, Alpert and his associates collected acoustic and linguistic measures from the speech of 10 patients diagnosed as schizophrenic while they participated in structured interactive tasks designed to investigate a number of communicative skills. Patients were examined while on therapeutic levels of neuroleptic medication and while drug free. The authors note that in previous research they found that prosodic aspects of the speech of schizophrenics changed when such patients were treated with drugs. These changes include decreases in productivity and increases in expressiveness. In the present study they found that medicated patients produced longer utterances that were more cohesive and that speech rate also increased. Drug-free patients produced shorter utterances that were more ambiguous and unclear, and their speech rate was lower than when they were medicated.

Patients produced more related and cohesive responses to the interviewer's questions while the patients were on medication. More bizarre, unclear, and ambiguous references were produced while patients were drug free. The information available to patients influenced referential choice. For example, all patients produced more situational references when the diagram features were labeled. However, only on medication could patients take advantage of the extra information to produce the most related responses. The authors found no significant differences for pausing behavior in speech across medication; nor were there any significant differences in dyadic measures of interaction, inflection, or emphasis.

These results, the researchers conclude, suggested that neuroleptics enhance attentional processes in linguistic performance and do not induce deficits in expressiveness. It appears that medication plays an important role in increasing pragmatic awareness and listener responsibility in patients with schizophrenia.

The authors refer to Chaika's characterization of the speech of schizophrenics as involving general problem in ordering and organizing. However, the authors found that the most unorganized and disruptive speech observed in their study was confined to those patients who were drug free and, that with medication and an active interactional partner, most medicated patients could produce meaningful task-oriented dialogues and perform well with the referential discrepancies. They found that communication problems were not due to general impaired interactional skills but to isolated attentional lapses, breakdowns in comprehension monitoring, and derailments involving memory intrusions from past experiences that they were unable to suppress, similar to the "faulty filtering" mechanisms found in Chaika's medicated patients.

The authors conclude by suggesting the potential utility of the speech-analysis methods they employed in clinical assessment. Although there are a number of precise and specific objective measures available to psychopathologists (e.g., attention, deployment, vigilance, eye tracking), they serve more to study pathogenetic mechanisms than to evaluate expressed pathology. It is not easy for clinicians to detect by ear the speech measures used in the research of Alpert and his colleagues. For example, with respect to pausal phenomena, the authors examined the ability of a clinician to estimate a patient's response latencies (Alpert, Sison, Pouget, Yahia, & Allen, 1992). Only 14% of the rating variance was associated with objective measures of switching pauses; there were larger contributions of halo effects and error to these ratings. Acoustic measures of the patient's voice could provide useful supplemental information for the clinician.

REFERENCES

Ach, N. (1921). *Uber die begriffsbildung: Eine experimentelle untersuchung*. Bamberg: C. C. Buchnero Verlag.

Alpert, M., Clark, A., & Pouget, E. R. (in press). The syntactic role of pauses in the speech of schizophrenic patients with alogia. *Journal of Abnormal Psychology, 102*.

Alpert, M., Merewether, F., Homel, P., Martz, M. R., & Lomask, M. (1986). Voxcom: A system for analyzing speech in real time. *Instruments and Computers, 18*, 267–272.

Alpert, M., Pouget, E., Lewine, R., Moskowitz, J., Kalus, O., Harvey, P., & Davidson, M. (1990, December). *Some effects of neuroleptic drugs on expressive and interactional behavior*. Poster presented at the meeting of the *American Academy of Neuropsychopharmacology*, Boca Raton, FL.

Alpert, M., Rosen, A., Welkowitz, J., Sobin, C., & Borod, J. (1989). Vocal acoustic correlates of flat affect in schizophrenia: Similarity to Parkinson's disease and right hemisphere disease and contrast depression. *British Journal of Psychiatry, 154*, 51–56.

Alpert, M., Sison, C., Pouget, E., Yahia, M., & Allen, E. (1992, May). *Clinical and acoustic measures of negative symptoms*. Poster presented at the meeting of the *New Clinical Drug Evaluation Units*, Boca Raton, FL.

Anderson, A. H., Clark, A., & Mullin, J. (1991). Introducing information in dialogues: Forms of introduction chosen by young speakers and the responses elicited from young listeners. *Journal of Child Language, 18*, 663–687.

Andreasen, N. C., Alpert, M., & Martz, M. J. (1981). Acoustic analysis: An objective measure of affective flattery. *Archives of General Psychiatry*, *38*, 281–285.

Arieti, S. (1955). *Interpretation of schizophrenia*. New York: Brunner.

Arieti, S. (1974). *Interpretation of schizophrenia* (2nd ed.). New York: Basic Books.

Bateson, G., Jackson, D., Haley, J., & Weakland, J. (1956). Toward a theory of schizophrenia. *Behavioral Science*, *1*, 251–264.

Bateson, G., Jackson, D., Haley, J., & Weakland, J. (1963). A note on the double-bind. *Family Process*, *2*, 154–157.

Benson, D. F. (1973). Psychiatric aspects of aphasia. *British Journal of Psychiatry*, *123*, 555–556.

Bleuler, E. (1911). *Dementia Praecox oder Grupper der Schizophrenien*. Leipzig: Deuticke.

Brown, R. (1958). *Words and things*. New York: Free Press.

Brown, R. (1973). Schizophrenia, language, and reality. *American Psychologist*, *28*, 395–403.

Cameron, N. (1938). Reasoning, regression and communication in schizophrenics. *Psychological Monographs*, *221*.

Cameron, N. (1963). *Personality development and psychopathology*. Boston: Houghton-Mifflin.

Carpenter, M. D. (1976). Sensitivity to syntactic structure: Good versus poor premorbid schizophrenics. *Journal of Abnormal Psychology*, *85*, 41–50.

Chaika, E. (1974). A linguist looks at "schizophrenic" language. *Brain and Language*, *1*, 257–276.

Chaika, E. (1977). Schizophrenic speech, slips of the tongue, and jargonaphasia: A reply to Fromkin and to LeCours and Varrier-Clement. *Brain and Language*, *4*, 464–475.

Chaika, E. (1990). *Understanding psychotic speech: Beyond Freud and Chomsky*. Springfield, IL: Thomas.

Chapman, L. J., & Chapman, J. P. (1973). *Disordered thought in schizophrenia*. Englewood Cliffs, NJ: Prentice-Hill.

Chapman, L. J., Chapman, J. P., & Daut, R. L. (1976). Schizophrenic inability to disattend from strong aspects of meaning. *Journal of Abnormal Psychology*, *85*, 35–40.

De la Garza, C. D., & Worchel, P. (1956). Time and space orientation in schizophrenia. *Journal of Abnormal and Social Psychology*, *52*, 191–195.

Docherty, N., Schmur, M., & Harvey, P. D. (1988). Reference performance and positive and negative thought disorder: A follow-up study of manics and schizophrenics. *Journal of Abnormal Psychology*, *97*, 437–442.

Ferreira, A. J. (1960). The semantics and the context of the schizophrenic's language. *Archives of General Psychiatry*, *3*, 128–138.

Forrest, D. V. (1968). Poiesis and the language of schizophrenia. In H. J. Vetter (Ed.), *Language behavior in schizophrenia* (pp. 153–181). Springfield, IL: Thomas.

Fromkin, V. A. (1975). A linguist looks at "A linguist looks at 'schizophrenic' language." *Brain and Language*, *2*, 498–503.

Garfinkel, H. (1967). *Studies in ethnomethodology*. Englewood Cliffs, NJ: Prentice-Hall.

Gerson, S. N., Benson, D. F., & Frazier, S. H. (1977). Diagnosis: Schizophrenia vs. posterior aphasia. *American Journal of Psychiatry*, *134*, 966–969.

Gerver, D. (1967). Linguistic rules and the perception and recall of speech of schizophrenic patients. *British Journal of Social and Clinical Psychology*, *6*, 204–211.

Glucksberg, S., Krauss, R. M., & Weisberg, R. (1966). Referential communication in nursery school children: Method and some preliminary findings. *Journal of Experimental Child Psychology*, *3*, 333–342.

Gold, G. (Ed.) (1974). *The White House transcripts*. New York: Bantam.

Goldman-Eisler, R. (1968). *Psycholinguistics: Experiments in spontaneous speech*. New York: Academic Press.

Goldstein, K. (1944). Methodological approach to the study of schizophrenic thought. In J. S. Kasanin (Ed.), *Language and thought in schizophrenia* (pp. 17–40). Berkeley: University of California Press.

Gottschalk, L. A., Gleser, G. C., Magliocco, E. G., & D'Zmura, T. L. (1961). Further studies on the speech patterns of schizophrenic patients: Measuring inter-individual differences in relative degree of personal disorganization and social alienation. *Journal of Nervous and Mental Disease, 132*, 101–113.

Halliday, M. A. K. (1978). *Language as a social semiotic: The social interpretation of language and meaning.* London: Arnold.

Halliday, M. A. K., & Hasan, R. (1976). *Cohesion in spoken and written English.* London: Longmans.

Harvey, P. D. (1983). Speech competence in manic and schizophrenic psychoses: The association between clinically rated thought disorder and cohesion and reference performance. *Journal of Abnormal Psychology, 92*, 368–377.

Harvey, P. D., Weintraub, S., and Neale, J. M. (1982). Speech competence of children vulnerable to psychopathology. *Journal of Abnormal Child Psychology, 10*, 373–388.

Heinrichs, R. W. (1993). Schizophrenia and the brain: Conditions for a neuropsychology of madness. *American Psychologist, 48*, 221–232.

Kraepelin, E. (1919). *Dementia praecox and paraphenia.* Edinburgh: Livingstone.

LeCours, A. R., & Vanier-Clement, H. (1976). Schizophasia and jargonaphasia: A comparative description with comments on Chaika's and Fromkin's respective looks at "schizophrenic" language. *Brain and Language, 3*, 516–565.

Lorenz, M. (1968). Problems posed by schizophrenic language. In H. J. Vetter (Ed.), *Language behavior in schizophrenia* (pp. 28–40). Springfield, IL: Thomas.

Maher, B. A. (1966). *Principles of psychopathology.* New York: McGraw-Hill.

Maher, B. A., McKean, K. O., & McLaughlin, B. (1966). Studies in psychotic language. In P. J. Stone et al. (Eds.), *The General Inquirer: A computer approach to content analysis* (pp. 469–503). Cambridge, MA: MIT Press.

McGhie, A. (1970). Attention and perception in schizophrenia. In B. A. Maher (Ed.), *Progress in experimental personality research* (Vol. 5, pp. 1–35). New York: Academic Press.

McGhie, A., & Chapman, J. (1961). Disorders of attention and perception in early schizophrenia. *British Journal of Medical Psychology, 34*, 103–116.

McGhie, A., Chapman, J., & Lawson, J. S. (1964). Disturbances in selective attention in schizophrenics. *Proceedings of the Royal Society of Medicine, 57*, 419–430.

Miller, G. A., & Selfridge, J. A. (1950). Verbal context and the recall of meaningful material. *American Journal of Psychology, 63*, 176–185.

Moran, L. J. (1953). Vocabulary knowledge and usage among normals and schizophrenic patients. *Psychological Monographs, 67* (No. 20).

Piaget, J. (1926). *The thought and language of the child.* London: Routledge & Kegan Paul.

Piaget, J. (1955). *The child's construction of reality.* London: Routledge & Kegan Paul.

Rochester, S. R., Harris, J., & Seeman, M. V. (1973). Sentence processing in schizophrenic listeners. *Journal of Abnormal Psychology, 3*, 350–356.

Rochester, S. R., & Martin, J. R. (1979). *Crazy Talk: A study of the discourse of schizophrenic speakers.* New York: Plenum.

Rosenberg, S. D., & Tucker, G. J. (1976, May). *Verbal content and the diagnosis of schizophrenia.* Paper presented at the 129th annual meeting of the American Psychiatric Association, FL.

Stone, J. P., Bales, R. F., Namenworth, Z., & Ogilvie, D. M. (1962). The General Inquirer: A computer's system for content analysis and retrieval based on the sentence as a unit of information. *Behavioral Science, 7*, 484–498.

Stone, J. P., Dunphy, D. C., Smith, M. S., & Ogilvie, D. M. (1966). *The General Inquirer: A computer approach to content analysis*. Cambridge, MA: MIT Press.

Storch, A. (1924). The primitive archaic forms of inner experiences and thought in schizophrenia. *Nervous and Mental Diseases Monograph*, *36*.

Truscott, I. P. (1970). Contextual constraint and schizophrenic language. *Journal of Consulting and Clinical Psychology*, *35*, 189–194.

Tucker, G. J., and Rosenberg, S. D. (1975). Computer content analysis of schizophrenic speech: A preliminary report. *American Journal of Psychiatry*, *132*, 611–616.

Ullmann, L. P., & Krasner, L. (1969). *A psychological approach to abnormal behavior*. Englewood Cliffs, NJ: Prentice-Hall.

Von Domarus, E. (1944). The specific laws of logic in schizophrenia. In J. S. Kasanin (Ed.), *Language and thought in schizophrenia* (pp. 104–114). Berkeley: University of California.

Weckowitz, T. E., & Blewett, D. B. (1959). Size constancy and abstract thinking in schizophrenia. *Journal of Mental Science*, *105*, 909–934.

Welkowitz, J., Bond, R., & Zelano, J. (1990). An automated system for the analysis of temporal speech patterns: Description of the hardware and software. *Journal of Communication Disorders*, *23*, 347–362.

7

The Double-Bind Concept
and Gregory Bateson

Sullivan (1944) has expressed the belief that language serves the vital function of preserving feelings of security among one's fellow human beings. The schizophrenic's peculiarities of language, he proposes, arise from an extreme need to feel secure. The schizophrenic does not believe that speech will help attain gratification; instead, it is used to counteract feelings of insecurity. The problem lies in recurrent severe disturbances in the schizophrenic's relationships with people that result in a confusion of the critical faculties concerning the structure of spoken and written language.

In a similar vein, Cameron (1944) suggests that the schizophrenic has somehow managed to become isolated from the common social environment. The language behavior and thinking of the organized adult are outgrowths of repeated social communication that depends on the development of an ability to take the role of other persons, to be able to reproduce their attitudes in one's own responses and thus learn to react to one's own behavior as others are reacting to it. The acquisition of this ability is what makes a social person. Cameron feels that schizophrenics are people who have never been able to develop role-taking skills and therefore have not been able to establish themselves firmly in the cultural pattern. In the face of emotional conflicts and disappointments the schizophrenic withdraws into fantasy life, which eventually dominates all thinking and excludes social life altogether.

Kasanin (1944) also maintains that the most important cause of disturbance in the language and thought of the schizophrenic is the disarticulation of the schizophrenic from the social context. It is obvious that early on the child or infant goes through some traumatic process that interferes with his or her relation to the outside world. The nature of this process involves the peculiar pattern of communicative behavior in the parent-child context to which the name *double bind* has been given.

The double-bind hypothesis, first advanced by Gregory Bateson and his associates (Bateson, Jackson, Haley, & Weakland, 1956), emphasizes the communication or interaction that occurs between parents and child. According to the theory, the parents (usually the mother) continually communicate conflicting or incongruent messages to the child because the mother for some reason has a fear of intimate contact with the child but is unable to accept this fear and denies it by overtly expressing "loving behavior." These two different and conflicting orders of messages are presented to the child at the same time.

The presentation of these incongruent messages poses a problem for the child. Since the mother is the primary love object, the child would like to be able to discriminate accurately between the messages received from her. However, if the child does this, he or she will be punished by the realization that his mother does not really love him or her. On the other hand, if the child does not discriminate accurately between the messages and accepts his mother's simulated loving behavior as real, he or she will then approach his mother. When the child does this, she will become hostile, causing him or her to withdraw. After the child withdraws, she will punish him or her verbally for withdrawing because it indicated to her that she was not a loving mother. Consequently, the child is punished whether he or she accurately or inaccurately discriminates between the messages. Hence, the child is caught in a double bind.

The only real escape for the child from this situation is to communicate with the mother about the position in which she has put him or her. However, if the child does this, she will probably take the communication as an accusation that she is not a loving mother and will punish the child for saying it. In other words, the child is not allowed to talk about the situation in an effort to resolve it.

Because this sequence of events occurs repeatedly in the child's home life, his or her ability to communicate with others about *their* communication to him or her is greatly impaired. As a result, the child is incompetent in determining what other people really mean when they communicate with him or her and also incompetent in expressing what he or she really means when he or she communicates with others.

Because of this impairment of the ability to relate to others effectively, the child may begin to respond defensively to others with incongruent responses when presented with the double-bind situation. In addition, the child may manifest withdrawal or other defense mechanisms that are part of the symptomatology of schizophrenia.

THE LOGICAL BASIS FOR DOUBLE BIND

Bateson (1955) reports that the basic conception of the double bind grew out of his observation of animals in a seminaturalistic setting. As part of a 10-year study of communication he was interested in the ways animals use signals in their interactions. The critical nature of these stimuli is best seen when animals are at play. When Bateson was invited to the Fleishhacker Zoo in California, he observed an interesting pair of otters that would not play with one another. One characteristic of otters is their playful nature; therefore, this pair was a rarity warranting closer examination. Bateson put together a string device to entice the otters to play with him, which they learned to do. When he withdrew, however, Bateson noticed that the otters would only play with one another for a limited amount of time: "The autism of his otters made him reflect anew on the mental disturbances of schizophrenic children and schizophrenic adults" (Rieber, 1989, p. 8).

Nearly as striking in the interaction is the fact that normal otters, like typical human children and/or adults, freely play with one another and seemingly know how to distinguish a menacing shove from a playful pat on the back. Such activity requires a surprisingly sophisticated message system that in effect communicates, "These actions, in which we now engage, do not denote what would be denoted by these actions which the actions denote" (Bateson, 1955). A playful bite must not be misperceived as an attack, even though it is the same in form as an attack. Two messages, the "bite" and "This is play," are on different levels of communication and are both required for play to occur. The first message denies the assertion of the second, and vice versa, and thus forms an Epimenides type of paradox.

In logic an example of this type of paradox is that as shown in Figure 7.1. Because the first statement is about the second statement, it is, by definition, on a different level of abstraction. And since each statement denies the assertion of another statement, the set of statements constitutes a paradox. It is a contradiction that follows a correct deduction from consistent premises. Bertrand Russell, in his *Theory of Logical Types* (Whitehead & Russell, 1913), was the first to "solve" this type of paradox with the general rule that whatever involved all of a collection must not be one of the collection. Therefore, the Epimenides type of paradox is an example of a type of reasoning, that is, an inappropriate use of concepts drawn from two levels.

Russell's approach accounted for antinomies, or paradoxes arising in formal logical systems; Carnap (1942) proposed a similar theory to account for hidden inconsistencies that arise from the structure of language ("paradoxical definitions"). By theorizing that there exist an object language and a meta-language about objects, a metalanguage about the metalanguage, and so on,

All statements within this frame are true

I love you   I hate you

FIGURE 7.1. Epimenidean paradox.

and by applying Russell's rule, paradoxes of the type "I am lying" can be defined as meaningless self-reflexive statements. This brief discussion of logic is necessary because Watzlawick, Beavin, and Jackson (1967) indicate that the paradox has pragmatic implications for everyday life. The fundamental conception of the double bind grows directly from these logical considerations.

INITIAL APPLICATIONS

Haley (1955) made some immediate extensions of Bateson's insights to fantasy, hypnosis, and psychotherapy. In 1956, Bateson, Jackson, Weakland, and Haley began to study schizophrenic communication. They hypothesized that the symptoms of schizophrenics were due mainly to an inability to assign the correct communicational mode to their own messages, to messages from others, or to their own thoughts and feelings. The notion behind the "communicational mode" was not defined, but it apparently referred to levels of communication: The schizophrenic seemed to be suffering from inner conflicts of logical typing à la Russell. Bateson et al. (1956) stated that, if their reading of the symptoms was correct and the hypothesized schizophrenia essentially resulted from familial interaction, it ought to be possible to arrive a priori at a formal description of those consequences of experience that would induce such a series of symptoms. The result of this deductive interactional approach to schizophrenia was the first explication of the double-bind hypothesis.

In Bateson et al. (1956) the stress was placed on the relationship between the schizophrenic victim and his or her anxious mother. The major elements of the double bind were (1) two or more people who have (2) repeated experience with a communication pattern consisting of (3) a primary negative injunction and (4) a secondary injunction conflicting with the first at a more abstract level, plus (5) a tertiary negative injunction prohibiting escape from the field. The complete set of ingredients is no longer necessary when the victim learns to perceive the universe in "double-bind patterns." In their discussion of schizophrenia per se, Bateson et al. (1956) add the concept of an intense relationship, defined as one in which the schizophrenic feels that accurate discrimination of the type of message being communicated is crucially important so that he or she may make the appropriate responses. Furthermore, the individual is unable to comment on the double bind so as to correct the misperception. Presumably, the motivational state inferred here guarantees the necessary repeated experience with the double bind, and the inability to comment is analogous to an inability to leave the field.

Lu (1962) and Ferreira (1960) objected to the dyadic emphasis in Bateson et al. (1956) and advanced the "quadruple bind" and "split double bind," respectively, to describe pathological communication patterns involving more than two family members. Around the same time, Weakland (1960) attempted a systematic extension of the initial conception to three-party interactions. Lu (1962) interestingly reports a double-bind pattern that is cultural in origin. The mothers of the schizophrenics in the study apparently attempted to make their children simultaneously dependent and independent; further, an analysis of "sick" versus "well" siblings indicated that the schizophrenics were the children who attempted to obey both injunctions. Unfortunately, the promised full analysis of Lu's sample of schizophrenics has never appeared in print.

Ferreira (1960) contends that the double-bind hypothesis has greater generality than as a theory of schizophrenia. He found that the families of delinquent boys tend to be characterized by bipolar messages from the parents to the children. These take the form:

1. *A* to *B*: "Thou shall not . . . *x* (or I will not love you)."
2. *C* to *B*: "Thou shall not . . . obey, hear, etc. . . . *A*'s message (or I will not love you)."

The child finds it impossible to obey both messages and is often pushed out of the field (i.e., the family interaction pattern). The major difference between this formulation and the one set forth by Bateson et al. (1956) is the lack of a tertiary negative injunction. It is possible that various "types" of double bind characterize various "types" of disturbed families and that schizophrenic, neurotic, delinquent, or homosexual behavior is simply an attempt to adjust to the peculiar demands of this type of environment. Mishler and Waxler (1965) report initial indications of considerable similarity among families that produce a variety of disturbed children.

Weakland (1960) emphasized that both individuals in the interaction were caught in the double bind and also that more than two individuals could be involved. He went on to postulate that the concealment, denial, and inhibition inherent in the basic contradictory pair of messages make the achievement of an adequate response nearly impossible. This was the first attempt to define some of the processes that prevent meaningful responses to paradoxical communications.

Jackson (1960, 1961) developed some of the themes of Haley's (1955) analysis of psychotherapy and formulated the concept of the therapeutic double bind, that is, that all forms of psychotherapy set up double binds through the requirements they place on the patient in the situation. Jackson and Haley (1963) explicated the double binds in psychoanalysis, and Haley (1963) extended the analysis to other types of therapy. A "cure" in this formulation comes about when the patient finally realizes the nature of the "game" the therapist is playing and refuses to play further. Watts (1961) stresses the "gamesmanship" aspects of this type of therapy and then attempts to picture the basic structure of society as a double bind consisting of rules that confer independence and in doing so take it away again. One of the unfortunate aspects of the double bind is that it can be applied fairly easily to almost any aspect of human behavior.

Watzlawick (1963) reviewed the literature on the double bind up to 1961 and commented that few of the references cited dealt with the essential component of the double bind, that is, the theory of logical types. He also stressed that the double bind was not equivalent to a failure to discriminate stimuli in an experimental situation. Pavlov's (1927) experiments on experimentally induced neuroses are an analog because the animal was first trained to discriminate the circle and oval. Behavior broke down when the discrimination was made impossible for the animal, not because of the ability to discriminate but because a previously established contingency pattern was broken.

In a short article, Bateson, Jackson, Haley, and Weakland (1963) reviewed their recently concluded research project and offered a series of observations and conclusions with respect to the double bind. The double bind, they stated, is a necessary but not a sufficient condition in accounting for the etiology of schizophrenic disorders. However, they make it plain that they regard the double bind as an inevitable byproduct of schizophrenic communication.

They emphasize that observable communicative behavior and relationships are the appropriate object of empirical and theoretical analyses involving the double-bind concept. They prefer to "conceptualize the conflicting definitions of the relationship" rather than a simple relationship involving a binder and a victim.

During the mid-1960s, the Palo Alto group dealt mainly with various aspects of schizophrenia and family therapy and only incidentally with the double bind. Only those papers that seem germane to a definition of the phenomenon are reported in the following sections of this chapter. Mishler and Waxler (1965) provide an excellent review of contributions to schizophrenia and a comparison of various theoretical approaches to family therapy.

Development of the Double Bind

A number of attempts have been made to define more precisely the double bind. Watzlawick (1965) provided the most comprehensive analysis of the relation between the double bind and logical paradoxes. He postulates a set of pragmatic paradoxes that are simply the semantic paradoxes (paradoxical definitions) that occur in one form or another in communication. Two of the most common types of pragmatic paradoxes are paradoxical injunctions (the core of the interactional double bind) and paradoxical predictions.

Paradoxical injunctions are statements that demand conflicting types of behaviors, such as "you ought to love me" or "don't be so obedient," which demand behavior that can only be spontaneous. This is the usual conception of the double bind and can presumably be handled by either commenting on the communication (metacommunicating), attempting to bind the binder, or retreating into a paradoxical (schizophrenic) mode of communication that enables a person to communicate that he or she is not communicating without actual communication taking place (Watzlawick, 1965).

The relation of paradoxical predictions to the double bind is not clear. The paradox in this case is based on the contention that "reason and trust do not mix." This is most clearly seen in the Prisoner's Dilemma game, in which trust of the other player and rational self-interest dictate alternative strategies so that the strategy usually adopted is the one involving minimal loss. In this case the paradox depends on the player's analysis of the situation conflicting with his/her analysis of another's intentions. Unfortunately in human interactions one subject must make predictions about another because the former cannot know the latter as the latter knows him- or herself. This raises the melancholy prospect that in at least some cases the victim may bind him- or herself as much or more than he or she is bound by others in an interaction situation. This conception also allows the prediction that an outside observer who has had some previous contact with the individuals in a communication situation will probably mislabel some straightforward interactions as double binds. The observer's previous experience could result in erroneous predictions about various metalevels of the ongoing communication.

Sluzki, Beavin, Tarnopolsky, and Veron (1967) made a pioneering effort to redefine the double bind in more experimentally meaningful terms. They postulated the existence of many different types of double binds, all based on differing paradoxical injunctions. They redefine Bateson et al.'s (1956) criteria in terms of disqualifying statements and attempt to indicate some of the common reactions to this "transactional disqualification." Their approach is important because it attempts to tie a specific type of double bind to a specific set of behaviors. Unfortunately, this study only presented clinical data, and the list of reactions is almost certainly too limited, but this is undoubtedly the only way to analyze the double bind in complex interaction situations. The theoretical literature on the double bind is replete with what are labeled examples of the double bind, but in many cases the bind is by no means as clear to the readers as it is to the writers. Even in the best collection of this material, a tape published by Watzlawick (1964), the nature of the bind is not always immediately apparent. When an entire family pattern is observed, analysis becomes incredibly complex (Jones, 1964). Haley (1963) admitted that the therapist frequently does not become aware of the binding nature of some interactions until considerable time has elapsed.

Bateson et al. (1963) have complained that the double bind is not the core of their work and have indicated that their major focus of interest was the development of a communicational approach to the study of behavior. The first full version of this theory was presented by Watzlawick et al. (1967), in which they offered a model for the analysis of the behavioral effects (pragmatics) of human communication. Basic postulates include the impossibility of *not* communicating (since even silence has some sort of communicative significance), the idea that every communication consists of a message and an *injunction* (metacommunication) that constrains behavior, and the notion that the nature of a relationship is contingent on the patterning of the communicational sequences between participants.

The fact that human beings can communicate both digitally and analogically is the source of many of the paradoxical features of human relationships.[1] The difficulties involve semantics, on the one hand, and syntactics, on the other hand. That is, digital language does not possess adequate semantic resources in the area of relationships, although it boasts a complex and versatile syntax. Conversely, analogic language has adequate semantics but lacks a logical and well-delineated syntax for dealing with relationships.

Watzlawick et al. (1967) present a modified and expanded formulation of

---

[1]*Analogic codification* involves communication via pictures or images of actual objects, people, or situations; *digital codification*, as exemplified by words and numbers, is a combination of specifically created and discrete entities that have representational or symbolic properties. Analogic communication can occur in an instantaneous, all-at-once fashion; digital communication, on the other hand, is sequential (Ruesch, 1961).

the double bind. First, it is essential that two or more people be involved in the kind of intense relationship (love, loyalty, dependence, etc.) that has a "high degree of physical and/or survival value" for them, individually or collectively. Second, a message is transmitted within this context that poses mutually exclusive interpretations, that is, if it is an injunction, it must be either obeyed or disobeyed. Third, constraints are present in the situation that prevent the individual from "leaving the field" by withdrawing or by means of metacommunication. This last stipulation is necessary if double binds are to be defined as paradoxes and not mere contradictions, since in contradictions, unlike paradoxes, an alternative is left open to the individual.

This definition of the double bind is both more explicit and easier to work with than those presented elsewhere. It should be fairly easy to set up a situation in a laboratory setting in which two people are in a fairly intense relationship. The experimental procedures developed in social psychology should be useful in this context. The wide list of situations mentioned should allow various different experiments that simply control the type of situation as an independent variable.

Simply stated, the second element of the double bind mentioned above indicates that any communication that in any way modifies another communication can potentially set up the binding situation. The two types of disqualification mentioned are probably part of a much larger set of binds that would require a set of investigations testing the effects of various ways of setting up mutually exclusive assertions. The conflicting messages could of course be introduced into the situation by a stooge, but it would probably be easier to use a set of standardized messages and structure the situation so that the individual feels it is essential to respond appropriately to the correct meaning of the message. An important line of research would deal with the ability of individuals to perceive double binds present in a larger set of communications and would also attempt to determine how people normally attempt to deal with paradoxical messages. The effects of varying the supposed source of the communication should also be tested, since a communication from a "significant other" should have an effect different from a communication from a less important source. Finally the effect of various operational definitions of the levels of communication must be evaluated.

The final element of the double bind, the restriction on metacommunication or withdrawal, may be difficult to set up in an experimental situation, but the initial instructions or the context of the experiment could probably control this. The definition offered by Watzlawick et al. (1967) is wide enough to allow various experiments but narrow enough to impose some regularity on the eventual results of such experimentation.

EXPERIMENTATION ON THE DOUBLE BIND

Most of the available material on the double bind is anecdotal in nature and there have been few well-designed studies. A review of the literature, however, seems to indicate that this pattern is changing, and more researchers are becoming interested in this area of inquiry.

Haley (1964), in a departure from his usual approach to family research, analyzed triads drawn from 40 healthy and 40 disturbed families. By simply measuring the order in which individuals talked he was able to significantly differentiate the two types of families. The addition of a fourth family member, however, changed the interaction patterns and washed out the difference (Haley, 1967).

Coser (1960) pointed out the importance of laughter in setting up double binds. Zuk, Roszormeny-Nagy, and Heiman (1963) were able to make a reliable count of the number of laughs in a family-therapy situation and report a significant inverse relationship between the number of times the parents and their schizophrenic daughter laughed. Zuk (1964) follows up this study and attempts systematically to relate laughter to the double bind. Zuk et al. (1963) and Haley's studies are important not because they buttress the double-bind concept but because they represent useful ways of studying interactions in situations in which double binds may be present.

Schuham (1967) reports on three doctoral dissertations (Ciotola, 1961; Potash, 1965; Loeff, 1966) that involved the double bind. Ciotola (1961) exposed schizophrenics and nonpsychotic psychiatric patients to an impossible auditory discrimination and then tested their reaction times to simply auditory discriminations. The fact that no differences were found is not surprising since, to satisfy the definition of the double bind, the order of presentation of discrimination tasks would have to be reversed. Also, since it is possible that the double bind may be involved in all types of behavior pathology, the comparison group should have more accurately reflected the general population.

Potash (1965) matched undifferentiated male schizophrenics and hospital employees on age, education, and intelligence and tested them in a two-person, three-choice game. It was hypothesized that the schizophrenics would choose more often to withdraw from the game, yet this was not confirmed. Why this game is not an analogy to the double bind is not clear from Schuham (1967), but an important part of the double-bind concept is that the schizophrenic cannot withdraw from the situation except through pathological communication. A more meaningful measure in this type of situation would have been the changes, if any, in the behavior of schizophrenics as they confront the situation. Nonschizophrenics should handle this situation in somewhat different ways.

A useful design is employed in Loeff (1966). He presented non-schizophrenics, schizophrenics, and delinquents with a set of metaphors in which the content and verbal affect were in direct conflict. Semantic differential scales (but not rating scales) significantly differentiated normal and combined pathological groups. The schizophrenics were not deficient in their perception of the metacommunication, and both pathological groups responded more to the affect than to the content level. As Schuham (1967) points out, both of these findings conflict with the Palo Alto group's conceptualization of schizophrenia. The differential results found with semantic differential and rating scales are interesting and bear directly on the question of how double binds are perceived. Variations on Loeff's design are likely to form a significant segment of future work on the double bind.

Berger (1965) developed a questionnaire consisting of 30 double-bind statements and applied it to patients with a history of communicational difficulties, nonschizophrenic hospitalized patients, ward attendants, and college students. The initial form differentiated schizophrenics and college students, and a form containing the 12 most discriminating items differentiated the two groups of hospitalized patients. The five items that best discriminated the schizophrenics from the other groups reflects either an affect/content or a father/mother conflict. The results indicate that it may be possible to develop a discriminating measure based on certain types of double-bind statements. Schuham (1967) objects to the procedure of requesting subjects to recall experiences on the grounds that such a procedure is unreliable. Berger (1965), however, reports a significant test-retest reliability when the questionnaire is given over a one-week period.

Perhaps the clearest example of the weaknesses of the double-bind concept can be found in two studies of letters to schizophrenics. Weakland and Fry (1962) postulated that such letters are typical of the communication patterns normally present between the sender and the recipient and as such are a "permanent and objective piece of data, on one level, unitary, condensed and easier to study." They arrived at their conclusions without study of non-schizophrenic letters, and in a number of cases their analysis of the sample letters is based more on their intimate knowledge of the patient than on what was actually written. Ringuette and Kennedy (1966) obtained 40 letters from parents to their schizophrenic children and also asked volunteers to write similar letters. The letters were rated on a seven-point scale (schizophrenic to nonschizophrenic): first-year psychiatric interns with experience in the double-bind theory applied Weakland and Fry's (1962) criteria; experienced informed and uninformed clinicians sorted the letters into schizophrenic and non-schizophrenic categories; and naive raters used a seven-point like/dislike scale. Only the naive raters and the interns with double-blind experience were consistent, while the "expert" and the "trained" judges were unable to differentiate the volunteer letters from the rest. Ringuette and Kennedy (1966) clearly indicates the uselessness of a global definition when one is trying to correctly perceive a phenomenon in a complex set of communications that are presumed to contain that phenomenon. The same processes that lead to the unreliability of clinical diagnosis are probably at work in this situation.

SUMMARY AND REDEFINITION

The work of Bateson, Haley, Jackson, and Weakland has already served the important purpose of shifting attention from psychic factors to the study of interactional processes through the analysis of communicational behaviors. Their interest, however, centers on the creation of a useful theory and not on the design of useful experiments to test that theory. Any attempt to investigate rigorously the pragmatic effects of communication must redefine the global definitions of phenomena now available into smaller, more carefully limited and operational statements that can be utilized in the design of experiments. In the specific case of the double bind this must involve recognition of the fact that, if the double bind exists, it is only the generic label for a large class of interactions satisfying some set of criteria drawn from logic and that the properties and effects of different "types" of double binds may well have different behavioral effects. The properties of these binds will in part depend on how the three aspects of the double bind are operationally defined.

The requirement of an "intense relationship" could, for example, be defined as a situation in which the individual is motivated to perceive correctly and/or respond appropriately to a set of communications. The experimental question then becomes: How can we set up experiments to initiate and maintain this "set"? If, by definition, any statement that refers to another statement is logically on a higher level than the first statement, then the process of setting up conflicting communications on different levels becomes clear. The various dichotomies (abstract/concrete, verbal/nonverbal, etc.) mentioned in the literature become different ways of operationalizing the basic concept and presumably have some validity and probably also differential effects. Finally, an experimental situation can be so structured as to limit metacommunication and leaving the field.

In conclusion, the experimental investigation of the double bind requires some major compromises between the desire of the Palo Alto group to extend a basic concept to large blocks of human behavior and the rather severe limitations and requirements of experimentation. This necessarily involves either the restriction of the concept to a limited range of behaviors or the breaking up of the concept into a number of categories that can be separately investigated.

CONCLUDING REMARKS

Chaika (1990) has recently challenged the double-bind theory, asserting, "There is no case history proof that all schizophrenics were ever caught in such a bind. Nor is there any evidence that normals have not been caught in such a double bind" (p. 4). She goes on to explain that schizophrenic speech is of an intermittent nature and thus "negates the double-bind theory" (Chaika, 1990, p. 4), given the contradiction resulting from the fact that schizophrenics *can* communicate at times, although not at all times. Chaika claims that schizophrenics, like others, must somehow and at some time have learned to communicate, and she further points out the important role played by peers in all learning processes. She emphasizes the established notion that the peer group is relevant to a child's language, basing this assertion on "sociolinguistic studies [which] have determined again and again that the peer group is the primary source of a child's language, not the parent" (Chaika, 1990, p. 4).

This criticism of the double bind, however, stems from a simplified view that fails unfortunately to make an effort to understand the very premises of the theory. Bateson's double bind does not address the speech processes that Chaika is concerned with, instead focusing on the communication that takes place between the mother and child "culture." Psychotic speech might have certain surface characteristics, many of which have been addressed throughout the earlier chapters, that are insightful in their own right. The double-bind theory, on the other hand, examines a much more deeply embedded process, and as such it takes a much broader perspective, or frame of reference, to accept the viability of the double-bind theory in explaining dysfunctional interaction systems.

An important point to underscore is that the double bind is a theoretical approach to explain a mental, or cognitive, problem and not a performance phenomenon. It is a theory that addresses the possible internal causes of outward behavior, which can be detected most readily in dysfunctional or otherwise abnormal linguistic patterns. In this respect, Bateson, in collaboration with Margaret Mead, advanced the notion of "*schismogenesis*" to describe "patterns of interchange between self and others that lead to a rapid escalation of behavior and a concomitant breakdown of social integration" (Rieber, 1989, p. 5).

Schismogenesis is a label for the circumstances in which the behavior of one individual serves as a signal to another to initiate more drastic behavior. This might in turn serve as a signal to the first to again react negatively, further arousing negative reactions on the part of the second individual. In such a possibly infinite cycle, a mere, slight, initial difference, perhaps a threatening gesture from one individual, igniting a feeling of threat in another, can cause the system to run rapidly out of control. The problem arises from the unbreakable loop in the cycle, almost resembling the way a computer might "get stuck" on a damaged application and run awry, not correcting itself until the power is switched off and usually losing some amount of information in the material that was being worked on. However, if the system is not turned off, the loop continues endlessly and hopelessly. In a way, the computer is caught in a double bind: If it is turned off, the information will be lost, but if no such action is taken, the loop will not automatically correct itself.

Little current research has focused on Bateson's ideas about the double bind. This could be due to the interdisciplinary and eclectic nature of the topics under the scope of Bateson's work, a characteristic of few researchers in any of these areas of study. However, the study of the mind encompasses more than that concocted in formal research settings. Indeed, our resources are limited with respect to formalized approaches to the study of communication. Yet we can gain exceptional insight from extraordinary individuals like Bateson in their unorthodox confrontations with questions pertaining to human cognition such as those we have been attempting to answer throughout this text.

REFERENCES

Bateson, G. (1955). A theory of play and fantasy. *Psychiatric Research Reports, 2*, 39–51.

Bateson, G., Jackson, D., Haley, J., & Weakland, J. (1956). Toward a theory of schizophrenia. *Behavioral Science, 1*, 251–264.

Bateson, G., Jackson, D., Haley, J., & Weakland, J. (1963). A note on the double bind. *Family Process, 2*, 154–157.

Berger, A. (1965). A test of the double bind hypothesis of schizophrenia. *Family Process, 4*, 198–205.

Cameron, N. (1944). Experimental analysis of schizophrenic thinking. In J. S. Kasanin (Ed.), *Language and thought in schizophrenia* (pp. 50–64). Berkeley: University of California Press.

Carnap, R. (1942). *Introduction to semantics*. Cambridge, MA: Harvard University Press.

Chaika, E. O. (1990). *Understanding psychotic speech: Beyond Freud and Chomsky*. Springfield, IL: Thomas.

Ciotola, R. (1961). *The effect of two contradictory levels of reward and censure on schizophrenia*. *Dissertation Abstracts International, 22*, 320. (University microfilms No. 2278, 61).

Coser, R. (1960). Laughter among colleagues. *Psychiatry, 23*, 81–95.

Ferreira, A. (1960). The double-bind and delinquent behavior. *Archives of General Psychiatry, 3*, 359–367.

Haley, J. (1955). Paradoxes in play, fantasy, and psychotherapy. *Psychiatric Research Reports, 2*, 52–58.

Haley, J. (1963). *Strategies of psychotherapy*. New York: Grune & Stratton.

Haley, J. (1964). Research on family patterns: An instrumental measure. *Family Process, 3*, 41–65.

Haley, J. (1967). Speech sequences of normal and abnormal families with two children present. *Family Process, 6*, 81–97.

Jackson, D. (1960). *The etiology of schizophrenia*. New York: Basic Books.

Jackson, D. (1961). Interactional psychotherapy. In M. Stein (Ed.), *Contemporary psychotherapies* (pp. 250–251). New York: Free Press.

Jackson, D., & Haley, J. (1963). Transference revisited. *Journal of Nervous and Mental Disease*, *137*, 363–371.

Jones, D. M. (1964). Binds and unbinds. *Family Process*, *3*, 323–331.

Kasanin, J. S. (1944). The disturbance of conceptual thinking in schizophrenia. In J. S. Kasanin (Ed.), *Language and thought in schizophrenia* (pp. 41–49). Berkeley: University of California Press.

Loeff, R. (1966). *Differential discrimination of conflicting emotional messages by normal, delinquent, and schizophrenic adolescents*. Dissertation Abstracts International, *26*, 6850–6851. (University Microfilms No. 1470, 66).

Lu, Y. (1962). Contradictory parental expectations in schizophrenia. *Archives of General Psychiatry*, *6*, 219–234.

Mishler, E., & Waxler, N. (1965). Family interaction processes and schizophrenia. *Merrill-Palmer Quarterly*, *11*, 269–315.

Pavlov, I. P. (1927). *Conditioned reflexes*. New York: Oxford University Press.

Potash, H. (1965) *Schizophrenic interaction and the conception of the double-bind*. Dissertation Abstracts International, *25*, 6767. (University Microfilms No. 2052, 65).

Rieber, R. W. (1989). In search of the impertinent question: An overview of Bateson's theory of communication. In Rieber, R. W. (Ed.), *The individual, communication, and society: Essays in memory of Gregory Bateson* (pp. 25–47). New York: Cambridge University Press.

Ringuette, E., & Kennedy, T. (1966). An experimental study of the double-bind hypothesis. *Journal of Abnormal Psychology*, *71*, 136–141.

Ruesch, J. (1961). *Therapeutic communication*. New York: Norton.

Schuham, A. (1967). The double-bind hypothesis a decade later. *Psychological Bulletin*, *68*, 409–416.

Sluzki, C., Beavin, J., Tarnopolsky, A., & Veron, E. (1967). Transactional disqualifications. *Archives of General Psychiatry*, *16*, 494–504.

Sullivan, H. S. (1944). The language of schizophrenia. In J. S. Kasanin (Ed.), *Language and thought in schizophrenia* (pp. 4–16). Berkeley: University of California Press.

Watts, A. (1961). *Psychotherapy east and west*. New York: Mentor.

Watzlawick, P. (1963). A review of double-bind theory. *Family Process*, *2*, 132–153.

Watzlawick, P. (1964). *An anthology of human communication*. Palo Alto, CA: Science & Behavior.

Watzlawick, P. (1965). Paradoxical prediction. *Psychiatry*, *28*, 368–374.

Watzlawick, P., Beavin, J., & Jackson, D. (1967). *Pragmatics of human communication*. New York: Norton.

Weakland, J. (1960). The double-bind hypothesis of schizophrenia and three-party interaction. In D. Jackson (Ed.), *The etiology of schizophrenia* (pp. 373–388). New York: Basic Books.

Weakland, J., & Fry, W. (1962). Letters of mothers of schizophrenics. *American Journal of Orthopsychiatry*, *32*, 604–623.

Whitehead, A. N., & Russell, B. (1910–1913). *Principia mathematica*. Cambridge: Cambridge University Press.

Zuk, G. (1964). A further study of laughter in family therapy. *Family Process*, *3*, 77–81.

Zuk, G., Roszormeny-Nagy, I., & Heiman, E. (1963). Some dynamics of laughter during family therapy. *Family Process*, *2*, 302–313.

8

Psychopathology and the Polyglot

The polyglot—the person who possesses linguistic competence in more than one language—presents a fascinating series of challenges and problems for both the psycholinguist and the clinical psychologist. When two or more linguistic codes are available, what factors determine the selection of one over the other in the encoding of psychopathological experiences? In terms of the Sapir-Whorf (linguistic relativity) hypothesis, does the possession of more than a single language code imply the possession of more than one *Weltanschauung*? Are delusional and hallucinatory formations susceptible to influences from competing linguistic systems within the bilingual individual? Does bilingualism contribute in any significant way to emotional instability? These and many more intriguing questions are raised by the phenomenon of multilingualism vis-à-vis psychopathology.

THE PHENOMENON OF BILINGUALISM[1]

Whether starting from a common origin or emanating from several sources, language has come, through a process of differentiation, to assume approximately 1,500 different forms. To this large number should be added

This chapter was written in collaboration with Eva M. Fernández, Linguistics Department, Graduate School and University Center, City University of New York.

[1]Although there are theoretical grounds for distinguishing between bilingualism and multilingualism (i.e., the practice of using alternately three or more languages), for the sake of convenience we shall use the terms indiscriminately in this chapter.

hundreds of dialects within various languages, some of which are as mutually unintelligible as separate language systems. Because of population movements through migration and conquest, and more recently, immigration, colonization, and annexations of territory, groups of people speaking different languages have been thrown together in daily contact and communication. The coexistence of two languages within the same political unit or geographic region has given rise to the phenomenon of bilingualism, the extent of which is probably greater today than ever before in human history because of the greater mixture of populations and easier means of communication in the present world.

Contact and convergence between two different languages or cultures results in a sociological situation in which the same individuals learn elements from a linguistic or cultural system other than their native system. Linguists refer to this learning situation as "language contact" and to the particular learning process as "bilingualization." Linguistic change resulting from such contact is called "interference," which Diebold (1961) explains as follows:

> in both language and cultural contact, there are two aspects to be considered, viz., a sociological learning process, viz., bilingualism and acculturation, and a result of that process: change in one or both of the systems, viz., linguistic interference and cultural borrowing. (p. 98)

Numerous examples of languages in contact suggest that bilingualism is seldom, if ever, mutually balanced between the two groups of speakers. It appears that more speakers from one of the speech groups becomes bilingual than the other. In most bilingual situations the two languages involved do not carry equal social prestige, "and this represents the complex psychological and sociological phenomenon of culture conflict. A truly bilingual situation where the two languages are on equal footing is rarely encountered" (Yamamoto, 1964, p. 476). One of the languages is usually more dominant, carries greater social approval, and is representative of the "superior culture." This situation is found especially in countries in which waves of immigration and periods of colonization have taken place or are still on-going.

How the individual copes with more than one language or one culture is a question of the utmost importance in this postmodern age. Faxes, modems, satellites, and fiberoptic telephone lines make communicating with the antipodes as easy as pushing a button on a machine—that is, easy so long as one is familiar enough with the language at the other end of the line, as well as with the operating instructions for the machinery being used. In New York City alone, dozens of language schools and translating agencies are currently in operation, training the employees of multinational corporations to speak the languages of their colleagues, as well as providing linguistically and culturally accurate translations of advertising brochures and company profiles. The clientele for these enterprises consists mainly of people looking to become as culturally aware as possible, or at least to pass off as such, and a multicultural atmosphere emerging in business capitals around the globe is a sign of a nascent world culture in which language must not be a barrier, particularly for the international business community. This idealistic situation, however, stands juxtaposed to the subcultures looming in the very same capitals of the world, not in the downtown business districts but rather in the ghettos, in which disproportionately immigrant populations are desperately trying to cohabit and stand on a par with the native speakers of their new land. The teaching of English as a second language (ESL) has become a primary concern in the public schools and other organizations throughout cities in the United States, although the situation is not limited to the United States; consider, for instance, the populations of Turks or Eastern Europeans in Germany and Austria, or North Africans and Middle Easterners in Spain and France. Learning a second language is now part and parcel of the Zeitgeist of this, the last quarter of the twentieth century. Language contact, interference, and bilingualization are no longer simply circumstances existing haphazardly in accordance with immigration or conquest but have rather become a part of everyday life in almost every corner of the globe and as such must be taken into account as a primary focus for research.

It is indisputable that this worldwide situation adds considerable stress not only to immigrant populations but also to populations of native speakers. It has been suggested that language contact speeds the internal changes that a given language is undergoing.[2] The change that may be manifested in a language community will therefore consist not merely of lexical borrowings but of shifts and transformations of the language itself, motivated by internal factors but accelerated by consistent exposure to and contact with a different language. If the extreme view of the Sapir-Whorf hypothesis is accepted such that one assumes (or believes) that the language spoken by a given community or group will affect this community's way of looking at and analyzing the world, then the phenomenon of accelerated language change in a situation of language contact will certainly also be assumed to have a psychological effect on the language community the implications of which must be accounted for and supported with empirical data.

SECOND-LANGUAGE ACQUISITION

Central to this discussion is the question of how an individual learns a second language and, more importantly, the psychological factors that may aid or retard such a process. Current theories of second-language acquisition (SLA)

---

[2]For an interesting discussion of Mexican Spanish in Los Angeles see Silva-Corvalán (1986).

rarely address factors other than the cognitive aspects of human psychology that play a role in language learning, while matters pertaining to human emotions as well as behavior or affective systems are often left aside.

It has been rather well established that the human brian loses plasticity after the onset of puberty, at which point language has become fully lateralized. Penfield (1953) was among the first experts to address this issue with respect to SLA. He asserted that "once functional localization of acquired skills has been established, the early plasticity tends to disappear" (p. 206), thereby concluding that "languages learned at the right age . . . may be learned perfectly, with little effort and without physiological confusion" (p. 209). This conclusion implies the existence of a critical period after which language will not be learned properly. However, it is rather common to find adults who have learned second—and third and fourth—languages, people who in their second language have seemingly achieved a certain level of competence as well as a level of performance almost indistinguishable from that of native speakers. Lenneberg (1967) pointed out that "a person *can* learn to communicate in a foreign language at the age of forty" and further proposed that this is feasible assuming that "the cerebral organization for language learning as such has taken place during childhood, and since natural languages tend to resemble one another . . . the matrix for language skills is [still] present" during adulthood (p. 176). It is therefore plausible to assert that the mechanisms responsible for relatively productive SLA are somehow tied to the principles of universal grammar (UG), which viewed from this perspective will be available to language learners both before and after the critical period.

Setting aside for the moment the possibility of human predisposition for language as postulated by nativists, it is interesting to consider that children have little predisposition for particular cultures or societies. When acquiring their first language, children might or might not have access to UG. What is clear, however, is that they do not have any previously formed social or psychological identity and that the psychological mechanisms geared to such can certainly be described as a "tabula rosa" containing little or no biologically encoded information. On the other hand, second-language learners have, in addition to their first language, a given social personality, social attitudes, customs, traditions, an ethical or moral code of sorts, a behavior code, and so on, all of which relate to their native language and background. Such extralinguistic factors may play a larger role in SLA than has traditionally been assumed, particularly considering the psychologically distressing reality of speaking a language at a level analogous to that of a three-year-old when one is in one's mid-30s. This situation could certainly be considered parallel to that of the schizophrenic's feelings of alienation when realizing, during a period of illumination, his/her inability to communicate coherently thoughts. Ellis (1990) has asserted that there ought not to be "a disjunction between a functional and a mentalist explanation of how a [second language] is acquired" (p. 389), and one might propose that the two sides of the UG debate on SLA can be reconciled by considering the role of psychological and psychosocial variables in adult SLA that seem not to have been given due attention in current empirical studies.

Adult SLA presents an interesting scenario on which to test the parameter-setting hypothesis. The pro-UG position taken by many theorists in regard to SLA (Cook, 1988, 1991; Gregg, 1989, 1990; White, 1990) also has as its basic underlying assumption that knowledge of language is innate, or rather that linguistic ability is organic. From this somewhat radical position have stemmed many divergent opinions as to the status of the knowledge of language in adult second-language learners. An extreme pro-UG position would hold that such knowledge of language is accessible to adults learning a second language as it is to children learning a first language. A less extreme position would consider the hypothesized critical period for language acquisition, namely, that after puberty, mere exposure to a second language will not result in a complete, nativelike dominance of a language, a position that has developed into models for SLA that account for the differences in language acquisition between children and adults (Bley-Vroman, 1989; Johnson & Newport, 1989; Schachter, 1989). Bley-Vroman has stated that first-language acquisition differs from adult SLA "in degree of success, in the character and uniformity of the resulting systems, in [SLA's] susceptibility to factors such as motivation, and in the previous state of the organism: The learner already has a knowledge of one language and a powerful system of general and abstract problem-solving skills" (Bley-Vroman, 1989, p. 41).

Social and Psychological Identity

Testing for the factors of social identity and psychological identity in SLA is realistically difficult, in contrast to testing for other factors of SLA, given the wide range of individual variation; such variation may perhaps be one of the reasons for the lack of empirical work in this area. Gregg (1989) asserts in this respect that "any attempt to construct a theory of acquisition in the domain of pragmatics or communication is going to be handicapped by the lack of a well-articulated formal characterization of the domain" (p. 24). Yet it seems that a theory of acquisition constructed merely on the domain of structural grammar will hardly account in a satisfactory fashion for the so-called logical problem articulated in Bley-Vroman (1989).

Johnson and Newport (1989) provide an insightful discussion of what they refer to as "experiential and attitudinal variables" tested in their study of

Chinese and Korean speakers of English as a second language who varied primarily in length of time living in an English-speaking environment. The study's results show that "age of arrival is the better measure over any of the attitudinal variables tested" (Johnson & Newport, 1989, p. 84). It was found nonetheless that variables such as self-consciousness and identification with the target culture did indeed play a significant role. Johnson and Newport (1989) propose that "greater self-consciousness and less identification would be *the result rather than the cause* of the performance problems" (p. 85; emphasis added). It is important, though, to establish empirically whether this is truly the case. If initial performance problems give rise to insecurity in and lack of identification with the target culture, then this insecurity and lack of identification may in turn be among the primary causes of fossilized forms or perhaps of a regression to a more elementary level of performance (the detrimental process referred to in the literature as "backsliding"). Dulay and Burt (cited in Ellis, 1985, p. 11) suggest that adult second-language learners have a "socioaffective filter" that acts somewhat as a selectively permeable membrane controlling the amount of input that actually reaches the language-processing device. When learners have fulfilled their needs for communication, the learning process comes to a halt.

Rather optimistically, Lenneberg asserted that "most individuals of average intelligence are able to learn a second language after the beginning of their second decade although the incidence of 'language learning blocks' rapidly increases after puberty" (Lenneberg, 1967, p. 176). This assertion is somewhat reminiscent of the explanation provided by Rosemsky (as discussed in Ellis, 1985) of the factors inhibiting natural-language learning in adults. Adults have a metawareness not yet developed in children, as evidenced in the former's flexibility of thinking, problem-solving cognitive schemas, and decentralized or objective Weltanschauungen. In addition, adults are subject to well-developed social attitudes as to the use of their native language and the target language that "may serve as blocks to natural language acquisition" (Ellis, 1985, p. 108) and may induce the learner to consider the language-learning task as a problem to be tackled by means of conventional strategies that might or might not lead to productive ends.

These learning blocks alluded to so often in the literature in some form or another ought perhaps to be considered as consequential of psychological and psychosocial processes and attitudes that have been inculcated in the individual over the years of development as both an autonomous individual and a member of a given societal group. The difficulties encountered by adult native speakers of English who are learning Spanish verb forms, which have both formal and informal persons, might partially stem from the fact that English only has one form of address that may be both formal or informal, having no morphological marker for either. Not knowing what social environment in which to use 'usted' (the formal second-person singular pronoun) or 'tú' (the informal counterpart of 'usted') adds confusion and stress to the learner and might in turn lead the learner to develop a block about Spanish verb morphology.

By far the most thoughtful hypothesis regarding the problem of social and psychological identity in the adult second-language learner is the one put forth by Schumann (1978) stemming from his assertion that interlanguages resemble the structure of pidginized languages.[3] He has proposed that "pidginization in second language acquisition can be viewed as initially resulting from cognitive constraints and later persisting due to social and psychological constraints" (p. 269). In his proposal Schumann advances a definition proposed by Smith (cited in Schumann, 1978, p. 260) dividing the function of language into three categories: communicative, integrative, and expressive. The most basic function, that of communication, serves the purpose of transmitting information of a referential or denotative nature. Language used for mere communication might resemble telegraphic speech, and at this level little emphasis will be placed on style, eloquence, perfection of accent, and so forth. Language serves the function of integrating when it relates the speaker to a particular language group with a particular set of attitudes, behavior codes, and so forth. According to Schumann (1978), to achieve fluency in the target language a speaker need only master the first two tiers of this hierarchical structure of language function. The upper-most level, that of language as a means for expression, is the one reached by the outstanding speakers of society, those who use language with exceptional creativity and ease. In the terminology of Gleitman and Gleitman (1970), speakers using language with the expressive function have in their grammar the "penumbral" features that distinguish them as elite users of the language.

Schumann (1978) suggests that a poor adult second-language learner, especially one who is socially and/or psychologically distant from the speakers of the target language, might have only mastered the communication tier, and he suggests that "restriction in function can be seen as resulting from social and/or psychological distance between speaker and the addressee" (p. 261). Putting this hypothesis into a larger framework concerning SLA in general, Schumann (1978) describes the process of second-language learning as follows:

---

[3] An interlanguage is an autonomous system for communication used by the second language learner in the elementary or intermediate phases of acquisition. Interlanguages, which obviously vary from speaker to speaker, are natural languages operating under their own set of rules and constraints, but they differ from both the native language and the target language in their permeability, consistency and stability. For a comprehensive analysis regarding interlanguages see Adjemian (1976).

Early second language acquisition would be characterized by the temporary use of a non-marked, simple code resembling a pidgin. This code would be the product of cognitive constraints engendered by lack of knowledge of the target language. The code may reflect a regression to a set of universal primitive linguistic categories that were realized in early first language acquisition. Then, under conditions of social and/or psychological distance, this pidginized form of speech would persist. (p. 269)

Language ought not to be considered merely in terms of the structural elements playing an admittedly important role in the models of language subscribing to the parameter-setting hypothesis and the principles of UG. Language acquisition, as well as language use, must be viewed as a Gestalt, and models of such ought to incorporate both the formal elements of language and the not-so-formal though much more complicated aspects that have to do with the psychological and psychosocial identity of individuals acquiring and/or using languages. To establish the function of psychological and psychosocial variables in the process of adult second-language learning, future research in the domain of the functional aspects of SLA ought to be aimed at further defining the social and psychological identity of the adult language learner. Theoretical linguistics, particularly in the domains of syntax and phonology, has for the most part not addressed issues of pragmatics that are extremely relevant to this discussion, resulting in a wide gap in the theory as to the problems raised by linguistic data generally put aside in the pragmatics "gutter" of unexplainable explananda. Building on psychological perspectives on language acquisition and language use, a better, more comprehensive model for SLA will be devised.

HYPOTHESES REGARDING BILINGUAL CONDITIONS

It is the mark of fluent bilingual individuals that they manage to keep their language generating essentially unilingual, although this assertion represents a hotly debated topic within the field of bilingualism. Weinreich (1953) observed that "the ideal bilingual switches from one language to the other according to appropriate changes in the speech situation . . . but not in an unchanged speech situation, and certainly not within a sentence" (p. 73). More recent research, however, has compiled extensive data of the code-switched speech of bilinguals and has provided interesting analyses of this linguistic phenomenon. Certain theories about code switching classify human activities into domains, and it is between these domains that code-switched utterances take place (Nishimura, 1986, p. 123). Other viewpoints distinguish between conversational and situational code switching, thus including the cases of code switching that may not be directly related to domains or contextual features of a given situation (Nishimura, 1986, p. 124). Code switching, nonetheless, is now generally accepted as being more than "a random phenomenon" (Nishimura, 1986, p. 124). Research focusing on the code-switched speech of bilinguals provides insight as to the internal coding of the bilingual's languages, for which reason it becomes of great interest to this discussion.

Currently there are two distinct trends in the approach to code-switching theory. The first point of view asserts that language assignment is not necessary for the production of code-switched utterances because of the universality of intrasentential code switching at certain constituent end points in an utterance. Woolford (1983) has advanced a model to account for the regularities in code-switched utterances that proposes that the two sets of phrase-structure rules for the bilingual's two languages might share certain aspects or components, such as elementary constituent structures. A hybrid phrase-structure tree is generated by the mixed phrase-structure rules in the bilingual's language processor: "This area of overlap between the two phrase structure components should be thought of as a sort of space warp that allows one speaker to be in two universes, or two grammars, at once" (Woolford, 1983, p. 522). The lexical items are kept separate, as are the word-formation components; the convergence lies in the phrase-structure rules, the overlapping elements of which provide and allow for the constraints that have been pointed out by researchers examining pertinent data, yielding well-formed code-switched utterances.

There is a certain amount of reticence in accepting such universal constraints as suggested by Woolford's model. Some researchers contend that code switching may be instead provoked by certain "trigger words" (Cline, 1987) that basically tell the speaker to switch to the other language. This point of view implies that language assignment plays an essential role in code switching, the occurrence of which will therefore depend on factors other than purely grammatical constraints, factors such as language dominance within the individual, interference, and integration.

An approach to understanding the coding of the bilingual's languages that takes the tenets of UG into account might prove to be theoretically sound, although its mentalist character will be difficult to support empirically, as evidenced in both the small amount of studies carried out in this respect and the heavy criticism of the few such hypotheses that have emerged. Notwithstanding such limitations, observations have pointed to some major organizing principle as yet unidentified by research that underlies the psychological separation of the bilingual's two languages. It may be that experiences are coded once, in common, and each of the bilingual's languages draws from this experience, or it may be that events are coded separately in the language in which they are experienced. Kolers (1963) points out:

If verbally defined past experiences were tagged, or coded, and stored in common, they would presumably be in some supralinguistic form such as "thoughts" or "ideas." . . . A bilingual's languages would then act as independent tape for this common storage, and experiences stored in one language could be retrieved and described directly in the other. . . . We will call this the *shared hypothesis*.

Alternatively, if verbally defined past experiences were tagged in a form specific to one language . . . a bilingual would have a different store of experiences to refer to for each language. It would be impossible to refer [in one language] directly to . . . an experience or event tagged in the other; such references would require an additional step of translation. We will call this the *separate hypothesis*. (p. 291; emphasis added)

To test the shared and separate hypotheses, Kolers (1963) performed a word-association experiment with three groups of bilingual subjects. Four test sequences were studied, namely, the stimulus word in English was responded to in (1) English or (2) the native language; and a translation of the word into the native language was responded to in (3) English or (4) the native language. There were five semantic categories of words.

Kolers's principal findings showed that subjects tended to give different associations to a word in their native languages from those they gave in English to its translation. "Further, when the test is made interlingually the stimulus in one language and the response in the other—again little similarity is found. . . . The present results suggest that an image can only be concomitant but cannot be an essential property of the cognitive referent of a noun" (Kolers, 1963, p. 297). The results seem to suggest, at least as far as word associations are concerned, that there are no fixed images acting as a basis for responses in both languages and thus lend support to the separate hypothesis.

Javier, Barroso, and Muñoz (1991) carried out a study testing the memory of bilingual subjects, assuming that "memory of events of either a personal or a non-personal nature can be assessed through the analysis of the individual's verbalizations of those events" (p. 4), having based this assumption on the premise that "language serves an encoding function which allows a person to organize better his or her experience into categories" (p. 4). This study examined the quantitative and qualitative differences found in the language produced by an autobiographical memory task performed by a number of bilinguals. This task involved the participants in a story-telling activity in which they were to narrate a past event in their lives, first in the language in which it occurred (the language of the experience), then—about one half hour later—in their second language. One of the hypotheses tested was whether "the nature of the linguistic organization of the experience [would] differ between languages" (Javier et al., 1991, p. 10), language being one of the primary media for encoding information in memory, although it is certainly not the only medium, as the authors of the study point out. The subjects were said to be coordinate bilinguals (see below for discussion of the coordinate-compound distinction), that is, individuals who in general operate equally well in both languages. The results suggest that

> there are in fact differences in the way memory of personal events are organized linguistically in bilinguals. The fact that the nature of the elaboration of the experience was richer in the first in comparison to the second monologue suggests that the communication of the memory of personal events are qualitatively different in the two languages in favor of the first monologue (the language of the experience). But the fact that important information (idea and thought units) remained language-specific, suggests the two languages may be processing the experience qualitatively and quantitatively different. (Javier et al., 1991, p. 23)

Thus one may conclude that bilinguals encode the linguistic memory information separately, to use Kolers's terminology, the primary language of encoding being the language of experience and not the dominant language. The authors of the study agree that further testing is necessary to lend further support to their results, given the small size of the population tested. Their conclusions nonetheless are in agreement with the general consensus that the bilingual's codes are somehow neatly kept separate.

Roger Brown (1965) points out that it is necessary to have some kind of standard grid or coordinate system that describes the reference domain. He then comments on the relationship of meaning and words in different languages:

> The findings of ethnoscience and comparative semantics suggest that it is a rare thing to find a word in one language that is exactly equivalent in reference to a word in an unrelated language. If each lexicon is regarded as a template imposed on a common reality, these templates do not match up. On the level of grammar, differences of meaning between languages are more striking and probably of greater significance. (p. 317)

Kolers examined another aspect of this question. In one of his studies (1964), he tested whether a language skill developed in one language necessarily transfers to a bilingual's second language. The principal finding was that a cognitive operation practiced on one set of materials does not necessarily transfer to another set. "While S can make information stored in one coding system available in another, what he can do with it seems to depend upon specific skills he has developed in each system, and, presumably, upon equally specific skills for transferring between them" (Kolers, 1964, p. 247). This observation also supports the separate hypothesis.

Neurological studies of aphasia in bilinguals are another compelling source of evidence for the separate hypothesis. According to Marcos and Alpert (1976), bilingual individuals exhibit differential impairment of their two languages after cerebrovascular accidents or during deteriorating chronic organic brain syndromes. A similar effect has been noted in bilingual psychiatric patients after electroconvulsive therapy (Marcos & Alpert, 1976, p. 1276).

There are, however, studies that support the shared hypothesis by establishing the possibility of a number of responses chained to a common stimulus. Research by Ervin-Tripp (1961) in the area of semantic shift has made use of the varied color-naming strategies of different cultures. She examined the color naming of Navaho bilinguals, in comparison with two monolingual groups. It was found that the categories for color used by the bilinguals differed systematically from the monolingual norms. The differences could be predicted on the basis of an assumption of verbal mediation by the response term that is most rapid. Ervin-Tripp concluded:

> If an implicit response occurs in the suppressed language, it mediates a response in the overt language. When two responses have often been emitted in the presence of the same external stimulus, they acquire a chained relation to each other, in the sense that one later may elicit the other without the presence of the external stimulus. (Ervin-Tripp, 1961, p. 234)

COORDINATE AND COMPOUND BILINGUALS

Weinreich (1953) classified bilingual systems as coexistent, partially merged, and completely merged. The first definition referred to a case in which two words from different languages have the same referent but different meanings. In partially merged systems, two words have the same referent and the same meaning, the two languages being interchangeable. When one of the words is lacking a referent and is used only to refer to a corresponding word in another language, then the systems are completely merged, with one system subordinate to the other. These categories are evidently similar to Kolers's separate and shared hypotheses concerning the codes of the bilingual.

Work by Marcos and Alpert (1976) suggests that Weinreich's first two categories (coexistent and partially merged) are characteristic of every bilingual system and are closely correlated with word function:

> In general, these studies suggest that words referring to concrete high imagery objects elicit more similar responses in the bilingual's two languages than do abstract words, which in turn tend to evoke more similar associations than words referring to feelings. Thus, for an English-Spanish proficient bilingual, the words "table" and "mesa" may generate approximately the same mental representation; "freedom" and "libertad" will arouse different ones; and the words "love" and "amor" will mean and feel quite different. (Marcos & Alpert, 1976, p. 1276)

It is also important to distinguish between bilinguals who learned both languages in the same cultural context (compound bilinguals) from those whose languages had different acquisition contexts (coordinate bilinguals), the difference between the two languages being greater for the coordinate bilinguals (Ervin & Osgood, 1954).

Compound bilinguals, individuals who have learned two languages as children, have "one system with a number of variable components between which [they] may switch at will" (Klein, 1986, p. 11). The coordinate bilingual, on the other hand, first knows one language and later assimilates the other, thus building two different systems and operating them in parallel. In this latter case, one language could be dominant and the other used only superficially (this extreme case is termed by Weinreich as "subordinate bilingualism").

This distinction was revised by Ervin and Osgood (1954) primarily by incorporating subordinate bilingualism into the coordinate category. They further expanded on the distinguishing factors, including in their definition more details about manner of acquisition. The coordinate bilingual acquires the two languages in two different contexts. Any other type of language acquisition yields compound bilingualism (Klein, 1986, p. 11). In other words, the coordinate bilingual has two different lexicons that have been learned in two different contexts. It is interesting to note, however, that certain aspects of the bilingual's lexicon may be coordinate and others compound. There are certain words that may be of relevance for a given bilingual in the two contexts that this person operates. Moreover, grammatical units such as prepositions, connectors, pronouns, and so forth are common to both languages yet phonologically and semantically different in each language. The compound-coordinate model fails to account for this phenomenon. Macnamara (1972) has described this model as a "quite inadequate . . . representation of the lexical structure which must be employed by anyone who speaks a natural language" (p. 64).

The compound-coordinate distinction thus seems to be a somewhat overintellectualized analogy of the differences between early and late acquisition. Since the compound-coordinate model is confined to lexical items, it provides no insight as to how the two codes of the bilingual work in terms of grammar, especially as far as syntax and semantics are concerned. To establish the capability of bilingual individuals to deal with their two linguistic codes as well as their organization of the same, further research concerning the compound-coordinate distinction and a radical revision of the model are certainly in order.

A more sound approach to understanding the bilingual's codes might take into account the Chomskyan distinction between competence and performance. The compound-coordinate distinction implies that bilinguals have internalized two distinct and completely separate language codes. It may be more precise to say that bilingual individuals' two codes "together constitute their linguistic competence in a singular sense, and their linguistic performance can draw

primarily upon [one language], primarily [upon the other] or upon a willy-nilly
mixture of the two" (Lance, 1972, p. 32).

The Language Barrier in Psychotherapy

Patients vary considerably in the fluency with which they speak a second
language. The phenomenon of subordinate bilingualism, in which an individual has an incomplete mastery of a second language, poses several challenges
for the psychotherapist. The "descriptive evaluation of the patient's appearance, motor behavior, speech and intellectual functioning" referred to as the
mental status of the patient is affected by the patient's difficulty in expressing
his/her thoughts. The language barrier acts as background noise, making it
difficult for the therapist to distinguish between patients' reluctance to disclose
information about themselves and their inability to do so. Another source of
difficulty stems from determining whether patients' anxieties are due to their
psychological state or to the frustration of being unable to express themselves
meaningfully and accurately. Marcos, Urcuyo, Kesselman, & Alpert (1973)
point out, "A number of vocal and paralinguistic aspects of verbal behavior
which may be interpreted as having clinical significance . . . derive from the
special problems posed for patients across the language barrier" (p. 655).

The authors note that subordinate bilinguals communicating in a nondominant language produced more hand movement than when speaking in their
native language. They also exhibited greater degrees of passivity, somatic
concern, motor tension, mannerisms, anxiety, hostility, depressive moods and
emotional withdrawal in the English language interviews. Speech disturbances
such as stuttering, repetition, omission, incoherent sounds, slips of the tongue,
and sentence correction were also more common in the foreign-language
interviews. Patients' use of indigenous words while speaking in a nondominant
language was recorded frequently among subjects. This last finding may have
interesting implications for psychoanalysis involving subordinate bilinguals.
For instance, it would be worthwhile to investigate whether indigenous words
used in foreign-language interviews are associated with key experiences affect-
ing the patient's psychological state or whether the patient uses such words
because of a lack of knowledge about their idiomatic equivalents. Further
research in this area is needed to discern whether such language mixing is due
to difficulties stemming from the language barrier or is of psychological
significance. Perhaps the most conclusive evidence that Marcos and Alpert
provide on the effects of the language barrier is a set of interviews with Spanish-
American bilingual schizophrenic patients that disclosed greater psychopathology when the patients were interviewed in English than when interviewed in

Spanish (Marcos, Alpert, Urcuyo, & Kesselman, 1973). When similar psychiatric interviews were conducted with other types of bilingual patients, similar results were found (Marcos & Alpert, 1976).

A recent article by Vásquez and Javier (1991) describes several case studies in which errors of communication, some of them with fatal results, occurred between doctors and patients during interviews conducted through the aid of an interpreter. Five common errors committed by interpreters are pointed out and discussed in the article: omission, addition, condensation, substitution, and role exchange. Vásquez and Javier (1991) emphasize the delicacy of the problem of interpreting in the case of psychiatric patients because of the amount and intensity of the "intrusion of distorted and confusing material" (p. 164).

> The interpreter must bridge two worlds that are not only different by virtue of their languages but also by virtue of the patient's communication pattern. This communication pattern is frequently fraught with tangentiality, hallucinatory and delusional material, or other pathological manifestations of mental illness. It is difficult to understand this type of verbalization and conceptualization even in English-speaking schizophrenic patients, let alone when such a verbalization is mediated by an untrained interpreter. (Vásquez & Javier, 1991, p. 164)

The case studies described by Vásquez and Javier provide a clue as to the extent of this problem. The article suggests that interpreters be trained extensively, although doctors' awareness of the intricacies of interpretation must also be elucidated.

PSYCHOTHERAPY AND THE POLYGLOT

Work with fluent bilinguals both poses a different set of challenges for psychotherapists and provides them with valuable insights into psycholinguistic processes. If one accepts the premise of the separate-code hypothesis outlined in the beginning of this chapter, then each language can be considered to have a unique set of cultural and idiosyncratic associations for a given individual. Various studies documenting psychotherapy with bilingual patients support this assumption as well as the notions that language "separateness" is not marked in the use of emotional words and in work with coordinate bilinguals.

Diagnosis of the Bilingual Patient

Areas of the bilingual's intrapsychic world may remain hidden and unexplored "due to the fact that they are independent of the language system in which the treatment is conducted" (Marcos & Alpert, 1976). Marcos and Alpert (1976) point out,

> The psychotherapist [should be] careful to estimate the potential for non-congruence of the two language systems. Factors that should be routinely explored include the age and developmental stage of the patient when the languages were acquired, experiential sorting of language contexts and nature of the object relationships associated with them, attitudes and values connected with each language. The therapist ought to explore and look for aspects that are shared by the two languages as well as events that seem unique to either one. This language evaluation will permit the therapist to assess the degree of language independence and to anticipate areas that may be unavailable in a particular language. (p. 1277)

The notion of "language independence" alluded to above by Marcos an Alpert is a simple and straightforward yet highly meaningful hypothesis about bilinguals. It has been suggested that language, being so intimately connected with culture and history of both large and smaller societal groups, carries more psychological meaning and psychosocial implications than reference to the world. Language viewed from this perspective serves as an aid to categorizing, regulating, and organizing the world (Javier, 1989) in a way that is not only culture specific but also language specific. This assumption has great implications in respect to the bilingual patient since "each language may be associated with different personality structures, especially if the individual learned the languages at a time when his or her personality structures were forming" (Javier, 1989, p. 520).

Javier (1989) describes the case of a Spanish-English bilingual patient who not only denied his Latino identity and tradition but also repressed traumatic events in his childhood aided by his refusal to speak Spanish, his parents' language. Whenever negative impulses emerged, this patient would avoid Spanish and turn to English, which in turn "represented an attempt to repress his past and the chaotic ego identity associated with [his] first language and an effort to establish a new identity where the demand of the superego was less intense" (Javier, 1989, p. 522).

A different Spanish-English bilingual patient, also described by Javier, found it difficult to express herself grammatically in Spanish, although she had not become proficient in English until she reached her 30s. She recovered her Spanish fluency only after "important interpretations were made regarding her sexual and sadistic fantasies toward her abusive and unavailable father and her weak mother" (Javier, 1989, p. 523). These two particular examples, along with many other similar cases, lend support to some form of the language-independence hypothesis. The importance of the study and careful analysis of the bilingual patient follows from the fact pointed out by Javier:

Language expresses conscious and unconscious mental contents through direct or indirect verbalization by the concatenation of associations, peculiarities of verbal choice, and slips of the tongue as well as through the peculiarities of pronunciation of language and the mannerisms of speech. In addition, for bilinguals, mental contents are also expressed through the operation of language choice. (Javier, 1989, pp. 523–524)

Bilinguals have the extra defense mechanism of language shift, which may be detrimental to the clinical diagnosis, just in case the clinician is not attuned to this possibility. However, there remains a likelihood that the therapeutic process may be aided and progress may be made by therapist-induced language shifting and/or code switching.

Unavailability

Several cases of language-related repression have been reported in the psychoanalytical literature. Greenson (1950) had as a patient a woman bilingual in German and English. During the first part of the treatment, she used both languages until a moment came when she could not longer bring herself to speak German. She explained that "in German, I am a scared, dirty child; in English, I am a nervous, refined woman." She felt that obscene words were "much easier to say and much cleaner in English" and that "talking in German I shall have to remember something I wanted to forget." Greenson (1950) concluded that German was the patient's pregenital tongue and was associated with cardinal unresolved conflicts. The woman preferred to use English because it allowed her to repress her infantile life and establish a new ego identity. Greenson used German during the subsequent interviews as a therapeutic technique aimed at bringing past conflicts to the surface and resolving the patient's neurosis.

Buxbaum (1949) recounted the psychoanalysis of two German women who emigrated to the United States as adolescents:

Both [women] spoke German and English fluently, but English was the treatment language. One patient suffered from a severe preoccupation with the penis. During the course of treatment she frequently associated about the word "sausages," but no therapeutic consequences resulted. Translation of that word into its German equivalent, "Blutwurst," released from repression a series of memories that helped to uncover fundamental sexual material from her infantile years. Although the other patient had dreamed repeatedly in the course of treatment about windows, she gave no association to them; when the word was translated into the German "Fenster," she verbalized a chain of relevant associations. (Marcos & Alpert, 1976, p. 1276)

Buxbaum concluded that, for these two bilingual patients, speaking in English meant avoiding the language of their key fantasies and memories, enabling them to detach themselves from significant psychic traumata.

Splitting

One of the primary characteristics of bilingual defense mechanisms is the use of a language devoid of emotional associations to describe affective experiences or activities. Krapf (1955) describes the treatment of a voyeur who was fluent in both Spanish and English. Although the interviews were primarily conducted in English, the subject spoke Spanish whenever he talked of his sexual activities. Krapf inferred that the patient's dual language skills made possible a psychic personality split. By speaking in Spanish, the man was able to avoid the overwhelming anxiety associated with his activities. Another case of "splitting" is reported by Marcos (1972), who tells of a bilingual patient lying about cardinal aspects of her personality for more than a year. The composure maintained by the woman while speaking English (her preferred language) gave way when she began to speak Spanish and her defensive lying became apparent. According to Marcos (1972), the patient chose the language that was less likely to provoke anxiety and conversely more likely to protect the ego against anxiety caused by the superego.

BILINGUAL TECHNIQUES IN THERAPY

Psychotherapy involving bilingual patients provides advantages as well as disadvantages. As we have already mentioned, bilingualism can be an asset in therapy, under the right conditions. When the patient and clinician are matched bilinguals, the clinician can utilize language switching to facilitate therapy. As Marcos and Alpert (1976) point out, language choice allows the therapist to explore areas of the bilingual patient's personality that are language specific. Used strategically, language switching may allow the patient to be introspective without the overwhelming anxiety that accompanies traumatic thoughts and feelings: "A hysterical patient whose intense affect interferes with attempts at objectifying issues may benefit from encoding experiences in the second, less emotional language" (Marcos & Alpert, 1976, p. 1277). Conversely, a patient who represses internal conflict by overintellectualization may be helped by verbalizing in the more intuitive, emotional language of the two (Marcos & Alpert, 1976).

There may also be dangers in therapy involving bilingual patients. First, the use of language switching is at the discretion of the therapist and is not well understood. It may in certain cases obscure the patient's psychic condition rather than clarify it. The power of language to compartmentalize experiences makes it a suitable vehicle for repression and avoidance for a bilingual subject, as evidenced in the cases discussed above.

Bilingualism and Psychosis

Robertson and Shamsie (1959) studied the gibberish produced by a multilingual schizophrenic patient. The patient, a 30-year-old native of India diagnosed as a chronic hebephreniac, spoke several languages. His mother-tongue was Gujerati, spoken by members of the Parsi religion to which the subject belonged. He spoke, read, and wrote both Hindi (the national language of India) and English with complete fluency and correctness. He also knew a small number of German and Norwegian words and phrases. Recordings were made of the subject's entire verbal production in responses to a series of tests and tasks administered under various conditions on three different occasions. Analyses of the data showed that "the phonological structure of B.'s gibberish was essentially English with general influences also present from his two Indian languages and a specific influence present from German" (Robertson & Shamsie, 1959, p. 7).

The report further indicated that the meanings of the findings were somewhat ambiguous. "It is not clear how far the circumstances that B. was multilingual was relevant to the fact that his thought disorder especially took the form of speaking gibberish. It is also not clear whether his gibberish is to be regarded as a *reversion to a linguistic stage of childhood*" (Robertson & Shamsie, 1959, p. 8; emphasis added).

This italicized comment above is an indirect reference to what Maher (1966) has called "one of the commonest hypotheses to be advanced regarding schizophrenic thinking" (p. 407). Maher goes on to point out that this hypothesis (called the regression hypothesis) was formulated first by Gardner in 1931 (Maher, 1966). The regression hypothesis regards schizophrenic thinking as representing regression to a previous, less mature level. "Schizophrenic thinking [and language], so this view holds, is essentially 'childish thinking' [and speech]" (Maher, 1966).

Lukianowicz (1962) has reported that some polyglot psychotics experienced auditory hallucinations in more than one language: "They usually hear the friendly voices in their native language, the hostile voices in a foreign tongue" (p. 274). Exceptions to this generalization, as we will see later, are explained by Lukianowicz on the basis of political circumstances in the home country that have a direct bearing on the patient as an individual.

Lukianowicz (1962) covers a broad span of time, geography, and culture:

> Multilingual auditory hallucinations disregard all geographical, racial, religious and national boundaries: we met them among some Asiatic tribesmen who served in the Russian Army, as well as among the so-called "European Voluntary Workers," whom German authorities brought from various European countries to work in the Third Reich during the war. After the war, we came across such hallucinations among the "D.P.s"

("Displaced Persons") in Austria, Germany and Italy, and we observed this phenomenon among some soldiers of the Polish Armed Forces treated in this country between
1947 and 1951. Finally the same pattern of auditory polyglot hallucinations was found
among some of the Hungarian Freedom Fighters, the most recent European refugees,
who came under our care in the U.K. in 1957. (p. 274)

Although the clinical picture varied considerably among this diverse
patient population, some consistencies in symptomatology, etiological background, and cultural origin could be discerned. The non-European patients
(mostly from Asiatic Russia, but including a Yoruba from Nigeria) presented a
"uniform type of schizophrenia-like reaction," while the European group
exhibited "the usual wide variety of clinical syndromes, ranging from an acute
anxiety reaction through a neurotic depression to a typical schizo-affective
picture" (Lukianowicz, 1962, pp. 274–275). Lukianowicz further classified the
patients into three categories: (1) the cultural group, (2) the political group, and
(3) the genetic group, which are defined and illustrated in the following pages.

The Cultural Group

It is postulated that the main causative factor in this group of cases was the sudden
impact of an unfamiliar culture and a strange, restless, highly mechanized civilization
upon subjects belonging to a more primitive civilization, often with a nomadic way of
life. An important additional precipitating factor was their home-sickness, exacerbated
by the patient's loneliness due to their cultural, social and linguistic isolation. These
traumatic conflicting forces were often frankly expressed in the contents of their
auditory hallucinations. (Lukianowicz, 1962, p. 275)[4]

Lukianowicz provides case histories of two Russian soldiers—both members
of eastern Russian ethnic minorities—who reacted to the stresses of "culture
shock" with symptoms resembling a typical catatonic pattern of initial excitement and subsequent extreme withdrawal. A similar reaction pattern is displayed by a 22-year-old Yoruba from Nigeria who came to England as a student
of economics:

At first he settled down well, attended lectures and mixed freely with fellow-students.
However after a few weeks he rapidly changed, went off food, lost sleep, became
suspicious and withdrawn. He stayed in his lodgings, was restless, and kept passing the
room, mumbling to himself in his native tongue. At night he continued to dash In his
room and was shouting out. A doctor was called, but R. refused to see him. In the
morning he left the house, and went to his friends in London. He was persuaded by them
to see a psychiatrist, and later to enter a psychiatric hospital, where he manifested
symptoms of schizophrenic excitement: he was restless, excited, his speech was

[4]This and all following excerpts from N. Lukianowicz are reprinted by permission of *Psychiatria et
Neurologia*, Basel, Switzerland.

disconnected, and he dashed about in an impulsive way, shouting out in English and in his native Yoruba. After two further days he became mute, immobile, incontinent, entirely withdrawn, and presented a typical picture of catatonic schizophrenia. This new syndrome disappeared after a few ETCs. The patient regained insight, and reported how he had heard "many voices" during his confusional episode. His English voices were stern and demanding "and they ordered me to stay here and to work hard; the Yoruba voices were sweet and soft. They promised to protect me from the White Man's Magic, and urged me to go home. All these voices kept quarreling in my head until I became muddled and didn't know what to do."—R. soon made an uneventful and a complete recovery, and was able to continue with his studies at the university. (Lukianowicz, 1962, pp. 276–277)

The Political Group

Lukianowicz (1962) subdivides this category into two subgroups: (1) prisoners of war and displaced persons "in whom the psychotic reaction was precipitated by certain factors of a political nature, causing an acute fear (of arrest, trial and death)" and (2) political refugees from various countries living in Britain. An example of the first type of patient is provided in the case history of a young Russian soldier, "W.R.," who was captured by the Germans in 1942.

A year later he joined the Free Russian Army, which was organized in Germany from Russian ex-prisoners of war. As long as this new anti-communist force was trained inside Germany, W.R. was quite happy; but when the time came for his brigade to move to the much feared Eastern Front, he deserted his unit. He obtained civilian clothes from his German girl-friend, and, pretending to be a Russian "East European Voluntary Worker", made his way to Austria, where some of his friends were living in one of the many camps for "European Voluntary Workers" on the outskirts of Vienna. His fair knowledge of German helped him to reach the desired camp unmolested, but there he unexpectedly met with a traumatic experience. As on the night of his arrival several young inmates absconded from the camp, a detachment of the Gestapo ("Geheime Staats-Polizei") was called in. The whole camp was placed under curfew and nobody was allowed to leave his hut before having been screened by the Gestapo and the camp commandant. W.R. became terrified, in case he might be recognized as a deserter, and court-martialled. But then, just when the Gestapo-men were entering his hut, the Allied bombers appeared overhead, dropping incendiary bombs, which started fires in several points at the same time. Hell broke out in the camp. People ignored the curfew and ran for their lives. W.R. luckily escaped unharmed and later, together with others, was admitted to a neighboring camp without anybody asking him for any documents. But there another shock was waiting for him. The commandant of the new camp was the former commandant of the camp where W.R. had been a prisoner of war before he joined the collaborator General Vlasov. The patient was convinced that this man will inevitably recognized in him the former P.O.W. and will hand him over to the Gestapo.—The same night he escaped from the new camp. Next day he was found in the near fields, confused, crying, and talking to himself. In the Observation Ward he remained restless and was conversing with his hallucinatory voices. (Lukianowicz, 1962, pp. 277–278)

The second group of patients, the political refugees, presents an interesting contrast to the prisoner-of-war and displaced-person group. All these patients suffer from homesickness, made more intense by letters from relatives behind the Iron Curtain, but they are also prey to intense fears of returning to their homelands. Says Lukianowicz (1962):

> The ensuing conflict is expressed in projected voices, heard in at least two languages, the native and one or more foreign tongues. However in such cases the originally "foreign" language (i.e., English) takes over the part of the "good" protective mother-language, while the original mother-tongue now represents the evil and threatening forces. (p. 279)

This pattern is exemplified in the case of "C.G.," a 25-year-old Hungarian university student who fled the country after taking part in the October 1956 revolt. Two years later in England, while recovering from an appendectomy, C.G. became depressed and developed fears of insanity and severe physical illness. At the same time he became homesick and insisted on returning to Hungary, in spite of the discouraging letters from his parents. Later he became suspicious and refused to see any of his Hungarian friends, suspecting them all to be "agents of the Hungarian Secret Police." After a few days of gloomy brooding he became "all mixed up" and began hearing voices. His English voices tried to dissuade him from returning to Hungary in a firm but friendly manner. His native Hungarian voices were of opposite kinds: some of them were friendly and warned him not to go back home, emphasizing their advice with such expressive words as "you silly ass," or "you idiot." The other Hungarian voices obviously personified the Hungarian secret police. They threatened to shoot C.G. "like a mad dog" and called him "a traitor, Judas, servant of the Imperialists, bastard," and many other rather uncomplimentary epithets (Lukianowicz, 1962, pp. 280–281).

The Genetic Group

This last group of cases consists of subjects whose psychosis was apparently of a genetic origin and was neither caused nor aggravated by any political factors. Yet, as these patients lived in a foreign country, their auditory hallucinations acquired a particular, quasi-political coloring, and their "good voices" used mostly their native languages, while the "bad voices" expressed themselves in the tongues of their new country. However, in some cases the opposite would take place (Lukianowicz, 1962, pp. 281–282).

In illustration of the "genetic" type of patient, Lukianowicz presents the case summary of "J.L.," a 45-year-old Polish laborer who exhibited an acute schizophrenic reaction with religious content.

> He alleged that, "A miracle occurred in Bristol the other night. The whole sky became illuminated by bright stars. It all was in the papers on the following morning. Everybody knows about it." [J.]L. heard "voices of Angels singing Polish hymns. Sometimes they were interrupted by loud screams under my windows. Later a black dog began to follow me to work on building-sites. He talked to me in a human voice, but as he did so in English, I could not understand him. But I knew that it was The Evil One himself, disguised as a dog, and pretending that he could not speak Polish."—In the ward the patient would spend hours reading his little prayer book and missal. He was cooperative and friendly, though for years he remained hallucinated. He heard "some English voices, calling out from Dundry Hill, and all over the fields. They are the voices of The Evil One," the "good" Polish voices were the voices of Angels, who encouraged the patient "to pray and to read the missal." (Lukianowicz, 1962, pp. 282–283)

Observations comparable to those of Lukianowicz were reported by Schaechter (1964). A group of 60 non-British female migrant psychotic patients hospitalized in Australia were studied from the standpoint of bilingual auditory hallucinations. Patients with acute psychoses of recent origin tended to hallucinate in English, while patients with chronic psychoses of less recent origin and more gradual onset tended to hallucinate in their mother tongue. It appeared that 23 of the 37 patients with persecutory hallucinations heard the persecutory remarks in English. This occurred whether the patients could or could not speak English; they "knew" that the voices were speaking in English.

Those patients who hallucinated in their mother tongue had regressed to an earlier form of language, since they were in an English-speaking environment. The fact that these patients were the ones with the most serious illness helps to make this finding agree with the regression hypothesis mentioned earlier in relation to Robertson and Shamsie (1959). There may be another explanation, however, of the refusal of these patients to live in the present. Haley (1959) describes the language of schizophrenics as consisting largely of efforts to negate relationships and communication. One wonders whether Schaechter's findings might not indicate an action on the part of the chronic patients to negate their existence in a situation that must, for any migrant, be deemed uncomfortable. As Lukianowicz (1962) points out, "The hearing of aggressive voices in a foreign language occasionally may be advantageous to the patient, as he may pretend 'not to understand' their hostile contents. . . . This may be regarded as a psychological defense mechanism, which may be expressed thus: 'You' (i.e., the foreign voices) 'can't really frighten me, because I don't understand you' " (pp. 292–293).

LANGUAGE INDEPENDENCE AND THE ROLE OF STRESS

We have pointed out the difficulties encountered when setting up experiments testing the role of extralinguistic factors on language production, and we have attributed the lack of empirical studies on psychological and psychosocial factors in SLA to such difficulties. It could be concluded that psycholinguistics needs to turn to other disciplines, such as cognitive science or psychopathology, to examine linguistic processes. This trend in the field is growing, as evidenced in most of the current research, some of which we have discussed here.

Linguists have analyzed the phenomenon of bilingualism primarily from the standpoint of purely linguistic factors, again lacking depth in extralinguistic factors of a psychological or psychosocial nature. We wish to point out now two recent studies of the effects of stress in the language processing of bilingual subjects that draw some interesting conclusions pertaining both to the language-independence hypothesis and indirectly to the regression hypothesis discussed above. Both experiments (Javier & Alpert, 1986; Javier & Marcos, 1989) tested a population of Spanish-English coordinate bilinguals who underwent differential conditioning while they listened to a series of words in both Spanish and English with a phonological, a semantic, or a neutral relation or similarity. The subjects' responses to the stimuli were measured with galvanic skin reflex electrodes. The most interesting aspect of these two studies is that they examine a given psychological—and extralinguistic—factor from a scientific and objective standpoint, unlike most analyses of bilingualism, which are primarily based on case studies of an observational and therefore somewhat subjective nature.

The results of the earlier study (Javier & Alpert, 1986) found a strong correlation between the subjects' responses to words semantically and phonemically related to the conditioned stimulus and a weaker correlation between the responses to words unrelated to the conditioned stimulus. This occurred in both languages, thus indicating that language-specific effects played no role in the study. Javier and Marcos (1989) elaborated on the same experiment design to further establish whether stressful conditions would intensify the occurrence of code switching and to clarify whether semantic or phonemic generalization would take place.

It was found that under circumstances of greater stress, phonemic generalizations, in contrast to semantic generalizations, were most frequent when the stimulus words were related. The conclusion drawn by Javier and Marcos (1989) in this respect is that stressful situations for a bilingual result in a primitivization of the bilingual's language processing. Furthermore, it was observed that a strong conditioning of a stimulus word in a given language "encouraged more generalization in the same language as the conditioned word . . . although the primary language of all subjects was Spanish, with English as their second language," whereas "the mild buzzer condition encouraged more generalization in the other language" (Javier & Marcos, 1989, p. 467). These results not only support the theory of coordinate bilingualism, given the distinct responses for strongly versus mildly conditioned stimuli in the two different languages. Further, the findings of this study also corroborate the regression hypothesis, since the authors concluded that "stress produced code switching, and hence, a primitivization of the subject's cognitive and linguistic functioning [was] assumed to have occurred" (Javier & Marcos, 1989, p. 449).

CONCLUSION

We have attempted to introduce some of the primary concerns in the current research regarding bilingualism and psychopathology. We have pointed out the lack of empirical work in the area of SLA as to matters pertaining to psychological and psychosocial factors that might affect the learning of a second language. It is feasible to assert that fluently learning a second language depends primarily on belonging to the group and on having a tight relationship with the native speakers of the target language, including a proper assimilation of the target culture. Coulmas (1981) describes the greatest difficulties encountered by the paradigmatically most meticulous students of a foreign language: spies. He stresses that the challenges for a nonnative speaker to pass as a native lie beyond "making sense" in the target language:

> Learning one's mother tongue as a child does not result in knowing much about it. . . . By contrast, the ideal spy to be cannot dispense with instruction and hence *knowing that* if he wants to acquire native like proficiency in the language. He lacks the natural environment and the conditions of language socialization characteristic of native development. His language acquisition process therefore passes through a stage of conscious learning, and his *knowing how* is mediated, in large measure, by *knowing that*. In other words, his command of the language is based on a high degree of linguistic awareness. (Coulmas, 1981, p. 359)

Thus, a perfect command of the language entails more than achieving an impeccable accent. It includes learning whether one says "black and white" or "white and black" when referring to old television sets, and certainly it involves learning to say "ouch!" instead of "ay!" or "itai!" when the car door slams on one's fingers. These processes, unconsciously acquired by the child, must be consciously learned by the adult. Linguistic production that is automatic in the speech of the native speaker is conversely calculated and premeditated in the speech of a nonnative. For our purposes it is interesting to consider the possibility that a nonnative speaker of a given language will never achieve full competence in the target language, no matter how many long hours are spent perfecting this ability. Coppieters (1987) conducted a study testing for differences in competence between natives and nonnatives when subjects spoke French, and his results point to a great divergence between the two groups, particularly in the functional and cognitive aspects of grammar, although all subjects in the study had been assessed as being equal in terms of language use and proficiency. This problem raised by the divergent competence, as evidenced in performance data, between natives and nonnatives is qualitatively similar to the problem raised by the divergent linguistic performances of individuals suffering from mental illness, putting aside the differences between the tangible nature of the two problems. The language of a psychopath, for example, differs greatly from the language of a healthy individual, although the differences are not so much structural as they are functional.

In this chapter we described the current understanding of the bilingual mind, including the compound-coordinate distinction and the language-independence hypothesis, as characterizations of the encoding of the bilingual's language processes. Evidence from studies of bilinguals and observation of bilingual patients tend to support the verisimilitude of the coordinate-compound distinction as well as it provides proof of the language-independence hypothesis. Further analyses of bilingualism and psychosis brought the regression hypothesis into the foreground, the findings of which we have attempted here to compare with the results of experiments dealing with stress and code-switching phenomena by Javier and Alpert (1986) and Javier and Marcos (1989).

REFERENCES

Adjemian, C. (1976). On the nature of interlanguage systems. *Language Learning, 26*, 297–320.
Bley-Vroman, R. (1989). The logical problem of foreign language learning. In S. Gass & J. Schachter (Eds.), *Linguistic perspectives on second language acquisition* (pp. 41–68). New York: Cambridge University Press.
Brown, R. (1965). *Social psychology.* New York: Free Press.
Buxbaum, E. (1949). The role of the second language in the formation of the ego and superego. *Psychoanalysis, 18*, 279–289.

Cline, M. (1987). Constraints on code switching: How universal are they? *Linguistics*, *4*, 739–764.

Cook, V. (1988). *Chomsky's universal grammar: An introduction*. Oxford: Blackwell.

Cook, V. (1991). *Second language learning and teaching*. London: Arnold.

Coppieters, R. (1987). Competence differences between native and non-native speakers. *Language*, *63*, 544–573.

Coulmas, F. (1981). Spies and native speakers. In F. Coulmas (Ed.), *A Festschrift for native speaker* (pp. 355–367). The Hague: Mouton.

Diebold, A. R. (1961). Incipient bilingualism. *Language*, *37*, 97–112.

Ellis, R. (1985). *Understanding second language acquisition*. Oxford: Oxford University Press.

Ellis, R. (1990). A response to Gregg. *Applied Linguistics*, *11*, 384–391.

Ervin-Tripp, S. M. (1961). Semantic shift in bilingualism. *American Journal of Psychology*, *74*, 233–241.

Ervin, S. M., & Osgood, C. E. (1954). Second language learning and bilingualism. In C. E. Osgood & T. A. Sebeok (Eds.), *Psycholinguistics (Journal of Abnormal and Social Psychology Supplement)*, *49*, 139–146.

Gleitman, L., & Gleitman, H. (1970). *Phrase and paraphrase*. New York: Norton.

Greenson, R. R. (1950). The mother tongue and the mother. *International Journal of Psychoanalysis*, *31*, 18–23.

Gregg, K. (1989). Second language acquisition theory. In S. Gass & J. Schachter (Eds.), *Linguistic perspectives on second language acquisition* (pp. 15–40). New York: Cambridge University Press.

Gregg, K. (1990). The variable competence model of SLA and why it isn't. *Applied Linguistics*, *11*, 364–383.

Haley, J. (1959). An interactional description of schizophrenia. *Psychiatry*, *22*, 321–332.

Javier, R. A. (1989). Linguistic considerations in the treatment of bilinguals. *Psychoanalytic Psychology*, *6*, 517–526.

Javier, R. A., & Alpert, M. (1986). The effect of stress on the linguistic generalization of bilingual individuals. *Journal of Psycholinguistic Research*, *15*, 419–435.

Javier, R. A., Barroso, F., & Muñoz, M. (1991). *Autobiographical memory in bilinguals*. Unpublished manuscript.

Javier, R. A., & Marcos, L. R. (1989). The role of stress on the language-independence and code-switching phenomena. *Journal of Psycholinguistic Research*, *18*, 449–472.

Johnson, J., & Newport, E. (1989). Critical period effects in second language learning: The influence of maturational state on the acquisition of English as a second language. *Cognitive Psychology*, *21*, 60–99.

Klein, W. (1986). *Second language acquisition*. Cambridge: Cambridge University Press.

Krapf, E. E. (1955). The choice of language in polyglot psychoanalysis. *Psychoanalytic Quarterly*, *24*, 343–357.

Kolers, P. A. (1963). Interlingual word associations. *Journal of Verbal Learning and Verbal Behavior*, *2*, 291–300.

Kolers, P. A. (1964). Specificity of a cognitive operation. *Journal of Verbal Learning and Verbal Behavior*, *3*, 244–248.

Lance, D. M. (1972). The codes of the Spanish-English bilingual. In B. Spolsky (Ed.), *The language education of minority children* (pp. 25–36). Rowley, MA: Newbury House.

Lenneberg, E. (1967). *Biological foundations of language*. New York: Wiley.

Lukianowicz, N. (1962). Auditory hallucinations in polyglot subjects. *Psychiatria et Neurologia*, *143*, 274–294.

Macnamara, J. (1972). Bilingualism and thought. In B. Spolsky (Ed.), *The language education of minority children* (pp. 60–76). Rowley, MA: Newbury House.

Maher, B. A. (1966). *Principles of psychopathology*. New York: McGraw-Hill.

Marcos, L. R. (1972). Lying: A particular defense met in psychoanalytic therapy. *American Journal of Psychoanalysis, 32*, 195–202.

Marcos, L. R., & Alpert, M. (1976). Strategies and risks in psychotherapy with bilingual patients: The phenomenon of language independent. *American Journal of Psychiatry, 133*, 1275–1278.

Marcos, L. R., Alpert, M., Urcuyo, L., & Kesselman, M. (1973). The effect of interview language on the evaluation of psychopathology in Spanish-American schizophrenic patients. *American Journal of Psychiatry, 130*, 549–553.

Marcos, L. R., Urcuyo, L., Kesselman, M., & Alpert, M. (1973). The language barrier in evaluating Spanish-American patients. *Archives of General Psychiatry, 29*, 655–659.

Nishimura, M. (1986). Intrasentential code switching: The case of language assignment. In J. Vaid (Ed.), *Language processing in bilinguals; Psycholinguistic and neuropsychological perspectives* (pp. 123–143). Hillsdale, NJ: Erlbaum.

Penfield, W. (1953). A consideration of the neurophysiological mechanisms of speech and some educational consequences. *Proceedings of the American Academy of Arts and Sciences, 82*(5), 201–214.

Robertson, J. P. S., & Shamsie, S. J. (1959). A systematic examination of gibberish in a multilingual schizophrenic patient. *Language and Speech, 2*, 1–8.

Schachter, J. (1989). *On the issue of completeness in second language acquisition*. Unpublished manuscript.

Schaechter, F. (1964). The language of the voices. *Medical Journal of Australia, 2*, 870–871.

Schumann, J. (1978). Second language acquisition: The pidginization hypothesis. In E. Hatch (Ed.), *Second language acquisition*. Rowley, MA: Newbury Press.

Silva-Corvalán, C. (1986). Bilingualism and language change: The extension of *estar* in Los Angeles Spanish. *Language, 62*, 587–608.

Vásquez, C., & Javier, R. A. (1991). The problem with interpreters: Communicating with Spanish-speaking patients. *Hospital and Community Psychiatry, 42*, 163–165.

Weinreich, U. (1953). *Languages in contact*. New York: Linguistic Circle.

White, L. (1990). Another look at the logical problem of foreign language learning: A reply to Bley-Vroman. *Linguistic Analysis, 20*(1–2), 50–63.

Woolford, E. (1983). Bilingual code switching and syntactic theory. *Linguistic Inquiry, 14*, 520–535.

Yamamoto, K. (1964). Bilingualism: A brief review. *Mental Hygiene, 48*, 468–477.

9

Conclusion
Repairing the Broken Connections

> . . . each venture
> Is a new beginning, a raid on the inarticulate
> With shabby equipment always deteriorating . . .
> Leaving one still with the intolerable wrestle
> With words and meaning . . .
>
> T. S. Eliot, East Coker

It seems appropriate to open this final chapter by restating as questions the two major objectives of most previous investigations of language behavior and communication in psychopathology. First, have we succeeded in obtaining precise descriptions of the way, or ways, in which the language behavior of individuals diagnosed as belonging to specific nosological categories differs from that of individuals in other diagnostic categories or from that of normals? Second, have studies of language behavior and communication advanced our understanding, to any appreciable degree, of the psychopathological processes involved in various psychiatric disorders? Once we have answered these questions as best we can, we will proceed to consider further issues that future research and theory may seek to confront.

Our assessment recognizes a major factor that has affected, and continues to affect, attempts at systematic investigation in this area of inquiry: The clinic rather than the laboratory is the primary locus of this research. Clinicians who are in daily contact with patients and who are obliged to cope with the problems of communication and interaction posed by psychotic language behavior as part of their ordinary round of activities can hardly be criticized for setting pragmatic goals that are likely to differ considerably from those of the scientific investigator. It is unavoidable that this symptom-oriented, functional approach to psychopathological language study has produced results that many researchers have found less than satisfying.

Only within recent years has the expertise of language specialists been brought to bear on problems of psychopathological language. Studies conducted by linguistic and psycholinguistic investigators have found their way into the professional literature during the 25 years since the publication of *Language Behavior and Psychopathology* (1969), and the products of such investigations, as we have already noted in the preceding chapters, have contributed to a clarification of some of the basic issues in psychopathological language development. This research, moreover, is informed by a point of view that assigns legitimacy of interest to psychopathological language phenomena per se as objects of scrutiny, quite apart from their purely clinical significance as symptoms of an underlying condition.

PHENOMENOLOGY AND SYMPTOMATOLOGY: IS THERE A DIFFERENCE THAT MAKES A DIFFERENCE?

The philosophical term, *phenomenology*, first used in the Husserlian tradition, has been applied to psychopathology in the Jasperian tradition, that is, stressing the symptomatology of the disorder. This interest in the phenomenological side of psychopathology emerged contemporaneously with the Kraepelinian influence on the DSM-III, which clearly had a behavioral-descriptive orientation rather than the more dynamic theoretical orientation contained in the DSM-II. The notion behind the potential usefulness of this concept lies in the assumption that this was a useful way to gain a better understanding of the manner in which patients experience their problems. It is looked on as a tool for description for European scholars in this field who wish to resurrect the Husserlian/Jasperian tradition.

After the appearance of the phenomenological approach to psychopathology, Berrios (1989) published a critique that questioned the usefulness of this approach for present-day psychiatry and psychopathology.

LANGUAGE DESCRIPTIONS AND PSYCHOPATHOLOGY

Complex methodological and conceptual issues abound in any attempt to answer the deceptively simple question: Have we succeeded to any significant extent in obtaining precise descriptions of language behavior in various psychiatric disorders? Psychiatric diagnosis is not widely reputed for its accuracy and precision. Diagnostic categories have been generated empirically over the years by thousands of clinical observations, and despite periodic efforts to sharpen them by means of revisions in the *Diagnostic and Statistical Manual* of the American Psychiatric Association, their use necessarily involves a range of variance.

Lack of precision in the formulation of diagnostic criteria has had a significant effect on the matter of sampling, which in turn has affected the generality of research findings. While the problems raised by sampling are present in most clinical research and are not specific to the study of language behavior and psychopathology, it cannot be denied that progress in this area of inquiry has consistently been hampered by small and nonrepresentative samples, one of the principal reasons research in this field has tended to be repetitive rather than cumulative.

Technological progress in the means for observing and recording language behavior in the psychopathological context (e.g., the camcorder) reminds us how far we have come since the days when "verbal behavior" of patients reached professional publication in the transcription of stenographic notes taken by the clinician during an interview. But apart from the issue of improvements in technology, it should be emphasized that those who observed such behavior were people who, for the most part, had been trained as psychiatrists or clinical psychologists. Lacking specific linguistic skills, their reports tended to reflect those aspects of language behavior that might range from the commonplace to the bizarre but with which their experience as clinicians made them familiar. What was included in such reports was often much less significant than what was left out, especially the entire range of paralinguistic phenomena.

Human speech consists of two simultaneous sets of cues. The first is the articulated sound patterns that form words, phrases, and sentences. These are characterized as a rapidly changing succession of stimuli presenting semantically meaningful material. The second set of cues includes the discriminable qualitative features of the voice itself. Soskin and Kaufmann (1961) describe the second set of cues as a "carrier" on which articulated sounds are superimposed. Within this carrier may be the major cues to the individual's emotional predisposition. Ostwald (1963) gives a graphic illustration of the distinction between carrier and semantic content. A psychiatrist asked a woman undergoing psychotherapy how she felt. With a tremulous voice and an anguished expression, she replied that she felt fine. There is a glaring discrepancy here between the denotative meaning of "feeling fine" and the emotive meaning inferred from the nonverbal acoustic sign. We must assume that the emotional import of the patient's utterance that is transmitted nonverbaly alters dramatically the meaning of the words themselves. Further research on language behavior in psychopathology must avail itself of the advances that have taken place in acoustic analysis and sound spectrography.

Psychotic speech, like nearly every other kind of speech, occurs within a context of human interaction. Patients talk to clinicians and to other patients. In addition, this interaction takes place in a specific setting, for example, a hospital ward or an office. However, most descriptions of psychotic speech in the professional literature are lacking in salient details with reference to both interactive context and setting.

Rochester (1980) observed that "there is no promising model of language use in schizophrenia" (p. 18), a fact commented on by every reviewer in the preceding decade. She attributed this to "the lack of broadly based, systematic observations" (Rochester, 1980, p. 19). Her comments have implications for research that range far beyond the analysis of schizophrenic speech and apply to all systematic study of language behavior and psychopathology. As Swartz (1993) points out, "broadly based, systematic observations" and "full analysis" require descriptions "based on extensive discourse samples and analyzed within a framework which allows for comparison with normal speech production. . . . Detailed analysis of context, including the effect of the listener on what is said, are an essential framework for the analysis of the discourse itself" (p. 6).

This point cannot be overstressed. Practically the entire corpus of psychopathological language phenomena available to us at present consists of texts without contexts, that is, spoken or written utterances by patients within clinical settings that are reported without sufficient accompanying information to permit clarification or interpretation of those utterances in significant ways. One of the frequent comments about psychotic speech is its lack of coherence. Swartz (1993) makes the point that incoherence is often in the ear of the beholder: "A text cannot be said simply to be incoherent; it is incoherent to a particular listener, in a specific situation" (p. 8).

She also notes the "striking lack of consideration of sociolinguistic variables in research on speech production of psychotic patients" (Swartz, 1993, p. 9). Ignorance of such variables in a psychiatric setting may lead to a situation in which misunderstanding is inappropriately attributed to mental illness. One of the authors recalls an experience that occurred while he was working at a large metropolitan psychiatric hospital. A patient had been admitted who had been apprehended by the police in the downtown section of the city. According to one of the officers, the man's speech was "incoherent" and he resisted vigorously when they attempted to put him into the police vehicle. Similar behavior was noted by the hospital admissions staff. Two days later, during visiting hours on Sunday, an elderly woman who was seeing one of her family members witnessed an altercation between the patient and attendants when the patient attempted to leave through the open area of the visiting room. She explained to one of the nurses on duty that the patient was a newly arrived refugee from a remote mountainous area in eastern Macedonia, where an obscure dialect was spoken. He had come to the United States and had missed connections with the people who were sponsoring his admission to the country. There was nothing incoherent about his speech to someone who spoke the same dialect.

In reply, therefore, to the question of whether we have attained precise descriptions of the way, or ways, individuals diagnosed as belonging to a specific nosological category differ from those in other categories or from normals, we are obliged to answer in the negative. Before real progress can be made toward answering this positively, it is our opinion that the shortcomings highlighted above will need to be rectified.

Analysis of Psychotic Speech: A Proposal

Swartz (1993) has recommended an "analytic package" that includes consideration of context, conversation analysis, cohesion analysis, and tone-unit analysis. This proposal for an approach to discourse analysis in psychiatric settings seeks to yield basic descriptions of psychotic speech in context. As we noted earlier, this approach represents an attempt to meet Rochester's (1980) requirement for "broadly based, systematic observations" as the potential basis for a "promising model of language use in schizophrenia." It also seeks to avoid further proliferation of decontextualized linguistic data and methods of analysis.

As a theoretical underpinning for her "analytic package," Swartz (1993) refers to *pragmatics*, "the systematic study of the relations between the linguistic properties of utterances and their properties as social action" (Ferrara, 1985, p. 138). It is the task of pragmatics to understand the relation between the "text" produced by the psychotic speaker and the context in which it was produced. In sharp contrast to the bulk of research that concentrates exclusively on texts, this analytical approach makes available a variety of information:

1. The patient's idiosyncratic style of speaking
2. Features of the linguistic community to which he/she belongs and by whose rules the discourse is, to some extent, bound
3. Features of discourse peculiar to a diagnostic category
4. Aspects of both the patient's and the interviewer's interpersonal functioning, reflected particularly in ways in which conversational rules are used (Swartz, 1993, pp. 8–9).

Swartz emphasizes that psychotic speech involves two speakers *in conversation*, regardless of how the discourse is elicited. A description of the setting would include the identities of the patient and the researcher, their relationship, social class, and cultural similarities or differences, and other cues of a nonverbal nature that might affect the form of the ensuing conversation. Contextual analysis deals with ways in which subjects seek to make sense out of situations in which they have been placed. Swartz describes an unstructured interview involving a female patient with a record of repeated hospital admissions for manic breakdowns. Although the patient's discourse was fragmented, it was noteworthy that the questions she asked Swartz were typical of those that might be asked by strangers seeking to clear a common ground for interaction. Coherence is constructed by interacting parties.

Ordinary conversation is bound by rules that are used across various discourse situations. These rules can be understood as predictable patterns of interaction. Turn taking, for example, involves the use of gaze and gesture to regulate the flow of speech. Adjacency pairing covers situations in which a specific type of utterance elicits a typed second: Questions elicit answers, greetings elicit greetings, apologies elicit disclaimers, and so on. Swartz suggests that such aspects of psychotic language behavior as pressure of speech, poverty of speech, and tendencies toward digression (e.g., tangentiality, derailment) might be understood in terms of failure of speakers to follow rules of topic maintenance and change.

Cohesion analysis, which we have already described in our discussion of language behavior in affective disorders, is a method of discourse analysis developed by Halliday and Hasan (1976). It measures one aspect of the coherence of speech: the way in which people relate sentences in order to make a coherent communication. The system involves the measurement of different kinds of links in the text known as "cohesive ties," "the means whereby elements that are structurally unrelated in the text are linked together" (Halliday & Hasan, 1976, p. 27).

Swartz (1993) observes that cohesion analysis is a useful way of exploring continuity in spoken discourse but is unable to provide data on the relation between discourse and its context. Nevertheless, she regards cohesion analysis as a research tool that "forms an important link between analysis of microelements of task (such as word choice) and the interactive perspective of contextual analysis and conversation analysis" (Swartz, 1993, p. 21).

Tone-unit analysis represents an additional approach to issues involving the intelligibility of texts. According to Halliday and Hasan, spoken discourse is segmented into "tone groups," each of which constitutes a single piece of information. Each tone group contains information presented by the speaker as new and other information given in the preceding text. Within the tone group or tone unit, new information is marked by being given intonational prominence. In the following examples of tone units, the encoded message changes according to which of the aspects is given prominence (new information is capitalized):

1. /I bought a CAKE/
2. /It's a cake I BOUGHT/

As Swartz points out, tone-unit analysis directs attention to three aspects of spoken discourse: (1) the length of the units used by the speaker to segment information, (2) the ration of new to given information in each unit, and (3) the relation between prosodic features of the discourse and the presentation of new and given information.

Swartz (1993) summarizes the values inherent in her analytical package, which studies different aspects of discourse:

> Firstly, all [of the approaches] focus to some degree on talk as a social activity. Interaction is central to context and conversation, and both cohesion and tone-unit analysis provide specific information about ways in which psychotic speakers fail as conversational partners. Secondly, all these forms of analysis are readily applicable to the interactions of clinical interviews, and are therefore likely to contribute directly to clinical descriptions of psychotic speech, and to the clinical work itself. Thirdly, by contextualising the discourse, and stressing the role of interaction in constructing coherence, the package examines in different ways the role of the interviewer in contributing to communication failure. (Swartz, 1993, p. 28)

We would like to express our opinion that the Swartz proposal marks a significant methodological advance in the systematic study of language behavior and psychopathology—one that takes a long stride toward meeting Rochester's goal of "full analysis."

UNDERSTANDING PSYCHOPATHOLOGY THROUGH LANGUAGE

Our second question is whether the systematic study of language behavior and communication has advanced our understanding of psychopathological processes in specific psychiatric syndromes. Let us refer to Andreasen's (1979) research finding that "the concept of thought disorder as pathognomonic for schizophrenic is incorrect" (p. 1329), a finding that was subsequently incorporated in the glossary of DSM-III. This conclusion was reached by means of an investigation that utilized definitions written "to describe speech and language behaviors commonly seen in psychiatric patients without any attempt to characterize the underlying cognitive processes unless they were reported by the patient (Andreasen, 1979, p. 1316).

Andreasen, like many other psychiatrists, appears to assume that the locus of dysfunction in psychotic speech is "thought disorder," which can be studied through the medium of language. Swartz (1993) refers to an editorial comment by Holzman on the 1986 special issue of *Schizophrenia Bulletin* devoted to thought disorder. Holzman referred to the development of "reliable scales for the measurement of thinking disorders" and commented on advances in cognitive psychology, which has made progress in "fashioning increasingly precise and subtle methods" (Holzman, 1986, p. 344). All these means of assessment, Swartz points out, use verbal tests or observations of language produced in clinical settings to arrive at conclusions about the presence of thought disorder. She specifically notes the "depressing circularity in arguments presented about schizophrenic thought" (Swartz, 1993, p. 5).

What are we dealing with here? Is it necessary to assume that language and thought are isomorphic to attempt inferences about the nature of the presumed "thought disorder" (or psychopathology) on the basis of language behavior? It is obvious from Andreasen's comments above that she does not believe so.

The identification of language and thought as one and the same is an ancient debate (pursued, e.g., by Müller, 1909; and Pick, 1973). The evidence against the identity of language and thought is considerable, and it is difficult to understand why the linguist Chaika (1990, p. 50) finds it necessary to engage in a lengthy polemic that seeks to prove that language and thought are not the same. Arnold Pick, in 1913 (Pick, 1973), made a substantial contribution to the resolution of this issue on the basis of the study of the nature of language itself. The structure of language, according to Pick, differs from that of cognition. Pick illustrates that in language the predicate comes after the subject, whereas in thought they come together. He further demonstrates that language may be illogical, while the thought behind it may not be so.

For some time there has been general agreement among language experts that language, at best, is imperfect and, at its worst, is even worse. The implication is that, in speaking of how psychological processes (e.g., cognition, emotion) operate, they are definitely more than simple language processes. Furthermore, different languages have widely different structures. It would be ridiculous to assert that thought in these different structures would be equally variable. To be sure, the words that we use in speaking are less than, and different from, the thought processes that take place. Language processes clearly permeate cognitive processes. Cognitive processes, in reciprocal fashion, permeate language processes. Even paralinguistic acts have been found to be dependent on verbal formulation or cues (Weisenburg & McBride, 1935). If language can be regarded as a mirror of the mind (because of its reflective nature), then cognition may be considered the scaffolding on which the mirror is constructed. Language reflects mind, which, in the final analysis, includes self-formation, that is, the cognitive, emotional, and volitional aspects of life. As one thinks, so one speaks. This reflective, reciprocal process is basic to interpersonal communication. The process is a dynamically patterned reciprocal act that helps define the nature of humankind and the individual's place within it.

The application of scientific knowledge in the area of the psychology of language and thought is useful to the extent that it provides an adequate and meaningful frame of reference for the explanation of the study of the mental life of the individual. Furthermore, it is beneficial to the practitioner as a belief system, which may serve to provide a sense of purpose, security, and faith in the methods used to bring about a change in the individual. Given that language and cognition are not separate entities but functions of an interacting mental Gestalt, it is still empirically necessary to determine what the full dynamic relation between these two processes comprises and how they operate. Even though this question is not fully answered, it appears clear from our perspective that the most useful theoretical frame of reference would be one that attempts to understand the reciprocal relation between language and cognition as a functional, dialectical one. From a primarily diachronic perspective, it is important that we appreciate the role that development plays in the shaping of the psychological relation between language and cognition, as well as the epistemological issues inherent in these two concepts.

One of the most significant issues in this field deals with the nature of the symbolic or semiotic functions inherent in the complex relation between language and communication. Although authorities may disagree with respect to the nature of symbolic function during the development of the organism, it is our opinion that symbolic function serves as a mediating device between actions (i.e., preverbal intelligence) and representations (i.e., verbal intelligence). There is even greater controversy among authorities concerning the origin or moment of acquisition of language and cognition in the course of their ongoing development. Basic to these considerations is the issue of continuity versus discontinuity. From a historical perspective, many controversies have surrounded this issue. At this time, there is a great deal of disagreement over the role that continuity and discontinuity play in human development. To clarify where and when continuity versus discontinuity may be useful in the description of the development of the human organism, it is essential to specify and be aware of the epistemological differences that emerge when one describes a particular event. In addition, it is crucial that we appreciate the differences that make a difference when we are describing similar things at various levels of abstraction (Weinberg, 1959).

Another related issue concerns the relation between inner language as opposed to interpersonal communicative discourse. Without a solid basis for inner-language events (cf. Vygotsky, Goldstein, et al.), the human organism would not easily develop interpersonal communications, which are essential to adequate socialization. In this sense we may better understand the concept of inner language as a by-product of the organism's personal representations of his/her own world. We may also more clearly comprehend the individual's interpersonal world in which cultural determinants play a significant role. Little doubt exists among most authorities that there is an intrinsic relation between verbal and nonverbal signals. To the extent that nonverbal language is a dominant mode of communication at earlier prelinguistic stages of development, this condition provides a hierarchical constant in the organism, with the consequence that one cannot have language without thought. Nevertheless, it is clear that cognition is always possible without language.

Several studies dealing with semantic associations and their context have been published since Eugene Bleuler's (1911) original observation that schizophrenic patients were unable to focus on the relevant meaning of words, which was suggested by the context in which they appeared. Chapman, Chapman, and Miller (1964) launched this approach, comparing responses made by schizophrenics to words with many different meanings to those made by nonschizophrenics. The intention here was to open the door to a better understanding of context dependency of associative processes.

Swinney (1984) demonstrated contextual ineffectivity in chronic schizophrenic patients. Using a cross-modal lexical priming technique, he found that presenting a polysemous word activated all its meanings (i.e., produced a semantic priming effect). This effect took place approximately one second later.

Recent German Research

Spitzer (1992) discusses three decades of research on word-association studies in psychopathology and provides a rationale for the revitalization of this approach in contemporary psychiatry and psychopathology. The notion was that a word-association paradigm in experimental psychiatry would facilitate a better understanding of the thought processes behind schizophrenia as well as other mental disorders. The strategy that was used involved the correlation of various experimental psychological test measures and the use of these measures, along with the symptoms, as a more fruitful means of establishing independent descriptions of clinical syndromes. A multifaceted approach combining many measures that could test various aspects of mental operations was seen as a more fruitful method for providing the scientific community with a "total picture" (i.e., a clinically significant index) of the problem.

Recently, an experimental method known as "semantic priming in lexical decision-making tasks" has been used to study the psychological processes as they relate to cognitive malfunctioning in schizophrenia. Moreover, research has indicated the presence of a larger semantic priming effect in thought-disordered schizophrenic patients (Kwapil, Hegley, Chapman, & Chapman, 1990).

Hoffman's Theory of Language Planning and Experience of Will

The problem of voluntary control in relation to cognitive planning and language behavior is central to any possibility of understanding abnormal communication in schizophrenic patients. Hoffman (1992) provides a "hypothesis of misdirection" by postulating that, at the syntactic-discourse level of language behavior, different cognitive-planning structures simultaneously compete with one another in the attempt to communicate. He further postulates that external speech provides the basis for inner speech, or the "language of thought," as it were. Plans that are produced by these structures are conceived as remaining below the conscious level of the individual. These unripened, unconscious, cognitive plans are seen as the core of the self-alien cognitive plans, as well as possible auditory hallucinations. In other words, Hoffman postulates that verbal and/or auditory hallucinatory behavior is derived from this dynamic form of language pathology.

CONCLUDING OBSERVATIONS

As we have seen, the more or less general pattern of psychopathological language research sought to identify recurrent linguistic and/or paralinguistic phenomena associated with various psychiatric disorders and to relate these phenomena to underlying psychopathological processes. Part of the research process was devoted to measuring the incidence of these phenomena among other nosological groups and normals. The aim was twofold: (1) to improve the accuracy of psychodiagnosis by recognizing these linguistic or paralinguistic phenomena as pathognomonic signs of particular syndromes and (2) to enhance understanding of the underlying pathological processes that manifested themselves in such phenomena.

The studies we reviewed have illustrated many of the shortcomings and problems involved in this standard approach. Much of this work can be relegated to the status of historical curiosity. We can view with amusement, for example, such efforts as the attempt to compile a "dictionary of schizophrenic speech." Other areas of inquiry have been overtaken by contemporary approaches that make increasing use of sophisticated research techniques that incorporate the latest advances in methodology and technology. Thus, the pattern for the future study of psychopathological language appears to emphasize objectivity, quantification, and precision.

Nevertheless, there remains a broad potential for the exploration of psychopathological language phenomena that depends on research methods of the type referred to above. Often such studies raise issues that can become the focus of more systematic and large-scale investigation. Let us conclude with a case in point: the original and insightful efforts of David Forrest (1969) on *poiesis* and schizophrenic language.

The author notes that schizophrenic speech may, in some cases, reflect forbidden thoughts; in others, it may reflect a general antipathy toward interaction. Sometimes it appears that a patient wants to communicate in the normal sense but cannot because of severe cognitive disturbances. Forrest cites one of Kraepelin's cases, in which, in response to the word "Bett," the patient replied, "Bett, Bett, Bett, dett, dett, dett, ditt, dutt, dutt, daut, daut, daut, dint, dutt, dett, datt. Wenn ich angefangen habe, fahre ich fort bis zu Ende" (Forrest, 1969, pp. 156–157). Says Forrest (1969):

> With his increased preoccupation with the form of words, the schizophrenic, like the poet, finds it more difficult to speak his mind, and may sometimes use his words to fill out a form at the expense of not having them express his thoughts. In other words, sometimes the meter displaces the argument. At this point the poet may revise his poem, or else be satisfied with the thought it says, although he did not intend to say it. He may even convince himself that the thought the words say was what he had in mind all along. (p. 157)

Forrest argues persuasively for the creativity of schizophrenic productions. Neologisms, "involving as they do distortions and condensations, may be of the intensity of good poetry which has always coined and rejuvenated words" (Forrest, 1969, p. 167). One of Bleuler's patients had been tormented by "elbow-people," which Forrest appreciates from his experiences on the New York subway. Bleuler himself (as quoted by Forrest) had commented on the similarity of schizophrenic and artistic productions, citing "the subordination of all thought-associations to one complex, the inclination to novel, unusual range of ideas, the indifference to tradition, the lack of restraints."

Forrest's analysis provided support for conclusions reached by Vetter's (1969) study of neologisms in psychopathological language, which produced no convincing evidence that new word coinage in schizophrenia involved any fundamental distortion at the morphological or morphophonemic level. Hundreds of samples of schizophrenic neologisms in several languages sustained Roger Brown's (1973) contention that most, if not all, neologisms conform to the phonological and morphological rules of the patient's native language.

With regard to more extended schizophrenic verbal productions, in all of the "word salads" that the present authors have been served by schizophrenic patients (usually those who would have been labeled "hebephrenic" by the older nosological terminology), we had never encountered any instances of the "severe agrammatism" to which older psychiatrists had referred. Indeed, we had never encountered any schizophrenic who took the kind of liberties with grammar that E. E. Cummings (1959) allowed himself in passages such as

> anyone lived in a pretty how town
> (with up so floating many bells down)
> spring summer autumn winter
> he sang his didn't he danced his did.

Nor had we ever met a schizophrenic patient who could supply an example of what Schneider (1930) called *Abwandlung* (switching grammatical functions of parts of speech) that compared with Cummings's haunting line: "but if a lark should april me."

Modern deviance theory affirms that a good deal of psychopathology is in the eye or ear of the clinician beholder. We have often wondered what might happen if, instead of schizophrenic verbal productions, an investigator were to use samples of writings by authors like Gertrude Stein, Gerard Manley Hopkins, Cummings, or James Joyce, who are famous for their linguistic inventiveness and originality. What kind of ranking on a five-point or seven-point scale of "schizophrenicity" would a clinician give such a selection by Stein as:

> Cut a gas jet uglier and the pierce pierce in between
> the next and negligent. Choose the rate to pay and
> pet pet very much. A collection of all around, a single person, a lack of langour and
> more hurt at ease.

Or James Joyce's:

> Dark ages clasp the daisy roots. Stop if you are a
> sally of the allies. Please stop if you are a B.C. minding missy, please do. But should
> you prefer A.D. stepplease. And if you miss with a venture it serves
> you girly well glad.

We suspect that there would be a significant level of agreement among judges that the above samples ranked high in schizophrenicity. Of much greater importance, of course, would be the demonstration that the relation between *poiesis* and schizophrenic language has hardly begun to be explored.

REFERENCES

Andreasen, N. J. C. (1979). Thought, language, and communication disorder: I. Clinical assessment, definition of terms, and evaluation of their reliability. *Archives of General Psychiatry*, *36*, 1315–1321.

Berrios, G. E. (1989). What is phenomenology? A review. *Journal of the Royal Society of Medicine*, *82*, 425–428.

Bleuler, E. (1911). *Dementia Praecox oder Gruppe der Schizophrenien*. Leipzig: Deuticke.

Brown, R. (1973). Schizophrenia, language, and reality. *American Psychologist, 28*, 395–403.

Chaika, E. (1990). *Understanding Psychotic Speech: Beyond Freud and Chomsky*. Springfield, IL: Thomas.

Chapman, L. J., Chapman, J. P., & Miller, G. A. (1964). A theory of verbal behavior in schizophrenia. In B. A. Maher (Ed.), *Progress in Experimental Personality Research* (Vol. 1, pp. 49–77). New York: Academic Press.

Cummings, E. E. (1959). *Poems 1923–1954*. New York: Harcourt.

Ferrara, A. (1985). Pragmatics. In T. A. Van Dijk (Ed.), *Handbook of discourse analysis: Vol. 2. Dimensions of discourse* (pp. 137–157). London: Academic Press.

Forrest, D. V. (1969). Poiesis and the language of schizophrenia. In H. J. Vetter (Ed.), *Language behavior in schizophrenia* (pp. 153–181). Springfield, IL: Thomas.

Halliday, M. A. K., & Hasan, R. (1976). *Cohesion in English*. London: Longman.

Hoffman, R. (1992). Language planning and alterations in the experience of will. In M. Spitzer, F. Uehlein, M. A. Schwartz, & C. Mundt (Ed.), *Phenomenology of Language and Schizophrenia* (pp. 197–210). New York: Springer.

Holzman, P. S. (1986). Thought disorder in schizophrenia: Editor's introduction. *Schizophrenia Bulletin, 12*, 360–371.

Kwapil, T. R., Hegley, D. C., Chapman, L. J., & Chapman, J. P. (1990). Facilitation of word recognition by semantic priming in schizophrenia. *Journal of Abnormal Psychology, 99*, 215–221.

Müller, M. (1909). *Three Introductory Lectures on the Science of Thought*. Chicago: Open Court.

Ostwald, P. F. (1963). *Soundmaking*. Springfield, IL: Thomas.

Pick, A. (1973). Aphasia. In J. W. Brown (Ed.), *Aphasia*. Springfield, IL: Thomas.

Rochester, S. (1980). Thought disorder and language use in schizophrenia. In R. W. Rieber (Ed.), *Applied psycholinguistics and mental health* (pp. 11–68). New York: Plenum.

Schneider, C. (1930). *Die Psychologie der Schizophrenen*. Leipzig: Thieme.

Soskin, W., & Kaufmann, P. E. (1961). Judgment of emotion in word-free voice. *Journal of Communication, 11*, 73–81.

Spitzer, M. (1992). Word associations in experimental psychology: A historical perspective. In M. Spitzer, F. Uehlein, M. A. Schwartz, & C. Mundt (Eds.), *Phenomenology of Language and Schizophrenia* (pp. 160–196). New York: Springer.

Swartz, S. (1993). *Some methodological issues in the analysis of psychotic speech*. Unpublished manuscript.

Swinney, D. (1984). Theoretical and methodological issues in cognitive science: A psycholinguistic perspective. In W. Kintch, J. R. Miller, & P. J. Poslon (Eds.), *Method and tactics in cognitive science* (pp. 42–58). Hillsdale, NJ: Erlbaum.

Vetter, H. J. (1969). *Language behavior and psychopathology*. Chicago: Rand McNally.

Weinberg, H. L. (1959). *Levels of knowing and existence: Studies in general semantics*. New York: Harper.

Weisenburg, T., & McBride, C. E. (1935). *Aphasia: A clinical and psychological study*. New York: Commonwealth Fund.

Author Index

Subject Index

ISBN 0-306-44757-6

90000